Advocates of what's called the 'New P
much to ponder in this work. Robert (
fresh arguments against the NPP inter|
in a way that makes the issues accessible to pastors who need informed
responses to this influential trend. I highly recommend it.

MICHAEL HORTON
J. Gresham Machen Professor of Systematic Theology and Apologetics,
Westminster Seminary California, Escondido, California

The new perspective isn't new anymore, but its influence is still
felt. Robert Cara directs our attention to the primary sources, to
what the texts themselves say. The claim that Second Temple Judaism is free from works-righteousness, Cara demonstrates, does not
accord with the sources. A sober look at the evidence reveals that
works righteousness was taught by some Second Temple Jews. Cara
also investigates later Pauline writings, which are often neglected
in the discussion. We see in Ephesians, 1 Timothy, and Titus a
polemic against works-righteousness. Cara vindicates his reading
with a careful exegesis of key texts in these letters. Cara writes in an
engaging and accessible style, showing that a Reformational reading
is faithful to Paul's theology.

THOMAS R. SCHREINER
James Buchanan Harrison Professor of New Testament Interpretation,
Associate Dean, The Southern Baptist Theological Seminary,
Louisville, Kentucky

Is there anything remaining to be said on the New Perspective on
Paul? The answer is an emphatic 'yes'. Robert J. Cara's *Cracking the
Foundation of the New Perspective on Paul* is a fresh response to one
of the most vigorous challenges to the Reformation's doctrine of
justification in the last quarter century. Demonstrating ease in the
Jewish sources, exegetical insight, and extraordinary pedagogical
clarity, *Cracking the Foundation...* makes a compelling case that the
New Testament writers were accurate in their assessment of Second
Temple Judaism. Students and scholars alike will benefit from this
fair-minded and firm engagement of the New Perspective.

GUY PRENTISS WATERS
James M. Baird, Jr. Professor of New Testament,
Reformed Theological Seminary, Jackson, Mississippi

In all the debates over the New Perspective on Paul, it is often forgotten that the whole system rests on the singular premise that first-century Judaism did not struggle with works righteousness. And if this premise were to be removed, then the whole system would collapse. And it is precisely this premise which Bob Cara so effectively challenges in this new book. With impressive analysis of the historical sources, and careful attention to overlooked texts, Cara shakes the foundation of what seemed to be an unshakable system.

MICHAEL J. KRUGER
President and Professor of New Testament,
Reformed Theological Seminary, Charlotte, North Carolina

R.E.D.S.
REFORMED,
EXEGETICAL
AND
DOCTRINAL
STUDIES

CRACKING THE FOUNDATION
OF THE
NEW PERSPECTIVE ON PAUL

COVENANTAL NOMISM VERSUS REFORMED COVENANTAL THEOLOGY

ROBERT J. CARA

SERIES EDITORS J.V. FESKO & MATTHEW BARRETT

MENTOR
Encouraging Christians to Think

Copyright © Robert Cara 2017

paperback ISBN 978-1-78191-979-8
epub ISBN 978-1-52710-013-8
mobi ISBN 978-1-52710-014-5

10 9 8 7 6 5 4 3 2 1

Published in 2017
in the
Mentor Imprint
by
Christian Focus Publications Ltd,
Geanies House, Fearn, Ross-shire,
IV20 1TW, Great Britain.
www.christianfocus.com

Cover design by
Pete Barnsley

Printed by
Bell & Bain, Glasgow

CONTENTS

Abbreviations

1QapGen	*Genesis Apocryphon*
1QH	*Thanksgiving Hymns* or *Hodayot*
1QIsa	Isaiah
1QpHab	*Pesher Habakkuk*
1QS	*Rule of the Community (Serek HayaHad)*
2 Bar.	*2 Baruch*
4QMMT	*Miqsat Ma'ase Ha-Torah*
11QT	*Temple Scroll*
AB	Anchor Bible
ABD	D. N. Freeman, ed., *The Anchor Bible Dictionary* (6 vols., 1992)
ABRL	Anchor Bible Reference Library
ANF	*Ante-Nicene Fathers* (10 vols.)
Ant.	Josephus' *Jewish Antiquities*
b.	Babylonian Talmud tractate
Barn.	*Epistle of Barnabas*
BDAG	W. Bauer, F. W. Danker, W. F. Arndt, and F. W. Gingrich, *A Greek-English Lexicon of the New Testament and Other Early Christian Literature* (3rd. ed., 2000)
BDF	F. Blass, A. Debruner, and F. W. Funk, *A Greek Grammar of the New Testament and Other Early Christian Literature* (1961)
BECNT	Baker Exegetical Commentary on the New Testament
BJRL	*Bulletin of the John Rylands University Library of Manchester*
BNTC	Black's New Testament Commentary
CBQ	*Catholic Biblical Quarterly*
CD	*Damascus Document*
CTQ	*Concordia Theological Quarterly*
DJG	J. B. Green and S. McKnight, eds., *Dictionary of Jesus and the Gospels* (1992)

DLNT	R. P. Martin and P. H. Davids, eds., *Dictionary of the Later New Testament and Its Developments* (1997)
DNTB	C. A. Evans and S. E. Porter, eds., *Dictionary of New Testament Background* (2000)
DPL	G. F. Hawthorne, R. P. Martin, eds., *Dictionary of Paul and His Letters* (1993)
DSD	*Dead Sea Discoveries*
DSS	Dead Sea Scrolls
EBib	Etudes bibliques
ECC	Eerdmans Critical Commentary
EJL	Early Judaism and Its Literature
EncJud	*Encyclopaedia Judaica* (16 vols., 1972)
GNS	Good News Studies
HTR	*Harvard Theological Review*
HUCA	*Hebrew Union College Annual*
ICC	International Critical Commentary
ISBE	G.W. Bromiley, ed., *The International Standard Bible Encyclopedia* (4 vols., 1979-1988)
JETS	*Journal of the Evangelical Theological Society*
Jos. Asen.	*Joseph and Aseneth*
JQR	*Jewish Quarterly Review*
JSNTSup	Journal for the Study of the New Testament Supplement Series
JSJ	*Journal for the Study of Judaism in the Persian, Hellenistic, and Roman Periods*
JTS	*Journal of Theological Studies*
Jub.	*Jubilees*
J. W.	Josephus' *Jewish War*
KJV	King James Version
LCL	Loeb Classical Library
LNTS	The Library of New Testament Studies
LXX	Septuagint
m.	Mishnah tractate

NIDOTTE	W. A. VanGemeren, ed., *New International Dictionary of Old Testament Theology & Exegesis* (5 vols., 1997)
NIGTC	New International Greek Testament Commentary
NPNF	*Nicene and Post-Nicene Fathers* (Series 1, 14 vols.; Series 2, 14 vols.)
NovT	*Novum Testamentum*
NovTSup	Supplements to Novum Testamentum
NPP	New Perspective on Paul
NRSV	New Revised Standard Version
NSBT	New Studies in Biblical Theology
NTC	New Testament Commentary
NTL	New Testament Library
NTS	*New Testament Studies*
NTT	New Testament Theology
OTP	J. H. Charlesworth, ed., *The Old Testament Pseudepigrapha* (2 vols., 1983-1985)
p.	*Pesher*
PNTC	Pillar New Testament Commentary
Pss. Sol.	*Psalms of Solomon*
RQ	*Römische Quartalschrift für christliche Altertumskunde und Kirchengeschichte*
RSV	Revised Standard Version
SBLDS	Society of Biblical Literature Dissertation Series
SBLMS	Society of Biblical Literature Monograph Series
SCS	*Septuagint and Cognate Studies*
SHBC	Smyth & Helwys Bible Commentary
Sib. Or.	*Sibylline Oracles*
SJT	*Scottish Journal of Theology*
SP	Sacra Pagina
t.	Tosefta tractate
T. Ab.	*Testament of Abraham*
T. Jud.	*Testament of Judah*
T. Levi	*Testament of Levi*

T. Sim.	*Testament of Simeon*
T. Zeb.	*Testament of Zebulun*
TrinJ	*Trinity Journal*
TPINTC	TPI New Testament Commentaries
TynBul	*Tyndale Bulletin*
WBC	Word Biblical Commentary
WCF	Westminster Confession of Faith
WLC	Westminster Larger Catechism
WSC	Westminster Shorter Catechism
WTJ	*Westminster Theological Journal*
WUNT	Wissenschaftliche Untersuchungen zum Neuen Testament
y.	Jerusalem Talmud tractate
ZECNT	Zondervan Exegetical Commentary on the New Testament
ZNW	*Zeitschrift für die neutestamentliche Wissenschaft und die Kunde der älteren Kirche*

To Jill Annette Cara,
my lovely wife.

Song of Solomon 4:7

Series Preface

Reformed, Exegetical and Doctrinal Studies (R.E.D.S.) presents new studies informed by rigorous exegetical attention to the biblical text, engagement with the history of doctrine, with a goal of refined dogmatic formulation.

R.E.D.S. covers a spectrum of doctrinal topics, addresses contemporary challenges in theological studies, and is driven by the Word of God, seeking to draw theological conclusions based upon the authority and teaching of Scripture itself.

Each volume also explores pastoral implications so that they contribute to the church's theological and practical understanding of God's word. One of the virtues that sets R.E.D.S. apart is its ability to apply dogmatics to the Christian life. In doing so, these volumes are characterized by the rare combination of theological weightiness and warm, pastoral application, much in the tradition of John Calvin's *Institutes of the Christian Religion*.

These volumes do not merely repeat material accessible in other books but retrieve and remind the church of forgotten truths to enrich contemporary discussion.

MATTHEW BARRETT

J. V. FESKO

PREFACE

In a real sense, I have been thinking about E. P. Sanders and the New Perspective on Paul since January 1990. Through the years I have lectured many times, wrote book reviews, etc. on this topic. I am pleased now to have my mature thoughts about a portion of that topic—works righteousness in Second Temple Judaism—come together in this book.

Of course, this is a polemical book. I trust I have argued in a truth-in-love manner (Eph. 4:15).

I want to thank the Board of Trustees of Reformed Theological Seminary and Dr J. Ligon Duncan, Chancellor, for encouraging me to continue to teach and write in the midst of my growing administrative duties. Thanks also goes to Rev. Jim Mitchell for reading this manuscript during the 2015 Christmas holidays and giving me suggestions for better clarity. He is my son-in-law and pastor of Sandy Plains Associate Reformed Presbyterian Church in Tryon, NC. Finally, I want to thank Drs Matthew Barrett and

J. V. Fesko, the editors of this series, for their many helpful suggestions and their love for Reformed theology.

I dedicate this book to my lovely wife, Jill A. Cara. We have been married since 1979, but we met as very young children in 1962 when her family began coming to 'my' church.

ROBERT J. CARA

Reformed Theological Seminary
Charlotte, North Carolina
April 2016

CHAPTER 1:

FOUNDATION OF THE NEW PERSPECTIVE ON PAUL

Alistair Begg, a famous evangelical pastor-scholar, lamented to me:

> Many evangelical pastors do not know how to respond when someone who is pro-New Perspective on Paul makes an argument from Second Temple Judaism. The pastors hardly know Second Temple Judaism documents and the tenuousness of arguments from them. Once someone makes a claim about Second Temple Judaism, the evangelical pastor feels inadequate to respond and the conversation simply stops.

Begg was aware that I was writing a book critical of the New Perspective on Paul (hereafter, NPP), but he was not aware of the particular focus of my book—engaging with the Jewish-background portion of NPP arguments. Needless to say, I was encouraged by his comments and sheepishly told him I was trying to remedy that situation. We then had a great discussion on aspects of Second Temple Judaism as he was very well informed.

INTRODUCTION

The *foundation* of the NPP is a new perspective on the soteriology of Second Temple Judaism. Once given this new perspective on Second Temple Judaism, the house of a new perspective concerning Paul is built. That is, the NPP involves two new perspectives. The first relates to Second Temple Judaism, and the second, based off the first, relates to Paul.

The debate about Second Temple Judaism and its resulting effect on Paul is important. Why? The main conclusion, as espoused by NPP authors, is that the traditional Protestant view of justification as understood by Calvin, Luther, most modern evangelicals, and even many critical scholars is simply wrong or at least needs serious modification. In fact, so argues the NPP, the Reformers read their battles over merit with Roman Catholicism into Paul's battles.[1]

Who are the leading lights associated with the NPP? For Second Temple Judaism, it is E. P. Sanders. For views of Paul based off the foundation of Sanders, there are a variety of perspectives and authors; however, James D. G. Dunn and N. T. Wright are the most well known and prolific.

BRIEF SUMMARY OF NPP AND JUSTIFICATION

Before discussing the focus of this book, a brief summary of the NPP's core commitments is presented below.

The NPP argues as follows: Second Temple Judaism 'was centered upon the gracious aspect of God's covenant with Israel' and was

---

1. So James D. G. Dunn in his famous article 'The New Perspective on Paul,' *BJRL* 65 (1983): 95-122. 'Since Paul's teaching on justification by faith seems to speak so directly to Luther's subjective wrestlings, it was a natural corollary to see Paul's opponents in terms of unreformed Catholicism which opposed Luther, with first century Judaism read through the "grid" of the early 16th century Catholic system of merit' (p. 98). While discussing exegetical options for justification by faith, Dunn opines 'far worse, to start our exegesis here from the Reformation presupposition that Paul was attacking the idea of *earning* God's acquittal, the idea of meritorious works, is to set the whole exegetical endeavour off on the wrong track' (p. 106, italics his).

not legalistic works righteous oriented as the traditional-Protestant view held.[2] This new conclusion about Judaism is then related to Paul's view of justification. Since the subject of justification in Paul comes up several times in contexts that include either first-century non-Christian Jews or Christian Jews (e.g., Rom. 2, Rom. 9-11, Gal. 3-5, Phil. 3), knowing what first-century A.D. Jews believed aids in understanding Paul's view of justification. This new view of Judaism helps to significantly better explain Paul's opponents and Paul himself.[3] Or so the NPP argument goes.

The NPP agreed that traditional Protestantism sees justification by faith as the opposite of legalistic works righteousness as a means for being declared righteous. Justification by faith is the legal declaration that Christ's work, and not the Christian's works, is the merit by which one is declared righteous. That is, if works righteousness is a human's work, then the opposite of that, grace, must not have any aspect of a human's work as the basis or ground of justification. Or to say it another way, the traditional Protestant view opposes two soteriological systems: justification by works of the law (works righteousness soteriology) versus justification by grace/Christ's work/faith (grace soteriology).

NPP rejects the traditional-Protestant view that Paul is opposing two soteriological systems. Why? Because a works righteousness soteriology did not exist during the first-century A.D.! In that light, here is the first main point we must consider: *NPP authors*

---

2. Frank J. Matera, *Galatians* (SP 9; Liturgical: Collegeville, MN, 1992), 30. Matera is pro-NPP and has an excellent, brief presentation of the standard NPP view on pp. 26-32.

3. On the other hand, I rebut that Paul also argues that some in OT Israel misunderstood justification (Rom. 9-11) and some understood it (Rom. 4); hence, Paul is not limited to first-century A.D. Jewish views. Anti-NPP authors with a high view of Scripture complain that many NPP authors tend to allow their Second Temple Judaism views to *control* the exegesis of Scripture. E.g., Guy Prentiss Waters, *Justification and the New Perspective on Paul: A Review and Response* (Phillipsburg: P&R, 2004), 154-55; and S. M. Baugh, 'The New Perspective, Mediation, Justification,' in *Covenant, Justification, and Pastoral Ministry: Essays by the Faculty of Westminster Seminary California* (ed. R. Scott Clark; Phillipsburg: P&R, 2007), 137-63, esp. 145-47.

agree that Paul was not arguing against a legalistic works righteousness view because it did not exist—that is, they accept Sanders' covenantal nomism.[4] Given this foundational starting point, the NPP further concludes that the expression 'works of the law' (e.g., Rom. 3:20, Gal. 2:16) in Paul cannot refer to legalistic works righteousness.[5] If 'works of the law' does not refer to legalistic works righteousness, then justification by faith which is contrasted with 'works of the law' cannot be the opposite of legalistic works righteousness. Consequently, justification by faith cannot be the traditional-Protestant view, which brings us to the second main point: *NPP authors agree on what justification is not—it is not the traditional-Protestant view.*[6]

How do NPP authors define 'works of the law' if not as works righteousness? The vast majority of NPP authors define 'works of the law' as technically the whole Torah, but primarily 'works of the law' in context as emphasizing the three Jewish boundary markers or badges, *Sabbath, circumcision, and food laws.*[7] It is these boundary markers that separate Jews from Gentiles. Therefore, Paul is contrasting grace, not against works righteousness, but against those who trust in their Jewish identity, or as Wright initially coined it,

---

4. Sanders' covenantal nomism is described below in the next section of this chapter.

5. So N. T. Wright, '[Paul's] polemic against "works of the law" is not directed against those who attempted to *earn* covenant membership through keeping the Jewish law (*such people do not seem to have existed in the 1st century*)' ('Justification,' in *New Dictionary of Theology* [ed Sinclair B. Ferguson and David F. Wright; Downers Grove: InterVarsity, 1988], 359-61, first italic his, second mine).

6. Some NPP authors, in their later works, have said that there is some level of compatibility between the traditional and NPP views of justification. See my discussion of this claim in the Dunn and Wright sections in Chapter 4, respectively.

7. So James D. G. Dunn, 'New Perspective View' in *Justification: Five Views* (ed. James K. Beilby and Paul Rhodes Eddy; Downers Grove: IVP Academic, 2011), 176-201, esp. 193-95. N. T. Wright agrees with Dunn (*The Climax of the Covenant: Christ and the Law in Pauline Theology* [Minneapolis: Fortress, 1991], 139 n. 10); also he still agrees in his latest work (*Paul and His Recent Interpreters: Some Contemporary Debates* (Minneapolis: Fortress, 2015), 92.

a trust in a 'national righteousness.'[8] Paul is proclaiming that one is justified by faith and not by Jewish boundary markers. Note, the NPP does not see these boundary markers as part of a larger category of works righteousness. Note also that 'works of the law' and 'works' never refers to general human deeds as many Reformers taught. Thus we come to the third main point: *NPP authors agree that 'works of the law' primarily refer to Jewish boundary markers, Sabbath, circumcision, and food laws.*

According to NPP authors, why would Paul be bringing up 'works of the law' (boundary markers) in Romans, Galatians, and Philippians 3? Why is this so important to him ? Yinger, a pro-NPP author, summarizes well:

> At issue was a question of social identity: 'Who belongs to the people of God and how is this known?' i.e., does one have to be Jewish—be circumcised, keep food laws, celebrate Sabbath, etc.—in order to inherit the promises of Abraham?[9]

Paul was an Apostle to the Gentiles. The issue of Gentile acceptance among Jewish Christians was very important to him. This leads us to the fourth main point: *NPP authors agree that Paul's mission to the Gentiles is the context for his teaching on justification.*[10] The context is *not* that some wanted to be justified by their works righteousness.

Finally then, what does justification by faith actually mean? NPP is clear and unified on what justification does not mean. However, NPP is unclear and not unified on what justification actually means. Is justification forensic? Is it transformative? Is it relational? Is it related to covenant? When does it happen? How does it relate to the 'righteousness of God'? Does it relate to getting

---

8. N. T. Wright, 'The Paul of History and the Apostle of Faith,' *TynBul* 29 (1978): 61-88, esp. 65, 71, 83. '[Israel] is guilty not of "legalism" or "works righteousness" but of what I call "national righteousness," the belief that fleshly Jewish descent guarantees membership of God's true covenant people' (65).

9. Kent L. Yinger, *The New Perspective on Paul: An Introduction* (Eugene, OR: Cascade, 2011), 30-31.

10. One of Dunn's four points of NPP is, 'The significance of Paul's mission is the context for his teaching on justification' ('New Perspective View,' 177).

into the covenant community (soteriology) or is it a confirmation that one is already in the community (ecclesiology)? Is it important? There are many differing NPP answers. However, it is useful to summarize briefly at least one standard NPP view.

Justification has two components, initial and final. Initial justification primarily concerns ecclesiology, that is, who is in the covenant community, not soteriology, how does one get in. Initial justification is related to grace, Christ's work, and faith. It is the status that one is in the covenant.[11] Final justification is at least partially based on one's works done in the Spirit.[12] Also, justification does not include the imputed righteousness of Christ—NPP is united and clear on this point![13] More specific details as to James D. G. Dunn and N. T. Wright's views of justification will be presented in the respective sections in Chapter 4. Finally, the fifth main point: *NPP authors are not united on justification. One standard view: Initial justification is by faith and recognizes covenant*

---

11. N. T. Wright, 'Justification in this setting [Paul's Jewish context], is not a matter of *how someone enters the community of the true people of God*, but of *how you tell who belongs to that community....* In standard Christian theological language, it wasn't so much about soteriology as about ecclesiology; not so much about salvation as about the church' (*What Saint Paul Really Said: Was Paul of Tarsus the Real Founder of Christianity?* [Grand Rapids: Eerdmans, 1997], 119, italics his).

12. N. T. Wright comments, 'Justification, at the last, will be on the basis of performance, not possession,' 'The Letter to the Romans: Introduction, Commentary, and Reflections,' in *The New Interpreter's Bible* (vol. 10; Nashville: Abingdon, 2002), 393-770, esp. 440. Similarly, 'Future justification, acquittal at the last great Assize, always take place on the basis of the totality of the life lived' ('The Law in Romans 2,' in *Paul and the Mosaic Law* [ed. James D. G. Dunn; WUNT 89; Tübingen: Mohr Siebeck: 1996], 131-50, esp. 144). Also see Wright's *Justification: God's Plan & Paul's Vision* (Downers Grove: IVP Academic, 2009), 186, 260 n. 11. To be clear, Wright sees these works done in the power of the Spirit. Similarly, James D. G. Dunn, 'Paul's theology of justification by faith alone has to be qualified as final justification by faith *and* works accomplished by the believer in the power of the Spirit' ('The New Perspective: whence, what and whither?,' in *The New Perspective on Paul* [rev. ed.; Grand Rapids: Eerdmans, 2008], 1-97, esp. 88, italics his).

13. Reformed theology affirms the imputation of Christ's righteousness, although not all modern evangelical affirm this. More on this in Chapter 4.

status (ecclesiology), while final justification is partially by works, albeit works produced by the Spirit.

I have summarized NPP, especially as it relates to the key doctrine of justification, with five main points.[14] The 'five points of NPP'[15] are repeated here:

1. NPP authors agree that Paul was not arguing against a legalistic works righteousness view because it did not exist— that is, they accept Sanders' covenantal nomism.

2. NPP authors agree on what justification is *not*—it is *not* the traditional-Protestant view.

3. NPP authors agree that 'works of the law' primarily refer to Jewish boundary markers, Sabbath, circumcision, and food laws.

4. NPP authors agree that Paul's mission to the Gentiles *is* the context for his teaching on justification.

5. NPP authors are not united on justification. One standard view: Initial justification is by faith and recognizes covenant status (ecclesiology), while final justification is partially by works, albeit works produced by the Spirit.

SANDERS' COVENANTAL NOMISM IS THE FOUNDATION OF NPP

The foundational new perspective on Second Temple Judaism is directly related to E. P. Sanders. In brief, E. P. Sanders' thesis is

---

14. Charles Lee Irons, an anti-NPP author, summarizes NPP with the metaphor of three pillars. His first pillar is Sanders and covenantal nomism (which matches my first two points). The second pillar is the 'social function of the law,' which is the Jewish boundary markers (which matches my third and fourth points). The third pillar is to interpret 'righteousness of God' as God's covenant faithfulness, which then relates to justification (part of my fifth point about the standard view). See his *The Righteousness of God: A Lexical Examination of the Covenant-Faithfulness Interpretation* (WUNT II/386; Tübingen: Mohr Siebeck, 2015), 2-8, esp. 3.

15. If I could just figure out an acrostic similar to 'Tulip'!

that Second Temple Judaism is not works righteousness oriented at all. It is a religion of grace and has a soteriological structure that he has termed 'covenantal nomism.'[16] Also, Sanders argues that this same soteriological structure existed across all varieties of Jewish groups in Second Temple Judaism. Details of Sanders' view are presented and critiqued in Chapter 2; part of the critique continues into Chapter 3.

The NPP authors themselves readily admit that Sanders' gracious covenantal-nomism is their foundation.

For example, N. T. Wright summarizes the core tenet of the Judaistic-background aspect of the NPP (specifically, E. P. Sanders' view[17]), 'Judaism in Paul's day was not, as has regularly been supposed, a religion of legalistic works righteousness. If we imagine that it was, and that Paul was attacking it as if it was, we will do great violence to it and him.' Wright continues and gives his view about this (Sanders') basic thesis: 'I do not myself believe such a refutation [of Sanders' basic thesis] can or will be offered, ... I regard his basic point as established.'[18]

Or consider Dunn, who lists 'four aspects' of NPP. The first is, 'The new perspective on Paul arises from a new perspective [Sanders] on Judaism.'[19] Yinger gives three 'main lines' of NPP. The first is, 'First-century Judaisms were not legalistic, but were

---

16. E. P. Sanders, *Paul and Palestinian Judaism: A Comparison of Patterns of Religion* (Minneapolis: Fortress, 1977), 422-23.

17. Wright is referring specifically to E. P. Sanders' book, *Paul and Palestinian Judaism*.

18. N. T. Wright, *What Saint Paul Really Said*, 18, 20. Wright has been consistent on this theme; in one of Wright's early works he states, '"Works of the Law" were not, as is usually thought, the attempt to earn salvation *de novo.*' He cites Sanders in this connection ('Justification: The Biblical Basis and its Relevance for Contemporary Evangelicalism,' in *The Great Acquittal: Justification by Faith and Current Christian Thought* [ed. Gavin Reid; Glasgow: Collins, 1980], 13-37, 109-19, esp. 18, 111 n. 18). While agreeing with Sanders' basic thesis, Wright does state that 'serious modifications are required' (*What Saint Paul Really Said*, 20). Wright's minor complaints about Sanders are found in *Paul and His Recent Interpreters*, 74-75.

19. Dunn, 'New Perspective View,' 177.

characterized by covenantal nomism—saved by God's grace and obligated to follow his ways.'[20]

McGrath in his well-known volume on justification discusses Sanders' covenantal nomism. If true, this has reoriented everything because the entire history of the church, although not agreeing on justification, did agree that Judaism had a works righteousness soteriology.[21] McGrath concludes his book by summarizing Sanders' potential impact and the possibilities that the NPP offers.

> The situation envisaged by Paul in formulating his doctrine of justification by faith is not universal human self-righteousness which makes Pelagian claims on God's favour, but a specifically Jewish concern about the covenantal limits of the people of God. If this is so, the traditional interpretation of the Pauline doctrine of justification, from Augustine through Luther and beyond, requires revision.[22]

FOCUS AND THESIS

I hold to a traditional Reformed view of justification and believe that the new perspective on Second Temple Judaism is substantially wrong. Similarly, I believe that the resulting NPP, at least as it concerns justification, is also substantially wrong.

There have been a reasonable number of good books by anti-NPP authors directly focused on Paul and defending the traditional-Protestant view of justification against the NPP.[23] There have been

---

20. Yinger, *The New Perspective on Paul*, 30.

21. Alister E. McGrath, *Iustitia Dei: A History of the Christian Doctrine of Justification* (3rd ed.; Cambridge: CUP, 2005), 30.

22. McGrath, *Iustitia Dei*, 420.

23. E.g., Thomas R. Schreiner, *The Law and Its Fulfillment: A Pauline Theology of Law* (Grand Rapids: Baker, 1993); Frank Thielman, *Paul & the Law: A Contextual Approach* (Downers Grove: InterVarsity, 1994); Mark A. Seifrid, *Christ, our Righteousness: Paul's Theology of Justification* (NSBT 9; Downers Grove: InterVarsity, 2000); Seyoon Kim, *Paul and the New Perspective: Second Thoughts on the Origin of Paul's Gospel* (Grand Rapids: Eerdmans, 2002); D. A. Carson, Peter T. O'Brien, Mark A. Seifrid, eds., *The Paradoxes of Paul*, vol. 2 of *Justification and Variegated Nomism* (Grand Rapids: Baker, 2004); Guy P. Waters, *Justification and the New Perspective on Paul*; Stephen Westerholm,

fewer books delving into the details of the Jewish-background arguments and making anti-Sanders arguments.[24] To supplement the imbalance, this book will focus on presenting and critiquing the foundational arguments related to Second Temple Judaism and Sanders' covenantal nomism. That is, the focus of this book will be the first of the 'five points of NPP.' That first point is 'NPP authors agree that Paul was not arguing against a legalistic works righteousness view because it did not exist—that is, they accept Sanders' covenantal nomism.' To say it another way, the central burden of this book is to show that works righteousness views did exist in the first-century A.D. To be clear: My view is *not* that every document or Jewish group was works righteousness oriented. I am simply trying to prove that some were. Once given this, then there is no need to deny that Paul's opponents had these views since this seems to be the straightforward way to take Paul's statements. In sum, if works righteousness views did exist in the first century A.D., then the core belief of NPP crumbles and the logic for a re-interpretation of Paul disappears.

However, there is a difficulty. I have been teaching NT at the same seminary for twenty-three years and know that the entering and graduating seminary students have not read much of the non-canonical ancient Jewish literature. On the other hand, they are well acquainted with the Bible. To aid those not as familiar with

---

Perspectives Old and New on Paul: The 'Lutheran' Paul and His Critics (Grand Rapids: Eerdmans, 2004); Cornelis P. Venema, *The Gospel of Free Acceptance in Christ: An Assessment of the Reformation and 'New Perspectives' on Paul* (Carlisle: Banner of Truth, 2006); John Piper, *The Future of Justification: A Response to N. T. Wright* (Wheaton: Crossway, 2007); R. Scott Clark, ed., *Covenant, Justification, and Pastoral Ministry: Essays by the Faculty of Westminster Seminary California* (Phillipsburg: P&R, 2007); and William B. Barcley with Ligon Duncan, *Gospel Clarity: Challenging the New Perspective on Paul* (Carlisle: EP, 2010).

24. Three excellent books are D. A. Carson, Peter T. O'Brien, Mark A. Seifrid, eds., *The Complexities of Second Temple Judaism*, vol. 1 of *Justification and Variegated Nomism* (Grand Rapids: Baker, 2001); Simon J. Gathercole, *Where is Boasting? Early Jewish Soteriology and Paul's Response in Romans 1-5* (Grand Rapids: Eerdmans, 2002); and Irons, *The Righteousness of God*.

non-canonical ancient Jewish literature and current scholarship's general views about it, I have included a lengthy appendix entitled 'Overview of Judaism's Literary Sources.' The question of works righteousness is *not* addressed in this appendix. This general background, including many primary-source quotes, should aid the reader in better evaluating the relative strengths of Sanders' arguments and my counter-arguments. Some readers should probably read the Appendix before reading Chapters 2 and 3.

To reiterate, the primary focus of this book will not be on Paul per se, but the focus will be the arguments related to the question of works righteousness in Second Temple Judaism. In addition, the meaning of 'works' in Eph. 2:8-10, Titus 3:4-7, and 2 Tim. 1:8-10 will be a secondary focus. Why include these Pauline texts? Although I affirm that these texts are genuine Pauline letters, many scholars do not and designate these as Deutero-Pauline. Hence, these three texts have received minimal attention in pro-and-con NPP debates. I want to fill in this gap.

Intriguingly, many scholars conclude that these three 'Deutero-Pauline' texts *do* contrast grace against works righteousness, and at the same time conclude that Galatians, Romans, and Philippians 3 do *not* contrast grace and works righteousness. I want to explore the implications of this on (1) the supposed uniformity of Sanders' covenantal nomism and (2) the NPP's interpretation of Galatians, Romans, and Philippians 3, especially as it concerns 'works of the law' and 'works.' Therefore, in terms of the 'five points of NPP,' this secondary focus will be on the third point ('works') and its implications for the fifth point (justification).

The primary thesis of this book, then, is that *there are many examples of works righteousness (Pelagian and semi-Pelagian versions) in Second Temple Judaism literature and, therefore, Sanders' uniform coven-antal nomism is mistaken.* Hence, the new-perspective-on-Judaism foundation crumbles and the NPP house comes crashing down. *The secondary thesis is that the NPP is especially vulnerable in its explanations and/or avoidance of Eph. 2:8-10, Titus 3:4-7, and 2 Tim. 1:8-10.*

Finally, I want to make clear that, the ultimate argument that vindicates the Reformed view of justification is made from the

Pauline corpus and other biblical texts themselves. Implications from non-canonical Second Temple Judaism texts may be useful, but they are only fallible aids.[25] Hence, I do not consider the primary thesis of this book as an ultimately adequate argument for justification. I do consider my secondary thesis as more directly related to defending Pauline justification, but I do not cover all of the biblical material. However, as I indicated above, I do believe that my primary and secondary theses considered from the standpoint of the NPP authors' own presuppositions logically destroy their conclusions.

NEW PERSPECTIVE OR NEW PERSPECTIVES?

It is common to say that there is not one new perspective on Paul, but many perspectives. Well, yes and no. For the 'yes' answer: Wright, one of the leading lights, comments that 'there never was a single entity called the "new perspective." It was always a loose movement containing sharply divergent presuppositions, aims, methods, and results.'[26] It is certainly true that there are significant differences among NPP authors. For example, authors differ on Pauline/Deutero-Pauline authorship, biblical inspiration, 'righteousness of God,' historical accuracy of the NT, forensic or participationist emphasis, importance of justification, Paul's consistency, Israel and 'exile' questions, Paul's intended contrast between Christ and Caesar, whether God exists at all (!), etc.

For the 'no' answer: Virtually all self-identified NPP authors agree to four of the 'five points of NPP.' The major divergence as to views only comes in the fifth point, the actual definition of justification—including also its relative importance and relationship to union with Christ. Admittedly, if we looked at other doctrines, the divergence would be expanded.

---

25. As opposed to Scripture interpreting Scripture which is an 'infallible' aid (WCF 1.9).

26. Wright, *Paul and His Recent Interpreters*, 64.

In my own mind, I see all NPP self-identified authors as following Sanders' covenantal nomism and the first four of the five points. Given that, I use Dunn and Wright as the most standard expression of the NPP. Dunn and Wright do not agree on everything and do have significant methodological differences; however, concerning justification (the fifth point), they are reasonably close. Given the standard Dunn/Wright view and placing them center-right on a NPP (or NPsP) continuum, I tend to categorize others to the left or right of Dunn/Wright. For example, I put Räisänen and Zetterholm far to the left and Yinger and Garlington moderately to the right of Dunn/Wright.[27]

Since this book focuses primarily on Sanders with whom all NPP authors substantially agree, the differing NPP views in other areas will not affect this focus. In Chapter 4 that concerns the three 'Deutero-Pauline' texts, I stick to the three NPP stars, Sanders, Dunn, and Wright.

There is an another group of scholars who are interested in Second Temple Judaism and agree with Sanders' covenantal nomism. But they do not put into print their views about Paul, or have significantly different Pauline views from both the traditional and NPP (e.g., 'Apocalyptic Paul,'), or are simply not interested in Paul (some Jewish scholars). In this book, I will simply refer to them as 'pro-Sanders.'

QUICK HISTORY OF NPP AND EVANGELICALISMS

NT scholarship was shaken in 1977 by E. P. Sanders' *Paul and Palestinian Judaism.* Soon after that Wright (1978) and Dunn (1983) published two articles that set the agenda for the NPP.[28] It

---

27. Heikki Räisänen, *Paul & the Law* (Philadelphia: Fortress, 1983); Magnus Zetterholm, *Approaches to Paul: A Student's Guide to Recent Scholarship* (Minneapolis: Fortress, 2009); Yinger, *The New Perspective on Paul*; and Don B. Garlington, *In Defense of the New Perspective on Paul: Essays and Reviews* (Eugene, OR: Wipf & Stock, 2005).

28. E. P. Sanders, *Paul and Palestinian Judaism: A Comparison of Patterns of*

was Dunn's article, 'The New Perspective on Paul,' that originally was more famous and from which the movement was named.[29]

Many self-identified NPP authors were waging war in the Pauline studies arena through the 1980s and 1990s in the English-speaking world. Two different foes were engaged: critical scholars with Bultmann/Lutheran tendencies and traditional Protestant evangelicals, although in print in the early days it was mostly the Bultmann/Lutherans. Standard quasi-evangelical commentary series were then including NPP authors. Dunn himself wrote the Romans WBC commentary (1988), Galatians BNTC commentary (1993), and Colossians NIGTC commentary (1996).[30] The preface to the impressive *Dictionary of Paul and His Letters* (1993), after noting Sanders' book and Dunn's article, suggests that every essayist in the dictionary ought to 'reflect their reaction, whether positive or cautious, to the "new look" on Paul's gospel.'[31] (I note that 'negative' was not mentioned as an option.[32]) Wright comments that in the early 1990s some NPP authors thought they had 'swept the board' of traditional Pauline views.[33]

The 'old perspective' scholarly backlash began in the 1990s and flourished in the first decade of the 2000s. D. A. Carson and Thomas R. Schreiner have been two shining lights here from the evangelical world, although the backlash was from more than

Religion (Minneapolis: Fortress, 1977); N.T. Wright, 'The Paul of History and the Apostle of Faith,' *TynBul* 29 (1978): 61-88; and James D. G. Dunn, 'The New Perspective on Paul,' *BJRL* 65 (1983): 95-122. Wright's early views were developed independently of Sanders, but Sanders' book confirmed them (N. T. Wright, 'New Perspectives on Paul,' in *Justification in Perspective: Historical Developments and Contemporary Challenges* [ed. Bruce L. McCormack; Grand Rapids: Baker, 2006], 243-64, esp. 243-48).

29. Wright and Dunn tell the story that Dunn actually got the name from a lecture by Wright that Dunn heard (*Paul and His Recent Interpreters*, 65 n. 4).

30. He also wrote a commentary on Acts in the non-evangelical series Narrative Commentaries by Trinity Press International.

31. *DPL*, ix.

32. To be fair, many anti-NPP authors contributed to this volume.

33. Wright, *Paul and His Recent Interpreters*, 107.

evangelicals. Carson gave an academic lecture on NPP at my seminary (Reformed Theological Seminary) in the spring of 2005. He told me then privately that he thought, at the academic level, the NPP had reached its high tide and was now retreating—and he was right, as usual! That is not to say that the NPP is going away soon, but its grip has lessened in the critical and evangelical academic world.

At the evangelical pastor/church level, there was much confusion in the 1980s through about 2005 due to the complicated nature of NPP views on justification. As opposed to other NPP scholars, pro-NPP evangelicals were/are especially attached to Wright due to his conservative historical methodology and conclusions, his orthodox theological views on most issues, and his engaging writing style.[34] Back then, many evangelicals personally told me that they agreed with Wright, but they also fully affirmed justification as presented in WCF 11. It was often claimed by pro-Wright evangelicals that the anti-NPP crowd did not fully understand Wright. We were not willing to give 'Wright a sustained and sympathetic reading.'[35] As the Dunn/Wright views became more clear, at least on justification, several American, conservative Reformed denominations adopted reports critical of the NPP between 2005 through 2010.[36]

As said above, the NPP is not going away soon. In 2013, Wright produced a massive, 1658-page volume on Paul, *Paul and the Faithfulness of God* and in 2015 its companion, *Paul and His Recent*

---

34. Clearly, Wright is an evangelical, or as I would term it, a 'left-leaning evangelical.'

35. This was claimed about me based on my distributed handouts from class lectures and conference addresses—and it was true as far as justification was concerned! See Rich Lusk, 'N. T. Wright and Reformed Theology: Friends or Foes?,' *Reformation & Revival Journal* 11/2 (2002): 35-52, esp. 35, 47 n. 2. To Lusk's point, I do agree that then many anti-NPP evangelicals did not fully understand Wright's complicated view of justification and its relationship to the Gospel. See Chapter 4 for more details of this relationship in the Wright section.

36. E.g., Orthodox Presbyterian Church (2006), Presbyterian Church in America (2007), and Associate Reformed Presbyterian Church (2009). I am an ordained minister in the latter denomination.

Interpreters.[37] Any scholar in the English-speaking world writing on Romans, Galatians, Philippians 3, and justification still has to, and should, deal with the NPP.

Currently, at the evangelical pastor/church level, pastors, no matter their stand on NPP, will be reading commentaries that interact with NPP; hence, they need to understand the general arguments. Also, pastors still need to be able to interact with other pastors and parishoners who ask questions about NPP.

From my perspective as an anti-NPP author, significant progress in refuting the NPP has been made in the Reformed Presbyterian and Reformed Baptist pastor/church worlds; however, there are still many evangelicals who are attracted to the NPP. A major reason I wrote this book is to clarify NPP issues for evangelicals especially as they relate to Sanders' covenantal nomism. Of course, I hope that all readers conclude that Sanders and the resulting NPP view of justification is misguided.

Finally, let me emphasize, as I often do in many different contexts, that my strong disagreements with the NPP relate to *justification*—and since I consider justification as very important for the health of the church, I have grave concerns about this. Otherwise, I truly enjoy reading Dunn, Wright, etc. as they are stimulating and have beneficial insights on a host of different micro-exegetical and global issues. Even when I disagree, I benefit from being forced to re-examine my own particular view against these well-nuanced foils that truly care about exegeiss and theology.

OUTLINE OF THE BOOK

Chapter 2 is entitled 'Works Righteousness: Reformed Theology and Covenantal Nomism Frameworks.' Before looking directly at the Second Temple Judaism primary sources, having a clear understanding of theological terms and competing theological frameworks is helpful. To accomplish this, an explanation of Reformed theology's broad covenantal framework is presented.

---

37. N. T. Wright, *Paul and the Faithfulness of God* (Minneapolis: Fortress, 2013); *Paul and His Recent Interpreters* (Minneapolis: Fortress, 2015).

Explanations are given of various Reformed terms/categories including works righteousness, covenant of works, covenant of grace, justification, second and third uses of the law, and final judgment.[38] Following this, an explanation of Sanders' ground-breaking *Paul and Palestinian Judaism* and his covenantal-nomism framework is included. Once given the understanding of the two frameworks, I begin the critique of Sanders. This critique concentrates not on specific documents but is a preliminary broad-brush analysis of 'conflicting data' within the covenantal-nomism framework. I present Sanders' explanation for the conflicting data and then mine.

Chapter 3, 'Works Righteousness in Jewish Literature?,' is the heart of my critique against Sanders. Using the two frameworks, I look closely at thirteen Second Temple Judaism documents with representatives from each of the literary categories. Each of these documents on the surface appears to confirm works righteousness. As in the previous chapter, I present Sanders' explanation (when available) and then mine for each document. I conclude that all thirteen documents confirm either a Pelagian or semi-Pelagian view of works righteousness. (This not to say that all of Second Temple Judaism was works righteousness oriented.) This chapter confirms that there is an abundance of works righteousness soteriology in Second Temple Judaism; therefore, covenantal nomism, the foundation of the NPP, has crumbled.

Chapter 4 evaluates 'works' in Eph. 2:8-10, Titus 3:4-7, and 2 Tim. 1:8-10 and is entitled, 'Works Righteousness in "Deutero-Paul"?' As mentioned previously, NPP authors are vulnerable here as to the implications on (1) the supposed uniformity of Sanders' covenantal nomism and (2) the interpretation of 'works of the law' and 'works' in Galatians, Romans, and Philippians 3. Concerning the three 'Deutero-Paul' texts, this chapter first presents the views of three non-NPP, non-Reformed scholars; second, my detailed exegesis; and third, the views of Sanders, Dunn, and Wright.

---

38. Of course, Reformed theology believes that these categories are biblical at the conceptual level.

Finally, my critical evaluation of Sanders, Dunn, and Wright's views concludes that Paul's use of 'works' in these three texts further confirms that works righteousness existed in Second Temple Judaism. In addition, I conclude that one's exegesis of justification by faith in Galatians, Romans, and Philippians 3 should reflect this.

Chapter 5, 'Summary,' brings together the arguments and conclusions of the book. The primary conclusion being that logically the foundation of covenantal nomism has crumbled and the house of NPP built upon that foundation has come crashing down.

The Appendix is entitled 'Overview of Judaism's Literary Sources.' This appendix orients the reader to historical issues, various movements, and the categories of literature of Second Temple Judaism. Also, specific discussions and quotes of selected documents are included. The design of this chapter is to prepare the reader to better understand the arguments pro-and-con related to Sanders' covenantal nomism. The question of works righteousness is bracketed out of this chapter. This appendix is included for those less familiar with Second Temple Judaism and should probably be read before reading Chapters 2 and 3.

CHAPTER 2:

WORKS RIGHTEOUSNESS: REFORMED AND COVENANTAL-NOMISM FRAMEWORKS

I once gave several NPP lectures at a large conference for minis-
ters. Before explaining Sanders, someone asked me, 'Isn't
Sanders' covenantal nomism and its emphasis on works *the same as*
the Reformed emphasis on the third use of the law?' I responded,
'Well ... I see why you might say that, but the same? ... no.'[1]
Another minister asked, 'I know I learned this in seminary, but
what is the third use of the law?'

---

1. Contrary to me, N. T. Wright does see the connection between Sanders
   and the third use as very close. Wright and I disagree on Sanders, not the
   definition of third use. '[In Sanders' system,] good works are simply gratitude,
   and demonstrate that one is faithful to the covenant—a sort of primitive
   version of the *tertius usus legis* [third use of the law]' ('The Paul of History and
   the Apostle of Faith,' *TynBul* 29 [1978]: 61-88, esp. 80).

INTRODUCTION

NPP authors claim that first-century Judaism was not works righteousness oriented. Any interpretation of Paul that assumes Paul is arguing against works righteousness is mistaken because a work-righteousness view did not exist in Paul's opponents. Consequently, especially concerning justification by faith, the traditional-Protestant view is wrong, and Paul needs to be re-interpreted.[2] It is this core belief about Judaism that unifies NPP authors.[3]

As stated in the previous chapter, the central burden of this book is to show that works righteousness views did exist in the first-century A.D. To be clear: My view is *not* that every document or Jewish group was works righteousness oriented. I am simply trying to prove that some were. Once given this, then there is no need to deny that Paul's opponents had these views since this seems to be the straightforward way to take Paul's statements. In sum, if works righteousness views did exist in the first-century A.D., then the core belief of NPP crumbles and the logic for a re-interpretation of Paul disappears.

Now to the point of this chapter. Before looking directly at the primary sources, a clear understanding of theological terms and competing broad-theological frameworks will be helpful. This will aid the reader to understand better my evaluation of the sources and allow the reader to compare and contrast my evaluation with

---

2. 'If the church developed in a matrix of Judaism and the mother was very different from what we have imagined and described, then we must reconsider the nature of the child' (George W. E. Nickelsburg, *Ancient Judaism and Christian Origins* [Minneapolis: Fortress, 2003], 3). Nickelsburg is a pro-Sanders author and in context is speaking about more than the interpretation of Paul.

3. Stephen Westerholm agrees, 'The conviction most central to the "new perspective on Paul" pertains in the first place to Judaism, not Paul' (*Perspectives Old and New on Paul: The 'Lutheran' Paul and His Critics* [Grand Rapids: Eerdmans, 2004], 178). Westerholm is an anti-NPP author. James D. G. Dunn lists four aspects of the NPP of which the first is 'The new perspective on Paul arises from a new perspective on Judaism' ('New Perspective View,' in *Justification: Five Views* [ed. James K Beilby and Paul Rhodes Eddy; Downers Grove: IVP Academic, 2011], 176-201, esp. 177).

NPP's evaluation. In addition to defining 'works righteousness,' I will present the Reformed framework and Sanders' framework, which he terms 'covenantal nomism.' Sanders' covenantal nomism is the NPP's grid for understanding Judaism's soteriology.

Again, I will admit my presuppositions.[4] I have a very 'high' view of the Bible and am convinced that traditional Reformed theology is the best understanding of the Bible. Concerning the below explanation of the traditional Reformed framework, I will not be defending it as much as simply explaining it. In the explanation of Sanders' covenantal nomism, I will also include a preliminary broad-brush critique. The specifics of the critique will be fleshed out in the next chapter in the evaluation of the primary sources.

DEFINITION OF LEGALISTIC WORKS RIGHTEOUSNESS

When I use the term 'works righteousness,' I am implying '*legalistic* works righteousness.' Others use synonyms such as 'self-righteous' or 'meritorious works righteousness.' Unfortunately, in the literature, the term 'works righteousness' and its synonyms are often used in a somewhat loose way. Hence, a clear definition is needed before proceeding.

In the 21st-century church contexts, the adjective 'legalistic' is used in several different ways. First, I will give three examples of how I am *not* using 'legalistic.' For example, one might say, 'Forbidding one from going to the movies is legalistic.' Here, the complaint is

---

4. For ultimate arguments, that is, those at the most basic level of one's worldview, I believe that some level of circularity is required. Cornelius Van Til states, 'To admit one's own presuppositions and to point out the presuppositions of others is therefore to maintain that all reasoning is, in the nature of the case, *circular reasoning.* The starting point, the method, and the conclusion are always involved in one another' (*The Defense of the Faith* [3d ed.; Philadelphia: Presbyterian and Reformed, 1967], 101, italics his). John M. Frame helpfully distinguishes between arguments that use 'narrow' (bad) and 'broad' (good) circles; broad-circle arguments will include significant amounts of data in addition to the presuppositions (*The Doctrine of the Knowledge of God* [A Theology of Lordship; Phillipsburg: Presbyterian and Reformed, 1987], 130-33). Or as I say it, 'Biases are not bad; bad biases are bad.'

that extra-biblical rules are being enforced and implying that they should not be.[5] A second example: 'Affirming that it is ethical to go five miles over the speed limit because the police only stop you for going ten miles over is a legalistic argument.' This use of 'legalistic' is similar to a casuistic argument—overly subtle distinctions usually intended to mislead or gain an advantage.[6] A third example: 'Your extreme concern over the quality of the communion plates is legalistic.' Here, the problem is on an over-emphasis on externals and rituals to please God as opposed to the heart.[7]

The above three uses of 'legalistic' are legitimate, but I am using 'legalistic' in the sense that it relates to laws and a law court. Legalistic works righteousness refers to works done to fulfill a law and works that are declared righteous by a judge. More specifically in our context, *a works righteousness theology means that one's works are, in part or the whole, the ground by which God the Judge declares one righteous (justification) and qualified to enter the afterlife.*

Note that included in my definition of works righteousness is 'in part or the whole.' That is, whether one's theology combines aspects of grace and works righteousness together ('in part') or is a crass complete-human-merit theology ('the whole') for justification, both of these are works righteousness theologies from a traditional-Protestant perspective.[8]

To use anachronistic terms, if justification is based on a combination of grace from God and human works, then it is considered

---

5. Rabbinic Judaism saw 'fences' around the law as good. Hence 'tradition' that went beyond the law was a 'fence' that prevented one from violating the law. See *m. Abot* 1:1, 3:13. Compare Mark 7:1-12, Matt. 15:1-9, and *WCF* 20, 'Of Christian Liberty, and Liberty of Conscience.'

6. Rabbinic Judaism is often accused of using casuistic arguments. For example, one is bound by a vow made by the utensils of the altar, but one is not bound by a vow made by Jerusalem (*m. Nedarim* 1:3). Compare Matt. 5:33-37, 23:16-22.

7. Again, Rabbinic Judaism is accused of concentrating on externals. The Bible often condemns this. See Isa. 29:13 // Matt. 15:8, Hosea 6:6, Micah 6:6-8, Matt. 5:21-30, 15:1-9, 23:25.

8. Of course, I would argue that the traditional-Protestant perspective is Paul's perspective!

semi-Pelagianism. If based on works-only, it is considered Pelagianism. Both are legalistic works righteousness.[9] To be more detailed, Warfield defines Pelagianism as a theological system that 'denies the native guilt, pollution, and moral impotence of man, and makes him independent of the supernatural assistance of God.' Semi-Pelagianism is an 'elastic system of compromise' between Augustinianism/ Calvinism and Pelaginism. Semi-Pelagianism 'admits man's original pollution but denies his native guilt … and refers the moral restoration of the individual to the co-operation of human and divine energy, the determining factor being the human will.'[10]

Why concentrate on the traditional Protestant definition of works righteousness? Primarily, because it is true! But in addition, pro-Sanders and NPP authors often condemn it in their writings.[11] Fair enough; however, I rarely get the sense that they fully understand it.[12] Usually what they are condemning is a Pelagian version of works righteousness and exhibit no or little awareness of the semi-Pelagian

---

9. Pelagius was a British theologian in the late 4th and early 5th centuries who clashed with Augustine over original sin and the place of works in salvation. Semi-Pelagianism is popularly used to designate theologies that combine grace and works. The Lutheran Formula of Concord condemns by name both of these (Epitome, Art. 2, negative 2-3).

10. B. B. Warfield, 'Calvinism,' in *Selected Shorter Writings: Benjamin B. Warfield* (ed. John E. Meeter; 2 vols.; Phillipsburg: P&R, 1970-1973), 2:411-47, esp. 411-12.

11. Don Garlington, a pro-NPP author, disagrees with me and claims that the NPP 'isn't an "attack" on the Reformation' (*In Defense of the New Perspective on Paul: Essays and Reviews* [Eugene: Wipf and Stock, 2005], 9-13, esp. 9). James D. G. Dunn also says that the NPP in general is not to be seen as 'hostile or antithetical to the "old perspective"' ('New Perspective View,' 176). However, concerning justification per se, it is antithetical to and an attack on traditional-Protestant theology because (1) there is no imputed righteousness of Christ to ensure that human works are not involved and (2) traditional-Protestant theology sees the doctrine of justification as very important as opposed to many, but not all, in the NPP who downplay justification (whatever way they define it). More on Dunn and Wright's views of justification in Chapter 4.

12. See Aaron T. O'Kelley, *Did the Reformers Misread Paul? A Historical-Theological Critique of the New Perspective* (Eugene, OR: Wipf & Stock, 2014).

version. N. T. Wright in *What Saint Paul Really Said* constantly refers to those who mistakenly see Judaism as 'Pelagianism,' 'moral bootstraps,' and 'Jewish self-help moralism.' However, there is no mention of semi-Pelagianism.[13] (Although, I agree that some do present Judaism in an unbalanced Pelagian manner.[14])

Also, many times the traditional Protestant view is dismissed with the footnotes relating not to Luther, nor Calvin, nor well-known creeds, nor modern evangelical authors, but instead to Rudolf Bultmann, who is in the critical-liberal Lutheran tradition.[15] Bultmann does have continuity with the traditional-Protestant view of justification, but he also has many idiosyncracies.[16] Finally, many NPP authors complain in broad-brush comments that the Reformers read their view of the theology of the Roman Catholic church back into the first-century A.D. situation.[17] Again, if aspects

13. *What Paul Really Said: Was Paul of Tarsus the Real Founder of Christianity?* (Grand Rapids: Eerdmans, 1997), 20, 32, 35, 113, 116, 119, 120, 121, 126, 129, 160. See James M. Hamilton's critique of this, 'N. T. Wright and Saul's Moral Bootstraps: Newer Light on "The New Perspective,"' *TrinJ* n.s. 25 (2004): 139-55. William B. Barcley with Ligon Duncan pick up on this also in Wright (*Gospel Clarity: Challenging the New Perspective on Paul* [Carlisle: EP, 2010], 61).

14. For example, see the critical-German scholar Eduard Lohse, *The New Testament Environment* (trans. John E. Steely; Nashville: Abingdon, 1976), 183-87.

15. In James D. G. Dunn's seminal article, he footnotes Bultmann and Käsemann and complains about the 'Lutheran hermeneutic' ('The New Perspective on Paul,' *BJRL* 65 [1983]: 95-122, esp. 99, 99 n. 14). E. P. Sanders also presents Bultmann as the paradigm of the view he is against (*Paul and Palestinian Judaism: A Comparison of Patterns of Religion* [Minneapolis: Fortress, 1977], 3-4, 39, 46, 493-94). According to Sanders, a line can be drawn from F. Weber's eighteenth-century views to Bultmann's (*Paul and Palestinian Judaism*, 33-46).

16. Rudolf Bultmann, *Theology of the New Testament* (trans. Kendrick Grobel; 2 vols.; New York: Scribner's, 1951, 1955), 1:270-79; and *Primitive Christianity in its Contemporary Setting* (trans. R. H. Fuller; London: Thames and Hudson, 1956), 59-71.

17. 'The Reformers' interpretation of Paul rests on an analogism when Pauline statements about Faith and Works, Law and Gospel, Jews and Gentiles are read in the framework of late medieval piety' (Krister Stendahl, 'The

of first-century A.D. Judaism are semi-Pelagian, then the parallel to Roman Catholic theology is apt from my perspective.[18] Also, the Reformers assumed that Judaism (and Roman Catholicism) contained crass versions of 'official' semi-Pelagianism that were Pelagian.

REFORMED FRAMEWORK

COVENANT OF WORKS AND COVENANT OF GRACE

Reformed theology's understanding of the history of redemption and the place of 'law' in that history is related to covenants. Traditional Reformed theology has two overarching covenants

---

Apostle Paul and the Introspective Conscience of the West,' *HTR* 56 (1963): 199-215, esp. 206-7). Similarly Sanders, 'We have here the retrojection of the Protestant-Catholic debate into ancient history, with Judaism taking the role of Catholicism and Christianity the role of Lutheranism' (*Paul and Palestinian Judaism*, 57); and James D. G. Dunn, 'Since Paul's teaching on justification by faith seems to speak so directly to Luther's subjective wrestlings, it was a natural corollary to see Paul's opponents in terms of the unreformed Catholicism, which opposed Luther, with first century Judaism read through the "grid" of the early 16th century Catholic system of merit' ('The New Perspective on Paul,' *BJRL* 65 [1983]: 95-122, esp. 98).

18. From my perspective, traditional Roman Catholic theology is semi-Pelagian. See Council of Trent, Decree of Justification, esp. chapter 16, canons 9, 11, 24; *Catechism of the Catholic Church*, Merit, esp. § 2006, 2010. B. B. Warfield calls the Trent system, 'semi-semi-pelagianism' (*Plan of Salvation* [Boonton, NJ: Simpson, 1989 {1915}], 30). The Lutheran Formula of Concord does connect 'Pharisaic and Papist confidence in their own works and merits' (Epitome 4, negative 2). Guy Prentiss Waters notes, 'While we must appreciate the differences between late-medieval soteriology and ancient Judaism, we must also recognize their fundamental soteriological identity: both are semi-Pelagian systems' (*Justification and the New Perspectives on Paul* (Phillipsburg: P&R, 2004), 58. Herman Bavinck complains that although Rome has in one sense rejected semi-Pelagianism, its use of prevenient grace has 'again smuggled [it] back in' (*Reformed Dogmatics* [trans. John Vriend; ed. John Bolt; 4 vols.; Grand Rapids: Baker, 2003-08 {2d. ed. 1906-11}], 3:514). R. Michael Allen notes that the 'Reformers sometimes referred to their opponents as semi-Pelagians [as opposed to Pelagians]' (*Justification and the Gospel: Understanding the Contexts and Controversies* [Grand Rapids: Baker, 2013], 109).

that both span the history of redemption, the Covenant of Works and the Covenant of Grace.[19] One of these overarching covenants, the Covenant of Grace, is progressively revealed in several sub-set covenants: post-fall Adam, Noah, Abraham, Moses, David, and New.

The Covenant of Works is a works righteousness covenant and related to biblical terms 'law,' 'do,' 'works,' 'righteousness of the law,' 'justified by works,' 'works of the law,' 'curse of the law,' etc. when Paul is contrasting two methods of salvation. The Covenant of Grace is a grace covenant and associated with biblical terms 'grace,' 'blood of Christ,' 'faith,' 'righteousness of faith,' 'righteousness of God,' 'justification,' 'righteousness apart from works,' 'gospel,' etc. when Paul is contrasting two methods of salvation (e.g., Rom. 3:22, 4:2, 4:6, 5:1, 5:9, 5:18, 10:3, 10:5-8, 1 Cor. 15:48, 2 Cor. 5:21, Gal. 2:16, 3:10-13, Eph. 2:8-10, Phil. 3:9, 1 Thess. 1:8, 5:9, 2 Thess. 2:16, 1 Tim. 1:15-16, 2 Tim. 1:9-10, Titus 2:11-14, 3:5-8, Philem. 3, 25).

Although differences exist, these two overarching covenants, the Covenant of Works and the Covenant of Grace, have many similarities with the Lutheran 'Law / Gospel' distinction as both Law and Gospel also span redemptive history.[20] Many modern-day

---

19. 'Two overarching covenants' is my terminology. Often this is referred to as 'bi-covenantal' or 'federal theology.'

20. 'The distinction between law and gospel is a particularly glorious light. It serves to divide God's Word properly and to explain correctly and make understandable the writings of the holy prophets and apostles' (Formula of Concord, Solid Declaration, 5). For a defense of the Law / Gospel distinction from a traditional Lutheran perspective, see John Theodore Mueller, *Christian Dogmatics: A Handbook of Doctrinal Theology for Pastors, Teachers, and Laymen* (St. Louis: Concordia, 1955), 470-85 and C. F. W. Walther, *The Proper Distinction between the Law and the Gospel: Thirty-Nine Evening Lectures* (trans. W. H. T. Dau; St. Louis: Concordia, 1928). The Reformed tradition also includes a Law / Gospel distinction, but this generally gets subsumed into the Covenant of Works and Covenant of Grace framework. Also, Reformed theology emphasizes the third use of the law which reduces the absoluteness of the 'law' portion of Law / Gospel. See L. Berkhof, *Systematic Theology* (4th ed; Grand Rapids: Eerdmans, 1941), 612-14 and J. van Genderen and W. H. Velema, *Concise Reformed Dogmatics* (trans. Gerrit Bilkes and Ed M. van

Evangelicals who are not as firmly rooted in either the Reformed or Lutheran traditions also have similarities to the two overarching covenants. They agree that throughout the OT and NT all are under the penalty of sin and Christ had to die for sin. No one is saved by works. Also, they agree that salvation is by grace through faith based upon the work of Christ, even for OT saints. These views have significant overlap with the Reformed view. Hence, even though I will be evaluating the primary sources through the grid of Reformed theology, my conclusions should resonate with traditional Lutherans and various Evangelicals.

Allow me a few more specifics on the Covenant of Works. In traditional Reformed theology, the term Covenant of Works (or Covenant of Life or Nature) refers to an agreement between God and man 'wherein life was promised to Adam, and in him to his posterity, upon condition of perfect and personal obedience.'[21] Therefore, this is a works righteousness covenant. Adam subsequently sins and all mankind falls with him. After Adam's sin, God makes a Covenant of Grace 'whereby [the Lord] freely offereth unto sinners life and salvation by Jesus Christ, requiring of them faith in him' (WCF 7.3).

Although after Adam's fall no human ('by ordinary generation'[22]) can fulfill the Covenant of Works as sin affects them, certain aspects of this covenant are still in force. All humans are still under the obligation to perfect obedience of the law and are

---

der Maas; Phillipsburg: P&R, 2008), 779. John M. Frame believes the Reformed tradition should eliminate the Law / Gospel terminology and emphasis (*The Doctrine of the Christian Life* [Phillipsburg: P&R, 2008), 182-91.

21. WCF 7.2, also see WLC 20, WSC 12, Belgic Confession 14, Sum of Saving Knowledge 1.2; Francis Turretin, *Institutes of Elenctic Theology* (trans. George Musgrave Giger, ed. James T. Dennison, Jr.; 3 vols.; Phillipsburg: P&R, 1992-97 [1679-85]), 1:574-78; L. Berkhof, *Systematic Theology*, 211-18; and John M. Frame, *Systematic Theology: An Introduction to Christian Belief* (Phillipsburg: P&R, 2013), 62-66.

22. A great phrase from the Westminster Standards to include all of humanity except Christ (e.g., WCF 6.3).

liable to the penalty of death for sin.[23] This obligation and penalty exist all through redemptive history, although the fulfilling of it is only theoretical for those infected by original and actual sins. The final judgment of works for unbelievers is based on the Covenant of Works. Even Christ is under the Covenant of Works, but He gloriously fulfills these requirements for the elect with His life and death. Therefore, by grace, based on the work of Christ, and through the instrument of faith in the person and work of Christ, a sinner moves from being under the curse of the Covenant of Works to the blessings of the Covenant of Grace (Eph. 2:1-10).

Given that the various sub-set covenants are part of the Covenant of Grace, is there a secondary sense that obligations in these covenants have works righteousness aspects? Or to ask it another way, is there some sense that the Covenant of Works is included, albeit in a secondary way, in the various covenants that are included in the Covenant of Grace? Usually, this question is most acute for the Mosaic Covenant. Although not uniformly, traditional Reformed theology has answered, 'yes,' there is some secondary sense that a works principle is in the Covenant of Grace.[24] This is confirmed by the NT's use of OT laws to present the requirements that are substantially in the Covenant of Works. WCF 7.2 foot-notes Paul's use of Lev. 18:5 ('do this and live') from the Mosaic Covenant in Rom. 10:5 and Gal. 3:12 to confirm the Covenant of Works with Adam. Paul argues that Lev. 18:5 is 'righteousness based on law' and contrasts this with 'righteousness based on faith'

---

23. 'After the fall, God lays a double claim on humans: that of the payment of a penalty for the evil done and that of perfect obedience to his law (satisfaction and obedience)' (Bavinck, *Reformed Dogmatics*, 3:226).

24. Brenton C. Ferry has an excellent summary of the significant variety of ways in history that Reformed scholars have characterized the relationship between the Covenant of Works and the Mosaic Covenant ('Works in the Mosaic Covenant: A Reformed Taxonomy,' in *The Law is not of Faith: Essays on Works and Grace in the Mosaic Covenant* [ed. Bryan D. Estelle, J. V. Fesko, and David VanDrunen; Phillipsburg: P&R, 2009], 76-106). As to my view, no, I do not believe in the 'republication' view, although my view has continuity with it. As will be seen in the next section, I prefer to use second and third use of the law as my primary grid.

(Deut. 30:14 // Rom. 10:6-8, Hab. 2:4 // Gal. 3:11) as two methods of salvation (note that *both* the law/works and faith options are proved from OT texts).[25] Jesus' use of the ten commandments in the Rich Young Ruler episode (Matt. 19:16-22) is often also cited as a works righteousness option in the NT.[26] Although hotly debated, many Reformed scholars see Rom. 2:13-15 ('doers of the law will be justified') as evidence of the continuing theoretical option of fulfilling the Covenant of Works.[27] Except for Christ, after Adam's fall, no one has the real option of fulfilling the Covenant of Works because of sin and because the ultimate purpose of the law was not to give life (Gal. 3:21).

The issue of the continuing relevance of the demands of the Covenant of Works relates to the 'second use of the law,' which will be my next topic.

SECOND AND THIRD USE OF THE LAW

Introduction

Important aspects of the Reformed framework for discussing works righteousness are the expressions 'second use of the law' and the 'third use of the law.'

Reformation scholars noticed that the NT writers tended to use 'moral' laws (e.g., do not murder, love your neighbor) in three different ways.[28] These moral laws could be from the OT or from the NT. The three uses are traditionally numbered as follows: (1st) magistrate or external restraint, (2nd) pedagogical or revealing sin (with the hope of driving one to Christ), and (3rd) guide to

---

25. N. T. Wright interprets righteousness of the law (Rom. 10:5) and righteousness of faith (Rom. 10:6) as *not* contrasting in Rom. 10:5-8 ('The Letter to the Romans: Introduction, Commentary, and Reflections,' in *The New Interpreter's Bible* [vol. 10; Nashville: Abingdon, 2002], 659-60).

26. E.g., Bavinck, *Reformed Dogmatics*, 3:226.

27. Footnote to WLC 92.

28. The three uses of the (moral) law is not to be confused with the standard categorization of OT laws into the 'moral' (e.g., do not lie), 'ceremonial' (e.g., sacrificial laws), and 'civil/judicial' (e.g., property laws). See WCF 19.3-5.

the Christian life.[29] The moral law also shows us aspects of God's character, but that is not in focus for the three uses of the law.[30]

The magistrate use refers to a government official using a moral law for a governmental law. For example, 'do not murder' should be a criminal law. Of course, not all moral laws can be made into governmental laws as 'do not covet' shows. Examples of the first use are not numerous in the NT (see Rom. 13:1-7, 1 Tim. 1:8-11, 1 Pet. 2:13-14). This first use will not be used in my subsequent analysis.

Second Use of the Law

The second use presupposes the requirements of the Covenant of Works, that is, one must be perfectly righteous to inherit eternal life and that a penalty awaits one who sins. The second use is designed to show us our sin and required penalty, and thereby it drives us to the need of Christ for our sinful state. Calvin says, 'While it shows us God's righteousness, that is, the righteousness alone acceptable to God; it warns, informs, convicts, and lastly condemns, every man of his own righteousness.'[31] Classic passages in Paul are Rom. 3:20, 7:7, and Gal. 3:19. Jesus' discussion with the Rich Young Ruler is another classic example (Matt. 19:16-22).

The second use of the law often operates as follows. Sally believes that she is a good person. She also vaguely assumes that if there is a God, she is righteous enough for heaven. She reads the ninth commandment, 'do not lie,' and is struck by how often she has lied and not cared about the God whose command she is violating.

---

29. The standard numbering system is based on Formula of Concord 6. Calvin has the same three uses but reverses the first two in the order of his presentation (*Institutes of the Christian Religion* 2.7.6-13).

30. In addition to telling us what we should do, the law 'do not lie' tells us about God's character, he does not lie. WLC 95 includes 'to inform [men] of the *holy nature* and will of God' as aspects of the moral law (italics mine).

31. Calvin, *Institutes of the Christian Religion*, 2.7.6. Translation from Ford Lewis Battles, *Calvin: Institutes of the Christian Religion* (Library of Christian Classics 20; ed. John T. McNeill; trans. Ford Lewis Battles; Philadelphia: Westminster, 1960), 354. Also see WLC 96 and Heidelberg Catechism 3.

This then leads to her questioning whether she is righteous enough for heaven. Hopefully, she sees that Christ is the answer. Her sin is legally imputed to Christ and Christ's righteous life is legally imputed to her. She repents and places her faith in Him.

As explained above, the second use relates to the unregenerate. However, it also relates to the regenerate, although not as under the Covenant of Works because the regenerate have moved to the Covenant of Grace.[32] Here, the second use of the law shows the regenerate his continuing sin and re-reminds him of Christ's work on his behalf. This produces repentance and further thankfulness to the Triune God.[33]

Third Use of the Law

The third use of the law is aimed at only the regenerate. Here, God's moral law from both the OT and NT is a guide to the Christian life.[34] A believer learns or is re-reminded of God's revealed will and is aroused to obedience. The believer has the correct motivations to fulfill God's law. He is not doing it for merit or to fulfill the Covenant of Works, but primarily out of love for God and thankfulness for God's past, present, and future redemptive work, along with the conscious knowledge that it is the Holy Spirit aiding him in his good works.[35] 'If you love me, you will keep my commandments' (John 14:15).

---

32. 'Although true believers be not under the law as a covenant of works, to be thereby justified or condemned; yet is it of great use to them' (WCF 19.6).

33. See WCF 19.6, WLC 97, Heidelberg Catechism 115.

34. For Calvin's discussion of the third use, see *Institutes of the Christian Religion*, 2.7.12. Also see Herman Ridderbos' classic discussion of the third use in Paul, *Paul: An Outline of His Theology* (trans. John Richard DeWitt; Grand Rapids: Eerdmans, 1975), 278-88.

35. The Bible contains many different motivations for obeying the third use of the law. One secondary motivation is to be a good worker for an unbelieving master so that name of God will not be reviled (1 Tim. 6:1). Of course, there are other more important motivations to be a good worker. John M. Frame gives three large categories of motivations to do good works: History of Redemption, Authority of God's Commands, and Presence of the Spirit (*Systematic Theology*, 1104-06).

One argument for the third use is that the NT quotes various OT 'moral' laws and simply assumes that a Christian is to obey them. For example, Paul tells children to obey their parents and then quotes the fifth commandment (Eph. 6:1-2). In a discussion of the Holy Spirit in a believer's life and obeying the 'whole law,' Paul quotes Lev. 19:18 ('love your neighbor as yourself') (Gal. 5:14-16, cf. Rom. 13:8-10). In Rom. 12:19-21, Paul uses the guidance of Prov. 25:21-22 to recommend a course of action for interacting with an enemy.

Back to Sally. She is now a Christian and is planning on doing her taxes in the afternoon. That morning she reads the 9th commandment ('do not lie') and meditates on its many applications to her life. She realizes the implications for her taxes. Although Sally was not planning on cutting corners to begin with, she asks the Holy Spirit to aid her and is confirmed and strengthened in her resolve to glorify God by completing her tax forms with integrity. This is the third use of the law.

How does one know if a moral law is to be used as third use or second use? I believe that every moral law has both second and third use implications depending on the reader. The same moral law having a variety of uses is not unusual. Paul uses the seventh commandment for all three uses of the law; first use, 1 Tim. 1:10; second use, Rom. 7:7, 2:22 with 3:20; and third use, Rom. 13:9. How does this work exegetically? I first determine the primary use of the moral law in its immediate context and assume that the other uses are secondary, but these secondary uses are still legitimate. For example, I consider the Sermon on the Mount as directed to believers and the commands (e.g., the 'golden rule,' Matt. 7:12) to be the third use of the law. However, if one is not a believer, or a believer who needs significant correction, the commands in the Sermon on the Mount are second use. Therefore, for me in this example, the second use is secondary in the Sermon on the Mount, but still legitimate. If I were preaching a sermon on the 'golden rule,' as a generality, I would emphasize the third use but definitely include the second use.

Second and Third Use: Equal Condemnation of the Lutherans and Reformed?

As noted previously, many comments are found in pro-Sanders and NPP authors condemning more of the Lutheran tradition, or at least the critical-liberal version, rather than the Reformed. How does this relate to the second and third use of the law?

Although the third use is in historic Lutheran creeds, the Lutheran tradition has always significantly emphasized the second use over the third use, and some in the Lutheran tradition, even the conservative Lutheran tradition, go further and deny the third use.[36] This emphasis or outright denial matches to the Law / Gospel distinction where Law is the second use of the law. In the critical-liberal Lutheran tradition, there is even more of a denial of the third use.

In the Reformed tradition, both the second use and third use are emphasized. The second use is included within the Covenant of Works, and the third use is included as part of the Covenant of Grace. Given that Lutherans de-emphasize the third use or deny it, the Reformed tradition, relatively speaking, emphasizes it.[37] Also, the Reformed tradition connects law to Covenant, and the Lutheran tradition does not.

---

36. The Lutheran Formula of Concord 6 explicitly affirms the third use, although Epitome 6.5 seems to soften it. From my perspective, Luther's Small Catechism and Larger Catechism are in essence third-use documents, although many Lutherans deny Luther agreed to the third use. For articles by traditional Lutherans arguing both for and against the third use, see *CTQ* 69 (2005): 187-308, especially see the excellent summary article, Lawrence R. Rast, 'The Third Use of the Law: Keeping Up to Date with an Old Issue,' *CTQ* 69 (2005): 187-90.

37. Calvin termed the third use as the 'principal use' (*Institutes of the Christian Religion* 2.7.12). For a comparison of Lutheran and Reformed emphases in the uses of the law from a Reformed perspective, see G. C. Berkouwer, *Sin* (trans. Philip C. Holtrop; Studies in Dogmatics; Grand Rapids: Eerdmans, 1971), 156-86. Historical scholars often note that Calvin developed his three uses of the law from Melanchthon's work (see Timothy Wengert, 'Biblical Interpretation in the Works of Philip Melanchthon,' in *The Medieval through the Reformation Periods* [ed. Alan J. Hauser and Duane F. Watson; vol. 2 of *A History of Biblical Interpretation*; Grand Rapids: Eerdmans, 2009], 319-40, esp. 328).

Again, why is there more condemnation and complaints by NPP authors of the Lutheran tradition than the Reformed? To be clear, as far as justification goes, both traditions are equally condemned. Concerning the second use of the law, which the NPP does not accept, Lutherans receive more complaints than do the Reformed because Lutherans are known to emphasize this. At some level, this is illogical as the NPP should equally condemn the Lutherans and Reformed for the second use of the law.

There are two other issues that tend to give the Reformed tradition more of a positive view among NPP authors.[38] One aspect of Sanders' covenantal nomism is to view 'doing of the law' as positive. On the surface, this has similarities with the third use of the law as emphasized by the Reformed tradition. Also, Sanders' covenantal nomism connects grace, covenant, and law. Again, on the surface, this has similarities with the Reformed connections between covenant, law, and redemptive history.[39]

These similarities between the NPP and the Reformed tradition are, however, only at the surface level. Without a clear view of justification, the agreement between the Reformed tradition and NPP on sanctification issues (e.g., third use, role of the Holy Spirit, covenant connections) will not be at a deep level.

Of course, there are real differences between some Lutherans and the Reformed tradition concerning the third use of the law. However, these issues are not the focus of this book.

---

38. N. T. Wright views Sanders' views as having 'resonance with the Reformed tradition of theology' (*Paul and His Recent Interpreters: Some Contemporary Debates* [Minneapolis: Fortress, 2015], 67).

39. N. T. Wright often associates himself with the Reformed tradition. He 'remember[s] with fondness' an anecdote concerning an 'angry' Lutheran review of his book *Climax of the Covenant*, which Wright had written for a Lutheran press. The reviewer complained that Wright was Reformed and the publishing house should not have published Wright's book. In context, Wright is relating this to his emphasis on covenant. Elsewhere in the same book, Wright includes extended praise of the Reformed tradition over the Lutheran tradition (*Justification: God's Plan & Paul's Vision* [Downers Grove: IVP Academic, 2009], 205, 71-74). Further, see his praise of the Reformed tradition in *Paul and His Recent Interpreters*, 28-33, 37, 51-62, 73.

FINAL JUDGMENT AND JUSTIFICATION

It is abundantly clear that the OT, NT, and various Second Temple Judaism sources include a final judgment of man by God.[40] However, there are significant differences between the Reformed view of the final judgment and Sanders' covenantal nomism and thus also with NPP authors. This makes sense. Since justification is related to the final judgment, if there is disagreement about justification, there will be disagreement about aspects of the final judgment. Of course, there are many aspects to the final judgment, I will only discuss the legal aspects and the relationship to justification.

In brief, the Reformed and traditional-Protestant view includes Christ's work as the sole basis for the declaration by God that a believer is justified. NPP authors do not agree to this view of justification. Also, NPP authors have differences among themselves as to exactly what justification is. But in the end, Sanders and NPP authors do include human works as part of what Paul terms justification at the final judgment.[41]

The following is a more detailed view of the Reformed view. The Reformed view believes that the legal requirement to enter the new heavens and earth is perfect righteousness (as required in the Covenant of Works). For believers, this legal requirement was accomplished by Christ's life and death and is applied to the

---

40. So much so, that Chris VanLandingham argues that the OT, Second Temple Judaism, and even Paul all believed in a final judgment that determined eternal life based on one's deeds. This was true for both believers and unbelievers (*Judgment & Justification in Early Judaism and the Apostle Paul* [Peabody: Hendrickson, 2006]. For my critique, see Robert J. Cara, review of *Judgment & Justification in Early Judaism and the Apostle Paul*, by Chris VanLandingham, *WTJ* 70 (2008): 388-92.

41. Sanders connects his covenantal nomism to Paul's justification at the final judgment that includes human works and concludes, 'Paul is in perfect agreement with what we found in Jewish literature' (*Paul and Palestinian Judaism*, 518, also 543). N. T. Wright in a rhetorical response to Piper says, 'Thus when Piper says that "Wright makes the startling statements to the effect that our future justification will be on the basis of works," I want to protest: it isn't Wright who says this, but Paul' (*Justification: God's Plan & Paul's Vision*, 260 n. 11).

believer when he comes to faith. Hence, the expected judgment of a believer's works at the final judgment as his basis for entering the new heaven and earth has been wonderfully declared during a believer's life. That is, a believer is actually declared justified by God when he first believes and not at the end of his life (Rom. 5:9, 8:1). This is possible because the justification of a believer is not based on a believer's works, but the work of Christ (Covenant of Grace). If the decision as to whether one entered heaven was based on one's own works, then the decision would have to be made after the completion of one's life. To repeat, believers can be declared justified *now* rather than at the final judgment because the legal basis is Christ's work, not ours. If it was ours, a legal decision by a judge would not be made until our lives were completed.

The classic Reformed definition of justification comes from the WSC 33, 'Justification is an act of God's free grace, wherein he pardoneth all our sins, and accepteth us as righteous in his sight, only for the righteousness of Christ imputed to us, and received by faith alone.' As is clear from this definition, a believer is justified based on the work of Christ and not his own works. The sin of the believer is imputed to Christ, and Christ's righteousness is imputed to the believer. A glorious double exchange! Hence, a believer has nothing to fear at the final judgment because the legal judgment has already been made when she put her faith in Christ.

The NT does speak of God making declarations about believers and believers' works being evaluated at the final judgment (1 Cor 3:13-15, 2 Cor. 5:10, Matt. 25:33-40, 2 Thess. 1:5, 11[42]). The Reformed view sees God at the final judgment 'openly acknowledg[ing]' his prior announcement of believers' justification based on the righteousness of Christ and presenting the good works of believers as *evidence* that they were and are truly connected to Christ.[43] However, to be clear, good works are not in any sense even

---

42. For further discussion related to the Second Thessalonians passages, see my comments in Robert J. Cara, *A Study Commentary on 1 & 2 Thessalonians* (EP Study Commentary; Webster, NY: EP, 2009), 180-81, 189-92.

43. WLC 90. Ridderbos, 'Works are indispensable as the demonstration of

a part of the basis for the declaration of justification. Keeping our good works separate from justification is a key point in Reformed soteriology.[44]

The NT also speaks of 'rewards' for believers (e.g., Matt. 5:12, 1 Cor. 3:14, 4:5-7, Col. 3:24, Heb. 10:35, a variety of Greek words are used for 'reward'). Assuming the context is not speaking of merit (e.g., Rom. 4:4), the Reformed tradition views these as *gracious* rewards.[45] The Belgic Confession 24 states, 'We do not deny that God rewards good works, but it is through his grace that he crowns his gifts.'[46]

What of unbelievers? An unbeliever is still under the requirement of the Covenant of Works, that is, he will be judged based on his works. At the final judgment, because of sin, he 'shall have the fearful but just sentence of condemnation pronounced against' him.[47]

The above Reformed view of the final judgment and justification dovetails well with most traditional Protestants. The exceptions would be the language of Covenant of Works and Covenant of

---

he true nature of faith and as the evidence of having died and been raised together with Christ' (*Paul: An Outline of His Theology*, 180).

44. For an excellent discussion of both Reformed creeds and Paul on 'justification and a final judgment according to works,' see Cornelis P. Venema, *The Gospel of Free Acceptance in Christ: An Assessment of the Reformation and 'New Perspectives' on Paul* (Carlisle: Banner of Truth, 2006), 257-92.

45. For an extended discussion of rewards from a Reformed perspective, see G. C. Berkouwer, *Faith and Justification* (trans. Lewis B. Smedes; Studies in Dogmatics; Grand Rapids: Eerdmans, 1954), 112-29. Also see Geerhardus Vos, *The Teaching of Jesus Concerning The Kingdom of God and the Church* (Phillipsburg: Presbyterian and Reformed, n.d. [1903]), 66-69; and Mark Jones, *Antinomianism: Reformed Theology's Unwelcome Guest?* (Phillipsburg: P&R, 2013), 71-76.

46. Belgic Confession 37, 'And for a gracious reward, the Lord will cause them to possess such a glory as never entered into the heart of man to conceive.' Heidelberg Catechism 63, 'The reward comes not of merit, but of grace.' Also see Second Helvetic Confession 16; WCF 16.6, 19.6; WLC 45. See discussion in J. V. Fesko, *Justification: Understanding the Classic Reformed Doctrine* (Phillipsburg: P&R, 2008), 328-31.

47. WLC 89. See 2 Thess. 1:8-9.

Grace, and some technicalities related to the 'active' component of Christ's imputed righteousness.

COVENANTAL NOMISM FRAMEWORK

INTRODUCTION

E. P. Sanders started the scholarly movement in the 1970s that became known as NPP. James D. G. Dunn, N. T. Wright, and he are the three most famous proponents of NPP.

Of course, NPP actually includes *two* 'new perspectives': (1) a new perspective on Second Temple Judaism's view of works related to salvation, that is, it was not works righteousness oriented, but had a covenantal nomism structure; and (2) a new perspective on Paul's view of justification. Within NPP, these two new perspectives are related. NPP sees traditional Protestantism as wrong on both issues.

It was Sanders' 1977 book, *Paul and Palestinian Judaism: A Comparison of Patterns of Religion*, that convinced a significant portion of the NT scholarly world of new perspective # 1 above. All NPP authors agree with Sanders concerning his view of Second Temple Judaism.[48] Concerning new perspective # 2 above, Sanders also had an explanation for Paul and justification. However, NPP authors did not agree to this and most followed Dunn and/or Wright for the more common NPP view(s) of Paul and justification.

PRECURSORS TO SANDERS

E. P. Sanders was not the first to argue that Second Temple Judaism was not works righteousness oriented. However, it was his 1977 book, *Paul and Palestinian Judaism*, that influenced much of the NT

---

48. For example, Wright, *What Saint Paul Really Said*, 18-20; and Timothy G. Gombis, *Paul: A Guide for the Perplexed* (New York: T&T Clark/Continuum, 2010), 87-90. James D. G. Dunn explicitly states that 'Sanders in effect gave NT scholarship *a new perspective on Second Temple Judaism*' ('The New Perspective: whence, what and whither?,' in *The New Perspective on Paul* [Rev. ed.; Grand Rapids: Eerdmans, 2008], 1-97, esp. 5, italics his.)

scholarly world in this direction.[49] Sanders himself readily admits that there were precursors to his view, especially in the scholarly world of Jewish studies.[50] Sanders primarily blames German critical-Lutheran scholarship (beginning with Weber in 1880s) for vigorously resisting these newer conclusions in Jewish studies.[51] It was German critical-Lutheran scholarship that significantly influenced NT critical scholarship for most of the twentieth century.[52]

The following is a very brief summary of a few of the precursors to Sanders. This will give the reader a bit of background before directly discussing Sanders' book.

C. G. Montefiore

C. G. Montefiore, near the turn of the twentieth century, wanted to defend Rabbinic Judaism as gracious and not legalistic. He agreed

---

49. Wright gives five reasons why, although Sanders was not the first to make these claims, it was Sanders' book that changed scholarship (*Paul and His Recent Interpreters*, 66-69).

50. Not that all Jewish writers agreed to downplaying works/ethics as part of a salvation requirement. Isidore Epstein flatly states that Talmudic 'Judaism makes salvation depend on right conduct.' This is in the context that both Jews and non-Jews enter heaven based on conduct. See his *Judaism: A Historical Perspective* (New York: Penguin, 1990 [1959]), 143. Similarly, Shaye J. D. Cohen, according to the rabbis 'the souls of gentiles did not need to be saved, because all righteous gentiles who observe certain basic norms of religion and ethics were guaranteed a share in the world to come' (*From the Maccabees to the Mishnah* [2d. ed.; Louisville: Westminster John Knox, 2006], 49, cf. 92). Jacob Neusner vigorously complains that Sanders has turned the Pharisees into liberal Protestants. 'His "Judaism" represented as *kosher* to Liberal Protestantism is only a caricature and an offence. With friends like Sanders, Judaism needs no enemies' ('Mr Sanders' Pharisees and Mine: A Response to E. P. Sanders, *Jewish Law from Jesus to the Mishnah*,' *SJT* 44 [1991]: 73-95).

51. Although, not all of German scholarship agreed. William Wrede, who saw justification as only a 'polemical doctrine' and 'nothing more than a weapon,' had a nuanced view of Judaism (*Paul* [trans. Edward Lummis; Eugene, OR: Wipf and Stock, 2001; repr. Boston: American Unitarian Association, 1908 {German 1904}], 123, 127). 'Some slight element of caricture enters into this [Paul's] conception of the Jewish religion; for it was not ignorant of grace; it even laid stress on grace. But the prevalent feature of that religion is nevertheless touched when the principle of its piety is found in performance of tasks or in earning of rewards' (p. 127).

52. Sanders, *Paul and Palestinian Judaism*, 6-12, 33-59.

that Paul was arguing against Jewish views that were legalistic. Therefore, Montefiore concluded, Paul must not have known the standard form of gracious Rabbinic Judaism, but a small branch of Judaism that was influenced by Hellenism.[53]

George Foot Moore

George Foot Moore was a Harvard professor who had studied in Germany. In 1921 he wrote a famous article, 'Christian Writers of Judaism,' in which he complained, similarly to Sanders, that German critical-Lutheran scholarship (beginning with Weber in the 1880s) had wrongly branded Second Temple Judaism as legalistic. Moore argued that older Protestant works of the 17th and 18th centuries were much more positive toward Judaism.[54]

Moore later wrote his well-respected three-volume book, *Judaism in the First Centuries of the Christian Era: The Age of Tannaim*.[55] Moore argues that Judaism is not legalistic but does agree that there are 'rewards' and 'merit' in this grace system. He blames the 'prejudice of many writers on Judaism against the very idea of good works and their reward, and of merit acquired with God through them' to Luther's polemic against Roman Catholicism.[56] Moore argues that Christianity and Judaism have a similar pattern of election and reward for obedience. Hence, 'if one is grace, so is the other.'[57] Moore, somewhat contradictorily from my perspective, did believe that Paul 'implie[d] that the salvation of the individual by the works of the law was the chief end of Jewish

53. C. G. Montefiore, 'Rabbinic Judaism and the Epistles of St. Paul,' *JQR* 13 (1900-1901): 161-217.

54. George Foot Moore, 'Christian Writers of Judaism,' *HTR* 14 (1921): 197-254, esp. 215, 228-31, 252. Sanders said that this article 'should be required reading for any Christian scholar who writes about Judaism' (*Paul and Palestinian Judaism*, 33).

55. George Foot Moore, *Judaism in the First Centuries of the Christian Era: The Age of Tannaim* (3 vols.; Peabody: Hendrickson, 1997 [1927-30]).

56. Moore, *Judaism in the First Centuries of the Christian Era*, 2:93.

57. Moore, *Judaism in the First Centuries of the Christian Era*, 2:95.

religiousness.' Moore concludes that Paul's implication was wrong about Palestinian Judaism at this point.[58]

Krister Stendahl

Another influential article on NT scholarship that was a precursor to Sanders was Krister Stendahl's 1963 article, 'The Apostle Paul and the Introspective Conscience of the West.'[59] Stendahl argued that Paul did not have an introspective conscience, was not concerned about his sins, and was little worried about individual salvation. In fact, Augustine was probably 'the first to express the dilemma of the introspective conscience.'[60] Luther later read into Paul problems from late medieval piety and theology.

More to the point of this book, Stendahl argued that Paul dealt with the problem of the Law for Gentile inclusion in the Church, not the problem of legalism. Also, Stendahl dismissed the concept of the second use of the law. Finally, he takes Bultmann to task for his emphasis on Paul's use of 'boasting.'[61] All of these views presuppose that Paul is not arguing against legalistic Judaism.

PAUL AND PALESTINIAN JUDAISM AND COVENANTAL NOMISM

As mentioned above, E. P. Sanders' *Paul and Palestinian Judaism: A Comparison of Patterns of Religion* (1977) is ground-breaking.[62] It

---

58. Moore, *Judaism in the First Centuries of the Christian Era*, 1:282.

59. Krister Stendahl, 'The Apostle Paul and the Introspective Conscience of the West,' *HTR* 56 (1963): 199-215.

60. Stendahl, 'The Apostle Paul and the Introspective Conscience of the West,' 203.

61. Stendahl, 'The Apostle Paul and the Introspective Conscience of the West,' 204, 206, 214-15.

62. Sanders also published *Paul, the Law, and the Jewish People* (Philadelphia: Fortress, 1983), which concentrated more on Paul. Then he published a survey of Judaism that was non-polemical, *Judaism: Practice and Belief 63 B.C.E.-66 C.E.* (Philadelphia: Trinity Press International, 1992). Much later, Sanders published *Paul: the Apostle's life, Letters, and Thought* (Minneapolis: Fortress, 2015).

is approximately 600 pages and well documented both for primary and secondary sources. From this book, the vast majority of both his overarching and smaller arguments concerning Judaism are still being used and assumed today by NPP authors.[63] Hence, a reasonable understanding of this book is necessary to fairly evaluate the NPP.

Paul and Palestinian Judaism consists of two parts. The first two-thirds relate to Palestinian Judaism. Here Sanders makes the argument that Second Temple Judaism is not a religion of legalistic works righteousness but instead has a gracious covenantal-nomism pattern. This pattern is consistent across all versions of Judaism. All NPP authors accept this view.

The final third of the book evaluates Paul (only seven undisputed letters[64]) based on Sanders' assumptions about Judaism. Sanders argued that Paul's *thought* first assumed Christ was the 'solution' and then Paul had to find a 'plight,' which was sin. Sanders acknowledged that Romans reads from 'plight to solution,' but that is not the structure of Paul's thought, which is 'solution to plight.' Sanders also does not see 'righteousness by faith' and 'justification' as key categories for Paul because they do not relate well to Paul's ethics (here following Schweitzer).[65] Since Sanders sees a high view of grace in Judaism and a high view of grace in Paul, he concludes famously, 'in short, *this is what Paul finds wrong in Judaism: it is not Christianity.*'[66] Virtually no NPP authors follow Sanders' view of Paul; hence, I will end my discussion of it here.[67]

Before laying out Sanders' arguments about Second Temple Judaism, a few preliminaries are in order. Why does Sanders include

---

63. See Wright's extended analysis of Sanders in *Paul and His Recent Interpreters*, 64-87.

64. Sanders, *Paul and Palestinian Judaism*, 431.

65. Sanders, *Paul and Palestinian Judaism*, 439-47.

66. Sanders, *Paul and Palestinian Judaism*, 552, italics his.

67. Frank Thielman countered Sanders' 'solution to plight' argument in *From Plight to Solution: A Jewish Framework for Understanding Paul's View of the Law in Galatians and Romans* (NovTSup 61; Eugene: Wipf & Stock, 2007 [1989]).

in his title 'Palestinian Judaism,' which is opposed to Hellenistic Judaism, when he is making the argument that all forms of Judaism have a covenantal nomism pattern? Sanders answers that this is 'basically practical; one cannot discuss everything at once.'[68] From his perspective, he primarily covers the Palestinian Jewish literature and only briefly covers the Hellenistic material. However, his conclusion applies to all Jewish groups.

What Jewish sources does Sanders use? He covers Rabbinic Judaism, the Dead Sea Scrolls, Apocrypha/Pseudepigrapha, and briefly Philo. Concerning Rabbinic Judaism, he limits this to the traditional Tannaitic material (rabbis who lived from 50 B.C.–A.D. 200) that is attributed to these rabbis in the standard Rabbinic works from the Mishnah to the two Talmuds, and even later midrashim such as the *Midrash Rabbah*.[69]

Covenantal Nomism Defined

Here is a brief overview of Sanders' 'covenantal nomism,' which he considers grace based. Sanders concluded that Second Temple Judaism was not works righteousness oriented. Sanders instead proposed that Second Temple Judaism had a soteriological 'pattern of religion' so that one entered into the covenant by election/grace and one stayed in the covenant by obedience to the law. This obedience, however, should not be considered merit or works righteousness (as Sanders is understanding these terms). He named this system 'covenantal nomism' ('nomism' comes from the Greek νόμος for 'law'). Sanders also colloquially used the terms 'getting in' and 'staying in' the covenant, and these are now standard terms in the scholarly literature related to covenantal nomism. Finally, he argued that covenantal nomism was the only pattern of religion for all of Judaism from 200 B.C. to A.D. 200.[70]

---

68. Sanders, *Paul and Palestinian Judaism*, 1-2.

69. Sanders, *Paul and Palestinian Judaism*, 59-60. Sanders had a fairly optimistic view that the traditional Tannaitic material truly reflects historic views during the Tannaitic period.

70. Sanders, *Paul and Palestinian Judaism*, 16-17, 419-28.

Allow me to add a little more detail directly from Sanders about covenantal nomism. 'Salvation is by grace but judgment is according to works; works are the condition of remaining "in," but they do not earn salvation.'[71] Elsewhere Sanders summarizes covenantal nomism as 'one's place in God's plan is established on the basis of the covenant and that covenant requires as the proper response of man his obedience to its commands, while providing means of atonement for transgression.'[72] Sanders' fullest definition of covenantal nomism is as follows:

> The 'pattern' or 'structure' of covenantal nomism is this: (1) God has chosen Israel and (2) given the law. The law implies both (3) God's promise to maintain the election and (4) the requirement to obey. (5) God rewards obedience and punishes transgression. (6) The law provides means for atonement, and atonement results in (7) maintenance or re-establishment of the covenantal relationship. (8) All those who are maintained in the covenant by obedience, atonement and God's mercy belong to the group which will be saved. An important interpretation of the first and last points is that election and ultimately salvation are considered to be by God's mercy rather than human achievement.[73]

Sanders' Various Explanations for Conflicting Data

To Sanders' credit, he does acknowledge that even from his perspective the Second Temple Judaism literature has, at first glance, some conflicting data relative to the arguments for covenantal nomism. Sanders notes these and then gives answers and explanations to show that these are not really problems for his views. In the following I will present his explanations for some of the conflicting data. I will not offer my critical comments here but in the next section and next chapter.

As we will see in the next chapter, there are many passages in Second Temple Judaism literature that at least appear to be

---

71. Sanders, *Paul and Palestinian Judaism*, 543 (italics in original).

72. Sanders, *Paul and Palestinian Judaism*, 75.

73. Sanders, *Paul and Palestinian Judaism*, 422.

works righteousness oriented. Sanders acknowledges this but simply assumes that other passages that speak of grace are more basic. Hence, the passage in question does not really indicate true works righteousness. For example, 'It is true that there are some sayings which do indicate that God judges strictly according to the majority of a man's deeds. But, as we have seen, this can by no means be taken as Rabbinic doctrine.'[74] Another angle to this argument is that these documents were not written by systematic theologians; hence, we should not expect consistency.[75] Similarly, 'homiletical exhortation should not be confused with basic belief,' that is, the exhortation to good works did present these works in a works righteousness manner but that is not the true belief.[76]

A large part of Sanders' argument is that God's election of Jews in the covenant is by grace. Sanders admits that except for Dead Sea Scroll documents, election and covenant are not prominent in the literature. However, by the very nature of Judaism and its presumed beginnings, covenant must be presupposed in any discussion of halakah and atonement.[77]

Repentance is often noted by Sanders to prove that 'staying in' is not a work. Repentance admits that a Jew does not have to be perfectly righteous to obtain final salvation and, according to Sanders, is proof of a non-works righteousness pattern. Sanders does admit that repentance sometimes appears as 'the condition on the basis of which God forgives,' but he concludes that 'God's election of Israel' discounts this from being works righteousness.[78]

Sanders does conclude that no Jewish groups were works righteousness oriented and that all operated with a covenantal-nomism

---

74. Sanders, *Paul and Palestinian Judaism*, 143. Also see pp. 124, 129, 139, 181, 228, 265, 291-2.

75. Sanders, *Paul and Palestinian Judaism*, 141.

76. Sanders, *Paul and Palestinian Judaism*, 181, 265.

77. Sanders, *Paul and Palestinian Judaism*, 236.

78. Sanders, *Paul and Palestinian Judaism*, 46, 177. Sanders is aware that Bultmann saw Jewish repentance as another aspect of merit (Sanders, *Paul and Palestinian Judaism*, 46; Bultmann, *Primitive Christianity*, 71).

pattern. On the other hand, Sanders admits that 4 Ezra is clearly a works righteousness document. Also, Sirach emphasizes obedience to the law but does not connect this to the covenant. Finally, Sanders admits that the polemic by Jesus in Matt. 23 against the scribes and Pharisees does present problems for his view. How does Sanders explain this conflicting data?

For 4 Ezra, Sanders notes that this works righteousness document is a polemical document explained by the pressures of the Roman oppression near A.D. 70. He complains that other scholars use 4 Ezra as the prime example of Judaism instead of seeing it as an exception driven by the polemical context.[79] Sirach does use works as a criterion to determine prosperity and suffering in this life; however, Sirach has no view of the afterlife. Thus the question of works for final salvation is moot.[80] The petty legalism of the scribes and Pharisees as presented in the Gospels (e.g., Matt. 23), although theoretically possible historically, should be discounted because a 'religion should be understood on the basis of its own self-presentations ... and not on the basis of polemical attacks.'[81]

Concerning the Rabbinic literature, Sanders admits there is an overwhelming amount of discussion of halakah or laws. However, according to Sanders, these laws were not burdensome to Rabbinic Judaism. This is so because the rabbis believed the laws came from God. Also, many of these laws were part of daily life similar to the modern world with its many laws. 'The Rabbinic halakah is analogous to modern law in that it aimed at providing regulations for all areas of life.'[82]

Sanders argues that the covenantal nomism pattern is uniform across Second Temple Judaism. This uniformity seems to be contradicted out of hand by the variegated nature of Judaism at the time. Sanders responds by noting that, yes, there are different

---

79. Sanders, *Paul and Palestinian Judaism*, 409-18, 427-428.

80. Sanders, *Paul and Palestinian Judaism*, 329-45, 420.

81. Sanders, *Paul and Palestinian Judaism*, 426.

82. Sanders, *Paul and Palestinian Judaism*, 111. This argument is used often, for example, Nickelsburg, *Ancient Judaism and Christian Origins*, 45.

theological conclusions and even sects that are much stricter than others in their definition of 'staying in.' But this is not an argument against a 'basic consistency in the underlying pattern of religion.' Are there different Judaisms? 'One can reply yes or no, depending on just what is meant [by Judaisms].'[83]

PRELIMINARY BROAD-BRUSH CRITIQUES OF COVENANTAL NOMISM

In this section, I will provide some preliminary broad-brush or big-picture critiques of covenantal nomism. Hence, the reader will have Sanders' explanations as just discussed above along with several counter explanations. Hopefully, this will provide the reader with an adequate grid to view the details of the next chapter. In the next chapter, I will present, from my perspective, multiple examples of works righteousness in Second Temple Judaism documents.

As a reminder, I do not view all of Second Temple Judaism as having a Pelagian works righteousness system. I believe that both Pelagian and semi-Pelagian systems existed. In addition, I believe that others in Second Temple Judaism understood that salvation was solely based on grace as they understood the OT correctly (Luke 2:25). Further, I believe that Paul was interacting with many who had (Pelagian and/or semi-Pelagian) works righteousness systems (Gal. 3:1-5), and he considered a large part of Jewish history to be infected with a (Pelagian and/or semi-Pelagian) legalistic works righteousness view (Rom. 10:3). Finally, as a good Protestant, I believe all humans, not simply those within Judaism, are infected with the desire to justify themselves.

Covenantal Nomism as Defined Appears To Include Works Righteousness

Many traditional Protestants read Sanders' definition of covenantal nomism and conclude that it is semi-Pelagian. The definition of 'staying in' includes both obedience and atonement.[84] By including

---

83. Sanders, *Paul and Palestinian Judaism*, 423.

84. Sanders, *Paul and Palestinian Judaism*, 422.

obedience, Sanders has included an aspect of legalistic self-righteousness. Eskola bluntly states, 'If legalism means that keeping the law affects eschatological salvation, then covenantal nomism is legalistic nomism by definition.'[85] Similarly Waters, 'Sanders has corrected the portrait of Judaism as a religion of pure Pelagianism, and has demonstrated that this religion is semi-Pelagian in nature.'[86]

How do Sanders and many NPP authors miss this? Silva answers that:

> Sanders operates with an understanding of 'legalism' that is at times fuzzy and ambiguous, at other times quite misleading. More to the point, Sanders (along with biblical scholars more generally) has an inadequate understanding of historical Christian theology, and his view of the Reformational concern with legalism does not get to the heart of the question.[87]

Silva's critique seems to be confirmed by the many passages in *Paul and Palestinian Judaism* where Sanders appears not to grasp the traditional-Protestant view of legalism even though part of his polemic in the book is to condemn this view.[88]

---

85. Timo Eskola, 'Paul, Predestination and "Covenantal Nomism"—Re-assessing Paul and Palestinian Judaism,' *JSJ* 28 (1997): 390-412, esp. 396, italics in orginal. Eskola then calls covenantal nomism a 'synergistic religion,' which matches to my use of semi-Pelagian. D. A. Carson notes that the 'covenantal nomism [Sanders] constructs is so flexible that it includes and baptizes a great deal of merit theology' ('Summaries and Conclusions' in *The Complexities of Second Temple Judaism*, vol. 1 of *Justification and Variegated Nomism* [ed. D. A. Carson, Peter T. O'Brien, and Mark A. Seifrid; Grand Rapids: Baker, 2001], 505-48, esp. 544-45).

86. Guy Prentiss Waters, *Justification and the New Perspectives on Paul*, 57. Similarly, William B. Barcley with Ligon Duncan, *Gospel Clarity: Challenging the New Perspective on Paul* (Carlisle: EP Books, 2010), 61; and Venema, *The Gospel of Free Acceptance in Christ*, 156-58.

87. Moisés Silva, 'The Law and Christianity: Dunn's New Synthesis,' *WTJ* 53 (1991): 339-53, esp. 348.

88. For example, see Sanders, *Paul and Palestinian Judaism*, 291-92, 338. Also see Sanders' discussion of the *Testament of Abraham* where he admits that 'everyone is judged by the same standard, whether the majority of his deeds be good or evil ... if righteous deeds predominate, the soul goes to life'

Are not 'works' in Sanders' covenantal nomism similar to the third use of the law in the Reformed Covenant of Grace? On the surface, yes, both systems do include works. However, the Reformed system clearly distinguishes between works done as part of the Covenant of Works (legalistic works) and works done as part of the Covenant of Grace. Sanders tends to confuse the two.

Final Judgment De-emphasized

Gathercole, an anti-NPP author, notes that the 'getting in' and 'staying in' scheme tends to downplay the importance of the final judgment in one's salvation. He notes this tendency in both Sanders and N. T. Wright.[89] Once one sees the importance of final judgment for Second Temple Judaism literature, the 'works' aspect takes on even more importance. Gathercole's thesis is that 'Jewish "soteriology" was based *both* on divine election *and* on final salvation by works, and that a number of Jewish groups express the belief that they would be vindicated on the basis of their works.'[90]

Election is not always Grace

In some Second Temple Judaism sources, the election of Israel is connected to the merit of the Patriarchs and others.[91] Why did God

---

('Testament of Abraham,' in *OTP*, 1:877-78).

89. Simon J. Gathercole, *Where is Boasting? Early Jewish Soteriology and Paul's Response in Romans 1-5* (Grand Rapids: Eerdmans, 2002), 23. Eskola earlier had noted Sanders' downplaying of final judgment ('Paul, Predestination and "Covenantal Nomism"—Re-assessing Paul and Palestinian Judaism,' 393-94). Douglas J. Moo considers this point very detrimental to NPP along with the variegated Judaism argument (*Galatians* [BECNT; Grand Rapids: Baker, 2013], 24 n. 32). Bruce W. Longenecker complains that Gathercole has over-emphasized this point ('On Critiquing the "New Perspective" on Paul: A Case Study,' *ZNW* 96 [2005]: 263-71). Wright responds that he *does* see Judaism as teaching a future judgment according to works, but so also does Paul (*Paul and His Recent Interpreters*, 72).

90. Gathercole, *Where is Boasting?*, 33, italics his.

91. E.g., *Sifre Deuteronomy* 170, 343, *Melkilta Pish*a 5, *Melkilta Beshallah* 3, Philo *On the Special Laws* 4.180-81, Josephus *Antiquities* 1.183, *Damascus Document* (CD) 3:1-4. Although I disagree with several of his ultimate conclusions, see VanLandingham's discussion of many passages that confirm that election

choose Israel? Sanders admits that some rabbis answer: 'Because of some merit found either in the patriarchs or in the exodus generation or on the condition of future obedience.'[92] His solution is simply to say that 'it was only an explanatory device' because ultimately election is unexplainable.[93]

This is an obvious problem for covenantal nomism as the emphasis on grace comes from election. Westerholm is typical in his complaint. 'Sanders's claim that salvation in Judaism is "by grace" is the claim that salvation is rooted in God's election of Israel and that election was an act of divine grace. Yet none of the explanations given for election in Rabbinic sources suggests the utter gratuity of God's choice.'[94]

Although this is a legitimate line of argument, I will not pursue it in this book.

Admission of Gentiles and Qumran Community

Since Sanders emphasizes the grace/election of Israel, what about the requirements for Gentiles 'getting in' to the Jewish covenant?[95] They were not simply born into the covenant. Similarly, the Qumran community had requirements for ethnic Jews to enter

---

was based on merit (*Judgment & Justification in Early Judaism and the Apostle Paul*, 23-49).

92. Sanders, *Paul and Palestinian Judaism*, 87. See pp. 87-101 for numerous Rabbinic quotes.

93. Sanders, *Paul and Palestinian Judaism*, 100.

94. Westerholm, *Perspectives Old and New on Paul*, 346. See John M. G. Barclay's critique of Sanders' election discussion (*Paul and the Gift* [Grand Rapids: Eerdmans, 2015], 154-55). He sees Sanders' problem as not having a full orbed definition of grace, 'priority grace' does not necessarily mean 'incongruity grace.' 'Incongruity grace' for Barclay would be similar to a Reformed view of grace. His complaint against Sanders is also applied to Sanders' covenantal-nomism scheme. 'Grace is everywhere in the theology of Second Temple Judaism, but not everywhere the same' (p. 565, cf. 2, 6). To be clear, Barclay favors much in Sanders and does 'not [want] to return to the theologically pernicious contrasts between Pauline grace and Jewish works righteousness' (p. 572).

95. For his discussion of Gentiles, see Sanders, *Paul and Palestinian Judaism*, 206-12.

their community. These 'getting in' entrance requirements tend to match 'staying in' requirements.[96] This shows that Sanders' emphasis on grace is exaggerated and works are more important than he allows.

Talbert looks at multiple Second Temple Judaism texts and concludes that 'in the cases both of proselytes and of righteous Gentiles, the soteriology sounds more like what has traditionally been called legalism than anything else.'[97] Concerning the Qumran community, Sprinkle complains that 'Sanders fails to recognize that God establishes this (new) covenant *with an obedient community already in existence*.'[98] See further discussion at *t. Sanhedrin* in Chapter 3.

Variegated Judaism

Sanders agrees that Second Temple Judaism is variegated but argues that covenantal nomism is consistent across it. In the Appendix, I review many types of Judaisms and note our tenuous understanding of most of these groups.[99] Based on this, Sanders' argument for a demonstrated consistent soteriological structure, let alone covenantal nomism, across all groups seems forced.[100] Watson complains about Sanders, 'What is problematic here is the

---

96. Eskola vigoriously opposes Sanders here. 'One cannot say that grace would have had anything to do with entering the [Qumran] community. The membership was not granted on the ground of nationality or circumcision. The covenant of God was a covenant of law. The sociological "getting in" had only to do with law' ('Paul, Predestination and "Covenantal Nomism"— Re-assessing Paul and Palestinian Judaism,' 405).

97. Charles H. Talbert, 'Paul, Judaism, and the Revisionists,' *CBQ* 63 (2001): 1-22, esp. 7.

98. Preston M. Sprinkle, *Law and Life: The Interpretation of Leviticus 18:5 in Early Judaism and in Paul* (WUNT II/241; Tübingen: Mohr Siebeck, 2008), 66, italics his. For Sanders' discussion of this problem, see *Paul and Palestinian Judaism*, 249-55.

99. Especially note the section 'Variegated Judaism: Parties and Movements.'

100. D. A. Carson summarizes a variety of articles related to variegated Judaism and covenantal nomism and states, 'One conclusion to be drawn, then, is not that Sanders is wrong everywhere, but he is wrong when he tries to establish that his category is right everywhere' ('Summaries and Conclusions,' 543).

assumption that an empirical account of a singular "Judaism" is attainable.'[101]

Or to say it another way, to make Judaism have one system, Sanders' definition of how works operate in covenantal nomism is so broad and undefined that it is not really useful to help us understand Second Temple Judaism and its relationship to Paul.[102]

Halakah Emphasis Tends Toward Works Righteousness

As a reminder, halakah texts are those that apply the law.[103] These are a significant portion of the Rabbinic literature and are included in the Dead Sea Scrolls. The Pharisees in the NT are portrayed with this emphasis also.

An noted above, Sanders and many others argue that this emphasis does not lead to legalism because these texts are analogous to a modern country's law code. My response is that concerning Rabbinic literature specifically, the difference is that Rabbinic Judaism venerated *religious* law documents (Mishnah and the Talmuds), making these a significant aspect of their religion, if not the main aspect. This emphasis on laws without a clear and consistent call within these documents toward grace, in my perspective, would tend to move one toward legalism. Schreiner remarks, 'Any theology that claims to stress God's grace but rarely mentions it and that elaborates human responsibility in detail inevitably becomes legalistic in practice, if not theory.'[104]

---

101. Francis Watson, *Paul and the Hermeneutics of Faith* (London: T & T Clark, 2004), 528 n. 8, also see 8 n. 14, 12-13. On the other hand, Watson does praise Sanders for 'marginaliz[ing] the previously dominant metaphor of "earning" or "meriting" salvation' (pp. 7-8).

102. N. T. Wright disagrees. 'Recent attempts to suggest a more variegated attitude to the Law than was allowed for by E. P. Sanders in *Paul and Paelstinian Judaism* are undoubtedly right to stress variety, and undoubtedly wrong to try to use that as a way of smuggling back an anachronistic vision of a Pelagian (or semi-Pelagian) or medieval works righteousness' (*Paul: In Fresh Perspective*, [Minneapolis: Fortress, 2005], 108-9).

103. For more explanation, see the 'Rabbinic Literature' section in the Appendix.

104. Thomas R. Schreiner, *The Law and Its Fulfillment* (Grand Rapids: Baker, 1993), 116. See his excellent discussion 'Was Palestinian Judaism Legalistic?' on pp. 114-21.

The NT presents aspects of Judaism as overly interested in the outward form of the law as opposed to inward motivation (Matt. 5:21, 23:23-28). This matches the emphasis on halakah. An outward emphasis on keeping the law may have a tendency toward works righteousness because it is easier to fulfill the outward law and thereby conclude that the law has been kept.[105]

For some in Judaism, this halakah emphasis probably resulted in a crass form of legalism (Pelagian), and for others, a softer form (semi-Pelagian). I believe that the Rabbinic literature bears this out. (As has often been pointed out by Reformed and Lutheran authors, a works righteousness tendency belongs to all humans due to sin—'legalism is but the human cry for personal autonomy.'[106])

Repentance and Works Righteousness

As mentioned above, Sanders argues that if a system includes repentance, then one does not have to be perfectly righteous to obtain final salvation, and this is a proof of a non-works righteousness system. Yes, non-meritorious repentance would indicate that one does not have to be perfectly righteous, but that does not necessarily mean that a soteriological system is not legalistic. A system could easily improperly combine repentance and works of merit.

Could it be that some NPP authors confuse aspects of the Reformed Covenant of Grace and Covenant of Works? One gets the impression that if it is shown that Second Temple Judaism did not believe that one had to be perfectly righteous, then the Reformed view of Judaism is shown to be wrong.[107] The Reformed

---

105. So also Geerhardus Vos, *Biblical Theology: Old and New Testaments* (Carlisle: Banner of Truth, 1975 [1948]), 396.

106. Silva, 'The Law and Christianity: Dunn's New Systhesis,' 339-53, esp. 349.

107. So James D. G. Dunn, 'The idea that the religion of Israel, or Second Temple Judaism, taught the need for perfect obedience is a kind of wish-fulfilment on the part of generations of Christian interpreters. That is, it most probably emerged as a necessary presupposition of the hypothesis of Jewish legalism, which has been such a dominant feature of Christian interpretation of Paul's theology of justification' ('Whatever Happened to the "Works of the Law"?,' in *The New Perspective on Paul* [rev. ed.; Grand Rapids: Eerdmans, 2008], 381-94, esp. 386-87).

view is that, yes, the Covenant of Works requires perfect obedience, but the Covenant of Grace includes non-meritorious repentance prompted by the second use of the law as well as third-use-of-the-law works. The Reformed view also believes that any soteriological system that includes any aspect of works righteousness would have to be considered under the Covenant of Works, and given that, one would have to be perfect under this Covenant. As Gal. 3:10 indicates, if one wants to gain eschatological life by including works, one is only cursed if he does *not* do '*all* things written in the book of the law.' In sum, both Pelagian and semi-Pelagian systems are inadequate.

Concerning another angle related to repentance, as noted above, even Sanders admits that some of the texts that include repentance and associated works of repentance appear to present repentance as a legalistic work. Also, there are examples where repentance does not gain eschatological life. The prime example is Manasseh. See discussion of *t. Sanhedrin* in Chapter 3.

Reliability of the New Testament for Second Temple Judaism Views

Some scholars object to using the NT to determine the views of Second Temple Judaism.[108] Their rationale is that (1) it is best to allow Judaism to explain itself, not to depend on an 'outsider's' view, and (2) the NT's description of Judaism is often in a polemical setting that renders the description suspect. Another issue is whether to use the 'Deutero-Paul' NT books, as most, but not all, NPP authors do not consider these prudent to use in a Pauline study. Do these books evidence that the 'author' is contrasting grace and works righteousness? As I will argue in Appendix and Chapter 4, my view of the Word of God encourages me to include the NT's views of Second Temple Judaism and to use the 'Deutero-Paul' books.

Several pro-Sanders authors do admit that the NT presents the Pharisees as legalistic, but this is dismissed because the NT is not

---

108. For further discussion, see the 'Include NT?' section of the Appendix.

an 'insider' and the context is polemical. As noted above, Sanders himself admits Matt. 23 is a problem for his view. The parable of the Pharisee and Tax Collector (Luke 18:9-14) on the surface indicates that works righteousness was evident in Palestine.[109] Nickelsburg, a pro-Sanders author, agrees that the NT portrays the Pharisees as legalistic but a polemical context and an 'outsider's' view are not to be trusted. He says,

> All four Gospels depict Jesus of Nazareth in repeated controversy with the Jewish establishment, notably the Pharisees and the scribes, whose detailed concern about the Law is emphasized in *stories* about Jesus and whose hypocrisy and self-righteousness are highlighted in *sayings* attributed to him. … Hypocrisy and 'self-righteousness' can be the dark underbelly of any religion that is deeply concerned with right conduct. In apologetic and polemical documents, however, such accusation against one's opponents and enemies are suspicious at the very least, and they do not constitute a sure foundation for a historical description of these opponents and enemies.[110]

Similarly, Magnus Zetterholm, another pro-Sanders author, complains that the Gospels' presentation of the Pharisees as 'hypocrites … must be viewed as a caricature.'[111]

Concerning 'insider/outsider' methodological assumptions, I agree that it is very helpful to note the portrayal that various Jewish

---

109. Even if one denies Jesus as the author of this parable, one would have to agree that the author of Luke viewed at least some Pharisees as self-righteous. See Frank Thielman's discussion that the Gospels present some first-century Jews as self-righteous and others as mercy based (*Paul & the Law: A Contextual Approach* [Downers Grove: InterVarsity, 1994], 67-68).

110. Nickelsburg, *Ancient Judaism and Christian Origins*, 29-30, 165, italics his.

111. Magnus Zetterholm, *Approaches to Paul: A Student's Guide to Recent Scholarship* (Minneapolis: Fortress, 2009), 15. Concerning the interpretation of Paul, Zetterholm sees three categories, (1) traditional Lutheran perspective, (2) NPP, and (3) 'radical new perspective.' He puts himself in the 'radical new perspective,' which sees little difference between Paul and Second Temple Judaism. In fact, Paul did not break with Judaism. He complains that NPP did not adequately follow the logic of Sanders' covenantal nomism. See pp. 231-40.

documents make of themselves ('insider's' view).[112] However, this does not necessarily exhaust the pertinent historical information as to the true nature of Second Temple Judaism.[113] Also, an 'insider's' view is not always without its own distortions.

Concerning polemical methodological assumptions, normally I am initially more cautious using a polemical source; however, since in the case above the polemical source is the Bible and given my traditional Reformed starting point, I take the NT description of various Judaistic views as completely accurate. Although, this does not mean that the NT is describing, for example, the views of every single Pharisee and/or explaining every aspect of Pharisaic theology.

As will be discussed in Chapter 4, some NPP authors do agree that 'works' in the deutero-Paul books is works righteousness, although they deny it for 'works of the law' in the 'true' or earlier Pauline books.

SUMMARY OF CHAPTER

One of the core beliefs of NPP is that Second Temple Judaism was not works righteousness oriented and instead had a soteriological structure termed 'covenantal nomism.' E. P. Sanders is the driving force behind this view of Second Temple Judaism.

In this chapter, I noted that many NPP authors do not have a clearly articulated definition of works righteousness, and if they do, it is a form of Pelagianism. I noted that traditional Protestants believe that Paul would have considered both Pelagianism and semi-Pelagianism as works righteousness.

---

112. Also see discussion in the 'Include NT?' section of the Appendix.

113. After commending Sanders for his emphasis of 'taking Judaism at its own valuation,' G. B. Caird complains that Sanders does not see the Gospels' comments as at least some form of evidence. 'Adverse criticism is not primary evidence or unbiased evidence, but it is evidence' and 'the [works righteousness] accusations may have been true' (review of *Paul and Palestinian Judaism: A Comparison of Patterns of Religion*, by E. P. Sanders, *JTS* NS 29 [1978]: 538-43, esp. 539-40).

Next, this chapter gave a brief overview of a Reformed framework for interpreting 'law' in the history of redemption. This included terms such as Covenant of Works, Covenant of Grace, second use of the law, and third use of the law. The purpose of presenting the Reformed framework was to compare and contrast it with Sanders' covenantal nomism.

Finally, I explained Sanders' covenantal nomism framework. 'Getting in' the covenant is by grace/election, and 'staying in' is by obedience to the law along with atonement/repentance. All this is by God's mercy. This framework is consistent across all Jewish groups in Second Temple Judaism.

I also included several broad-brush critiques of covenantal nomism. They are (1) covenantal nomism as defined includes a semi-Pelagian soteriology, (2) covenantal nomism's structure of 'getting in' and 'staying in' de-emphasizes the final judgment, (3) even election is not always clearly by grace in Second Temple Judaism sources, (4) the variegated nature of Second Temple Judaism argues against a uniform covenantal nomism, (5) the admission of Gentiles into Judaism and the admission of Jews into the Qumran community undercuts the supposed consistent grace emphasis of 'getting in,' (6) the halakah (law) emphasis tends toward works righteousness, (7) a soteriological system with repentance does not necessarily preclude a works righteousness component, and (8) the rejection of the NT as reliably providing important evidence.

In the next chapter, I will present various primary sources and show, from my perspective, that many Jewish literary sources have a works righteousness soteriology.

CHAPTER 3:

WORKS RIGHTEOUSNESS IN JEWISH LITERATURE?

Over coffee, I was networking with a young NT professor at the annual meeting of the Evangelical Theological Society. After several discussions of various issues, I innocuously enquired about his view of NPP. He paused, probably not knowing my view, and finally said, 'I don't get it. In my Ph.D. program I read all of the Apocrypha, OT Pseudepigrapha, and the DSS. There is lots of works righteousness there. To be honest, I am not the least bit interested in the NPP because the starting point with Sanders seems so wrong. Does that offend you?' Obviously, it did not.

INTRODUCTION

The primary argument for NPP being wrong on justification is the Pauline texts themselves. However, this book concerns secondary arguments related to Second Temple Judaism that NPP authors rely upon so heavily. Knowledge of these secondary arguments will dovetail with the primary Pauline argument to enhance one's understanding and ability to defend the traditional view of justification.

The NPP argument has two parts or two 'new perspectives': the Judaistic-background part and the explicitly Paul part. The first part of the argument is that Second Temple Judaism across all groups was not works righteousness oriented. This is the 'new perspective on Judaism' and is strongly tied to E. P. Sanders. The second part of the argument relates to Paul based on this 'new perspective on Judaism.' The implication related to Paul, according to NPP, is that Paul's opponents could not have been works righteousness oriented given that this did not exist in Second Temple Judaism. This then further implies that the traditional Protestant view of justification is wrong because it presupposes that when Paul contrasts 'works' and 'faith,' 'works' is equal to works righteousness. Up to this point, all NPP advocates agree. So what does Paul positively mean by 'justification' according to NPP authors? Here the NPP turns into multiple new perspectives on Paul. See Chapter 4 for more detail on Dunn and Wright's views of justification.

The purpose of this chapter will be to present various Second Temple Judaism documents that, in my view, have either a Pelagian or semi-Pelagian view of works righteousness. Once given this, the argument that all groups in Second Temple Judaism are not works righteousness oriented falls. Hence, the statements in Paul that on the surface appear to be arguing against works righteousness must truly be that, arguments against works righteousness. And further, justification in Paul must then be that God declares one righteous based on the work of Christ and not the works of the elect.

For convenience, I will proceed by looking at various documents in the order of Apocrypha, OT Pseudepigrapha, DSS, and Rabbinic literature.[1] (I will not include Philo nor Josephus because of the limitations of space.) For significantly more background on these groups, including Philo and Josephus, see the Appendix.

---

1. As a point of interest, E. P. Sanders in *Paul and Palestinian Judaism: A Comparison of Patterns of Religion* used the order of: Rabbinic literature, DSS, and Apocrypha/Pseudepigrapha, with the most emphasis on Rabbinic literature (Minneapolis: Fortress, 1977).

As will be seen in the following discussion, I believe that many documents are works righteousness oriented. However, that is not to say that I have the same level of exegetical certainty for all of them. My primary point is to show that *some* documents had a works righteousness soteriology and/or could easily have been taken that way by some readers. Also, I am not presenting every document that I think is works righteousness oriented, just significant examples.

APOCRYPHA [2]

The Apocrypha refers to sixteen books/additions written between approximately 180 B.C. and A.D. 100. I am using the modern-scholarly definition of the Apocrypha that has a slightly expanded list of books relative to Roman Catholic and Eastern Orthodox churches. [3]

4 EZRA

4 Ezra includes chapters 3-14 of a longer work known as 2 Esdras. [4] The extant text is in Latin and several other languages, but scholars assume that the original Jewish document, 4 Ezra 3-14, was written in Hebrew or Aramaic near A.D. 100. 4 Ezra is unusual as an Apocryphal book in that it is an apocalypse.

4 Ezra includes seven visions given to Ezra while he is in Babylon during the exile. Ezra asks questions of God, and God sends an angel to answer Ezra. Most of Ezra's questions relate to sin, suffering, and God's justice in the purported context of Israel's destruction in 587 B.C. but are actually related to the Temple's destruction in A.D. 70. The third vision, 4 Ezra 6:35-9:25, concerns the final judgment. My discussion and quotes will concentrate on the third vision.

---

2. All English translations of the Apocrypha are from *The Apocrypha of the Old Testament: Revised Standard Version: Expanded Edition Containing the Third and Fourth Books of the Maccabees and Psalm 151* (ed. Bruce M. Metzger; New York: OUP, 1977).

3. For an overview of the Apocrypha, see the 'Apocrypha' section of the Appendix.

4. 2 Esdras is sixteen chapters long of which scholars see chapters 1-2 and 15-16 as Christian interpolations to an original Jewish document consisting of chapters 3-14.

Below are quotes from 4 Ezra that relate to the question of works righteousness.

> For God strictly commanded those who came into the world, when they came, what they should do to live, and what they should observe to avoid punishment. (4 Ezra 7:21)

> For you have a treasury of works laid up with the Most High. (4 Ezra 7:77)

> Now this is the order of those who have kept the ways of the Most High ... they laboriously served the Most High, and withstood danger every hour that they might keep the Law of the Lawgiver perfectly. (4 Ezra 7:88-89)

> The day of judgment is decisive and displays to all the seal of truth. ... For then everyone shall bear his own righteousness or unrighteousness. (4 Ezra 7:104-5)

> For the righteous, who have many works, laid up with you, shall receive their reward in consequence of their own deeds. (4 Ezra 8:77)

As can be seen from the above text, 4 Ezra has a clear works righteousness view of salvation for individuals.[5] There is one text in 4 Ezra that is confusing and at first glance appears to offer both a salvation by works option and a salvation by faith option.

> And it shall be that everyone who will be saved and will be able to escape on account of his works, or on account of the faith by which he has believed. (4 Ezra 9:7, cf. 8:36)

---

5. Bruce W. Longenecker concludes a discussion of the author's view of covenant, 'Confidence in God's justice and faithfulness is the mainstay of the author's covenantal perspective, but it is a perspective that seems to be characterized by two other factors: (1) a somewhat skeptical attitude towards the people's ability to keep the law with the kind of rigorous and exacting standards that are required, and (2) the virtual absence of a robust theology of grace' (*2 Esdras* [Sheffield: Sheffield Academic Press, 1995], 100). In an early work, Longenecker states, 'The author of *4 Ezra* has advanced a new understanding of the character of Jewish existence without the temple: salvation is not a national privilege but an individual responsibility worked out with great effort by works of merit. Divine grace is, for all purposes, absent in his scheme, except as an eschatological reflex to those who have saved themselves anyway by their works' (*Eschatology and the Covenant: A Comparison of 4 Ezra and Romans 1-11* [JSNTSup 57; Sheffield: Sheffield Academic Press, 1991], 152).

As Stone notes, this is not teaching two methods of salvation. 'While not asserting that these two concepts, faith and works, are identical, we may say that they were not very clearly differentiated and are used interchangeably.'[6]

As noted in Chapter 2, Sanders agrees that 4 Ezra is a works righteousness document.[7] However, he argues that the works righteousness of 4 Ezra is not representative because it is a polemical document produced by the pressures of the Roman oppression near A.D. 70.[8] If difficult times produced a works righteousness document, could not one argue that other types of difficulties would also produce works righteousness attitudes?

SIRACH (ECCLESIASTICUS, WISDOM OF JESUS THE SON OF SIRACH)

A summary of Sirach is included in the Appendix. Following are quotes from Sirach that relate to the works righteousness question.

> For kindness to a father will not be forgotten, and against your sins it will be credited[9] to you. (Sir. 3:14)

> Water extinguishes a blazing fire: so almsgiving atones for sin. (Sir. 3:30)[10]

> For it is easy in the sight of the Lord to regard a man on the day of death according to his conduct. (Sir. 11:26)

---

6. Michael Edward Stone, *A Commentary on the Book of Fourth Ezra* (Hermeneia; Minneapolis, Fortress, 1990), 296. Similarly, see Simon J. Gathercole, *Where is Boasting? Early Jewish Soteriology and Paul's Response in Romans 1-5* (Grand Rapids: Eerdmans, 2002), 138-39.

7. Sanders, *Paul and Palestinian Judaism*, 409.

8. Sanders, *Paul and Palestinian Judaism*, 427.

9. Greek is προσανοικοδομέω; 'credited' could be more mechanically translated 'built up.'

10. Tob. 12:9 has a very similar statement, 'For almsgiving delivers from death, and it will purge away every sin.' Gathercole sees both Sirach and Tobit as having works righteousness views that are for 'this' world (*Where is Boasting?*, 37-40).

He will make room for every act of mercy; every one will receive in accordance with his deeds. (Sir. 16:14)

Store up almsgiving in your treasury, and it will rescue you from all affliction. (Sir. 29:12)

Who has been tested by [love of gold] and been found perfect? Let it be for him a ground of boasting. ... His prosperity will be established and the assembly will relate his acts of charity. (Sir. 31:10-11)

So if a man fasts for his sins, and goes again and does the same things, who will listen to his prayer? (Sir. 34:26)

Do your work before the appointed time, and in God's time he will give you your reward. (Sir. 51:30, the final verse in the book)

Sanders argues that the author 'believes that a man is rewarded in this life strictly according to his merits.'[11] However, since the author does not believe in an afterlife, the question of works for final salvation is moot.[12] I am not convinced that Sirach does not believe in an afterlife (Sir. 11:26); however, even if he did not, one reading Sirach who did believe in an afterlife would certainly understand it as advocating either a Pelagian or semi-Pelagian view of works righteousness. It is not a far step from works righteousness for this life to works righteousness as a basis for the afterlife.

OLD TESTAMENT PSEUDEPIGRAPHA[13]

The OT Pseudepigrapha is a scholarly name given to approximately sixty books primarily written between 200 B.C. and A.D. 200.[14]

---

11. Sanders, *Paul and Palestinian Judaism*, 341.

12. Sanders, *Paul and Palestinian Judaism*, 420.

13. All English translations from the OT Pseudepigrapha are from *The Old Testament Pseudepigrapha* (ed. James H. Charlesworth; 2 vols.; Garden City: Doubleday, 1983-1985).

14. For an overview of the OT Pseudepigrapha, see the 'Old Testament Pseudepigrapha' section of the Appendix.

2 BARUCH

A summary of *2 Baruch* is included in the Appendix. The following are quotes from *2 Baruch* that relate to the works righteousness question.

> For the righteous justly have good hope for the end and go away from this habitation without fear because they possess with you a store of good works which is preserved in treasuries. (*2 Bar.* 14:12)

> For behold, the days are coming, and the books will be opened in which are written the sins of all those who have sinned, and moreover, also the treasuries in which are brought together the righteousness of all those who have proven themselves to be righteous. (*2 Bar.* 24:1)

> For behold, I see many of your people who separated themselves from your statutes and who have cast away from them the yoke of your Law. . . . Their time will surely not be weighed exactly, and they will certainly not be judged as the scale indicates. (*2 Bar.* 41:3, 6)

> Behold, your Law is with us, we know that we do not fall as long as we keep your statutes. (*2 Bar.* 48:22)

> Miracles, however, will appear at their own time to those who are saved because of their works and for whom the Law is now a hope. (*2 Bar.* 51:7)

> [Concerning the approaching Assyrian army and Hezekiah's request to God], Hezekiah trusted upon his works, and hoped upon his righteousnesses. (*2 Bar.* 63:3)

> [Jewish forefathers] intervened for us with him [God] who has created us since they trusted in their works. And the Mighty One heard them and purged us from our sins. (*2 Bar.* 85:2)

2 Baruch intends to give comfort to the reader. Even though Israel was punished (Babylonian Exile // Roman destruction of Jerusalem) and not all Israelites will reach heaven, those who live by the Law will. This is works righteousness. Klijn bluntly gives the author's view, 'He who chooses to live according to the Law will receive eternal life.'[15] Among other things, note the several references above

---

15. A. F. J. Klijn, '2 (Syriac Apocalypse of) Baruch: A New Translation and Intro-

to a treasury of works (*2 Bar.* 14:12, 24:1) and scales (*2 Bar.* 41:6). Gathercole comments, 'The stores [treasury] of good works are the deeds done by these righteous in obedience to Torah, and these same works are an instrumental cause of their final salvation.'[16]

TESTAMENT OF ABRAHAM

The *Testament of Abraham* is a fascinating story. Righteous Abraham is told by the angel Michael that God wants Abraham to give a testament and then to give up his soul (die) by following Michael to heaven. Abraham refuses (*T. Ab. A* 1-7) and offers a compromise. Abraham wishes to see all of the inhabited world before he dies. God grants this request (*T. Ab. A* 8-9). Michael takes Abraham up into the clouds so he can see the whole world. Abraham now sees all the evil in the world and condemns it without mercy (*T. Ab. A* 10). God stops the tour and has Michael take Abraham to the entrance of heaven to see how God determines who gets in, which includes a balance of good and evil works (*T. Ab. A* 11-14). After this, Abraham still refuses to give up his soul (*T. Ab. A* 15). God now sends Death to get Abraham's soul. Through some trickery, Abraham finally dies, and his soul goes to heaven (*T. Ab. A* 16-20).

The *Testament of Abraham* is extant in multiple Greek manuscripts, and the current scholarly consensus is that the original language was Greek. Given that and the lack of specific Jewish ceremonial works, the original provenance is assumed to be Egypt with a date range from A.D. 50–110. The work exists in two Greek recensions, the longer one labeled 'A,' and the shorter, 'B.' Most consider 'A' as closer to the theoretical original.[17]

For our purposes, it is interesting to note that Abraham is considered perfectly righteous, but his method of judgment is improper

---

duction,' in *OTP*, 1:619. He lists several proof texts, *2 Bar.* 32:1, 38:1, 48:22, 51:3, 4-7, 54:15.

16. Gathercole, *Where is Boasting?*, 140.

17. See George W. E. Nickelsburg, *Jewish Literature Between the Bible and the Mishnah: A Historical and Literary Introduction* (rev. ed.; Philadelphia: Fortress, 1987), 248-53; and James R. Mueller, 'Abraham, Testament of,' *ABD*, 1:43-44.

—it has no mercy. More importantly, *T. Ab. A* 11-14 describes the judgment process that includes three gates being overseen by Adam. The first that leads to heaven is for those who are clearly righteous. The third that leads to destruction is for those who are clearly evil. The middle gate includes a balance held by an angel where one's good and evil deeds are weighed to see whether one goes to heaven or destruction. This middle gate is the one that Abraham was not considering. The following are quotes from *T. Ab. A.*

> [Michael says to God,] Master, Lord, let your might know that I cannot announce the mention of death to the righteous man [Abraham] because I have not seen upon earth a man like him— merciful, hospitable, righteous, truthful, God-fearing, refraining from every evil deed. (*T. Ab. A* 4:6)

> [God said to Michael,] For behold, Abraham has not sinned and he has no mercy on sinners. (*T. Ab. A* 10:14)[18]

> The two angels on the right and on the left recorded. The one on the right recorded righteous deeds, while the one on the left recorded sins. The one who was in front of the table, who was holding the balance, weighed the souls. (*T. Ab. A* 12:12-13)

> The Commander-in-chief said, 'Hear, righteous Abraham: Since the judge found its sins and its righteous deeds to be equal, then he handed it over neither to judgment nor to be saved, until the judge of all should come. ... If [one] could acquire one righteous deed more than one's sins, one would enter in to be saved.' (*T. Ab. A* 14:2-4)

As Abraham is watching the balancing, the situation occurs where the sins and righteous deeds perfectly balance. Abraham says a prayer for the person, and this tips the scale in favor of that person going to heaven (*T. Ab. A* 14:1-8).

Clearly the *Testament of Abraham* has a works righteousness view. God allows the perfect to go to heaven, and in 'mercy,' God also allows those with more good deeds than sins to go to heaven.

---

18. Confusingly, Abraham when talking to Michael calls himself a 'sinner' (*T. Ab. A* 9:3). Later after seeing the method of balance, Abraham states that he has 'sinned' (*T. Ab. A* 14:12).

Both of these scenarios are presented in a Pelagian manner. Yes, the book teaches that one does not have to be perfect to go to heaven, but it still teaches that one gets to heaven by performing works. As VanLandingham notes, 'The only criterion for this judgment relies on deeds—Gentiles are not damned because they are Gentiles, and neither are Jews saved because they are Jews.'[19]

How does Sanders respond to this? He says nothing in *Paul and Palestinian Judaism*; however, he wrote the article 'Testament of Abraham' in the *OTP*.[20] He states, 'The judgment on the basis of deeds is standard, both in Jewish and Christian literature ... the efficacy of repentance and God's merciful inclination to delay the death of sinners until they repent are noteworthy.'[21] Upon reading the article, I am not sure if Sanders sees the *Testament of Abraham* as teaching works righteousness or not. Gathercole assumes he does and further assumes that since the provenance is Hellenistic, Sanders does not see it as pertinent.[22] Possibly Sanders does not admit to works righteousness here, as repentance is a key theme for him.

In any event, the *Testament of Abraham* is a Second Temple Judaism document that clearly has a works righteousness soteriology.

PSALMS OF SOLOMON

A summary of the *Psalms of Solomon* is included in the Appendix. The following are some pertinent quotes related to the question of works righteousness.

> I considered in my heart that I was full of righteousness, for I had prospered and had many children. (*Pss. Sol.* 1:3)

---

19. Chris VanLandingham, *Judgment & Justification in Early Judaism and the Apostle Paul* (Peabody: Hendrickson, 2006), 169. Nickelsburg notes, 'Although the author ascribes to the patriarch some of the virtues traditionally attributed to him (righteousness, hospitality), he has glaringly omitted the most celebrated of these: Abraham's obedient faith' (*Jewish Literature Between the Bible and the Mishnah*, 251).

20. E. P. Sanders, 'Testament of Abraham,' *OTP*, 1:871-902.

21. Sanders, 'Testament of Abraham,' 1:878.

22. Gathercole, *Where is Boasting?*, 27-28.

He atones for (sins of) ignorance by fasting and humbling his soul, and the Lord will cleanse every devout person and his house. (*Pss. Sol.* 3:8)

May God remove from the devout those who live in hypocrisy; may his flesh decay and his life be impoverished. May God expose the deeds of those who try to impress people; (and expose) their deeds with ridicule and contempt. (*Pss. Sol.* 4:6-7)

Our works (are) in the choosing and power of our souls, to do right and wrong in the works of our hands, and in your righteousness you oversee human beings. The one who does what is right saves up life for himself with the Lord, and the one who does what is wrong causes his own life to be destroyed; for the Lord's righteous judgments are according to the individual and the household. (*Pss. Sol.* 9:4-5)

And whose sins will he forgive except those who have sinned? You bless the righteous, and do not accuse them for what they sinned. And your goodness is upon those that sin, when they repent. (*Pss. Sol.* 9:7)

The Lord is faithful to those who truly love him, to those who endure his discipline, to those who live in the righteousness of his commandments, in the Law, which he has commanded for our life. The Lord's devout shall live by it forever; the Lord's paradise, the trees of life, are his devout ones. (*Pss. Sol.* 14:1-3)

As the above quotes show, *Psalms of Solomon* includes statements with both mercy and works of righteousness required for eschatological salvation.

The clearest statements that deeds are required for eschatological salvation are *Pss. Sol.* 9:1-5 and 14:2-3. 'The one who does what is right saves up life for himself with the Lord' (*Pss. Sol.* 9:5). *Psalms of Solomon* 14:2-3 includes an apparent quote, or at least an allusion, of Lev. 18:5.[23] Eschatological life is connected to the righteous deeds of the Law.

Of course, some of these works statements could be taken in the sense of the third use of the law. However, since I do not see a clear

---

23. For a detailed discussion of Lev. 18:5 and *Psalms of Solomon*, see Preston M. Sprinkle, *Law and Life: The Interpretation of Leviticus 18:5 in Early Judaism and in Paul* (WUNT II/241; Tübingen: Mohr Siebeck, 2008), 87-100. Paul uses Lev. 18:5 in key works righteousness passages, Rom. 10:5, Gal. 3:12.

and overwhelming grace pattern in *Psalms of Solomon*, I consider this document semi-Pelagian. I agree with Gathercole's summary of *Psalms of Solomon*, 'The role of works in final vindication cannot be ruled out simply by asserting that the mercy of God is basic for life and salvation: both viewpoints are held simultaneously.'[24]

Sanders has long discussion on the *Psalms of Solomon*. He notes both the mercy passages and the works passages. However, he emphasizes the supposed covenant background and concludes that 'God's covenant is the basis of salvation, and the elect remain in the covenant unless they sin in such a way as to be removed.'[25] As noted in the previous chapter, if Sanders sees any mercy from God due to repentance, he assumes the document has no works righteousness. For me, Sanders' analysis overplays his assumed covenant background and ignores the category of semi-Pelagian.[26]

Psalms of Solomon 4 is a famous chapter denouncing hypocrisy. The author is condemning others who were acting as if they followed the Law but were violating it in secret. Clearly, to condemn hypocrisy is not a works righteousness act (Matt. 6:2, 23:13, Mark 7:6). However, the author is aware of others who are acting hypocritically. To act hypocritically is not necessarily done because of works righteousness motives, but many times it is. And if it is,

---

24. Gathercole, *Where is Boasting?*, 67. For a view between Sanders and me, see Daniel Falk, 'Prayers and Psalms,' in *The Complexities of Second Temple Judaism*, vol. 1 of *Justification and Variegated Nomism* (ed. D. A. Carson, Peter T. O'Brien, and Mark A. Seifrid; Grand Rapids: Baker, 2001), 35-51.

25. Sanders, *Paul and Palestinian Judaism*, 408. For the entire discussion, see pp. 387-409.

26. Charles Lee Irons argues that 'righteousness' language in the *Psalms of Solomon* includes both 'ethical righteousness' and 'God's judicial righteousness (*iustitia distributiva*).' In context, Irons is arguing against the Cremer/Dunn/Wright view of righteousness as the 'the covenant faithfulness of God.' More directly to our topic, Irons notes, 'Yes, there is mercy for those who repent, but repentance is turning oneself back to the Law. It is a way of getting back onto the path of righteousness. In the final analysis, righteousness by Law-keeping is still the necessary means of obtaining eschatological life' (*The Righteousness of God: A Lexical Examination of the Covenant-Faithfulness Interpretation* [WUNT II/386; Tübingen: Mohr Siebeck, 2015], 222-25).

then we have another piece of evidence that works righteousness views historically existed in Second Temple Judaism.

DEAD SEA SCROLLS [27]

The Dead Sea Scrolls (DSS) are a collection of more than 850 documents (many fragmentary) found in eleven caves just northwest of the Dead Sea. The writings date from 150 B.C. (or maybe even 250 B.C.) to A.D. 68.[28]

The document 1QH (*Thanksgiving Hymns* or *Hodayot[29]*) is a compilation of thirty full and partial poems similar to biblical psalms.[30] Many of these begin with 'I thank you, O Lord,' which explains the document name (*hodayot* means 'thanksgiving'). There are numerous examples of praising God's mercy and the admission of sin. Also included is strong predestination language.[31] 1QH will not be discussed further as only documents that emphasize works are. However, it is clear that at least there are some documents in the library of the DSS that praise God's grace and mercy. How 1QH dovetails with the documents below, if at all, is an open question.[32]

---

27. All English translations from the DSS are from Geza Vermes, *The Complete Dead Sea Scrolls in English* (rev. ed.; New York: Penguin, 2004).

28. For background on the DSS, see the discussions in sections 'Essenes and Qumran Community' and 'Dead Sea Scrolls' of the Appendix. For a broad critique of Sanders' covenantal nomism related to Qumran entrance requirements, see 'Admission of Gentiles and Qumran Community' in Chapter 2.

29. הודיות.

30. For an overview, see E. M. Schuller, 'Thanksgiving Hymns (1QH),' *DNTB*, 1214-18. For the most recent up-to-date translation, see Eileen M. Schuller and Carol A. Newsom, *The Hodayot (Thanksgiving Psalms): A Study Edition of 1QHa* (EJL 36; Atlanta: SBL, 2012).

31. Sanders also notes the strong predestination language in these hymns (*Paul and Palestinian Judaism*, 257-70).

32. I. Howard Marshall, an anti-NPP author, concludes, 'The Qumran community, for example, is just one group which was able to emphasize God's grace and at the same time require righteous deeds as the means of forgiveness. For them and for other groups the problem was not one of "staying in" the covenant people but of regaining entry by fulfilling the

To give the reader a sense of these wonderful hymns, a few quotes are provided below.[33]

> As Thou hast said by the hand of Moses, Thou forgives transgressions, iniquity, and sin, and pardons rebellion and unfaithfulness. (1QH IV, 10)

> I know that the inclination of every spirit [is in Thy hand]; Thou didst establish [all] its [ways] before ever creating it, and how can any man change Thy words? (1QH VII, 14)

> By Thy mercies and by Thy great goodness, Thou has strengthened the spirit of man in the face of the scourge and has purified [the erring spirit] of a multitude of sins that it may declare Thy marvels in the presence of all Thy creatures. (1QH IX, 33)

> For I remember my sins and the unfaithfulness of my fathers.... I lean on Thy grace and on the multitude of Thy mercies, for Thou wilt pardon iniquity, and through Thy righteousness [Thou wilt purify man] of his sin. Not for his sake wilt Thou do it ... For Thou has created the just and the wicked. (1QH XII, 37)

> I thank Thee, O Lord, for Thou hast upheld me by Thy strength. Thou has shed Thy Holy Spirit upon me that I may not stumble. (1QH XV, 6)

RULE OF THE COMMUNITY (1QS)

A summary of the *Rule of the Community* is included in the Appendix. The *Rule of the Community* included many directives about entering and staying in the group and ends with a long, psalm-like hymn praising the grace of God. To enter the community is to enter the true 'Covenant of God.'[34] Those not in the community are not

---

appropriate conditions laid down by the particular group' ('Salvation, Grace and Works in the Later Writings in the Pauline Corpus,' *NTS* 42 [1996]: 339-58, esp. 357).

33. Vermes' numbering system follows Peuch's.

34. Craig A. Evans concludes after evaluating 'covenant' in the DSS, 'Simply put, the distinctive feature of the understanding of Covenant at Qumran is the reduction of the number of elect' ('Covenant in the Qumran Literature,' in *The Concept of the Covenant in the Second Temple Period* [ed. Stanley E. Porter and Jacqueline C. R. de Roo; Supplements to the Journal for the Study of Judaism 71; Atlanta: SBL, 2003], 55-80, esp. 80).

destined for salvation (1QS V, 7-19). The *Rule of the Community* is probably the most important document for understanding the Qumran community. One's view of this colors much of one's view of the rest of the DSS.

The following are quotes related to the question of works righteousness.

> He shall admit into the Covenant of Grace all those who have freely devoted themselves to the observance of God's precepts, that they may be joined to the counsel of God and may live perfectly before Him in accordance with all that has been revealed. (1QS I, 7-8)

> They shall not depart from any command of God concerning their times; they shall be neither early or late for any of their appointed times, they shall stray neither to the right nor to the left of any of His true precepts. ... [They] shall enter into the Covenant before God to obey all His commandments. (1QS I, 15)

> Let him then order his steps (to walk) perfectly in all the ways commanded by God concerning the times appointed for him, straying neither to the right nor to the left and transgressing none of His words, and he shall be accepted by virtue of a pleasing atonement before God and it shall be to him a Covenant of the everlasting Community. (1QS III, 9-12)

> But when a man enters the Covenant to walk according to all these precepts that he may be joined to the Holy Congregation, they shall examine his spirit in community with respect to his understanding and practice of the Law. ... And they shall examine their spirit and deeds yearly, so that each many may be advanced in accordance with his understanding and perfection of way, or moved down in accordance with his distortions. (1QS V, 20-24)

> Whoever has deliberately deceived his companion by word or by deed shall do penance for six months. (1QS VII, 5)

> [Council of the Community] shall preserve the faith in the Land with steadfastness and meekness and shall atone for sin by the practice of justice and by suffering the sorrows of affliction. (1QS VIII, 3-4)

> And no man among the members of the Covenant of the Community who deliberately, on any point whatever, turns aside from all that is

commanded, shall touch the pure Meal of the men of holiness or know anything of their counsel until his deeds are purified from all injustice and he walks in perfection of way. (1QS VIII, 17-18)

[Members of the Community] shall atone for guilty rebellion and for sins of unfaithfulness, that they may obtain loving-kindness for the Land without the flesh of holocausts and the fat of sacrifice. And prayer rightly offered shall be as an acceptable fragrance of righteousness, and perfection of way as a delectable free-will offering. (1QS IX, 4-6)

I will declare His judgment concerning my sins, and my transgressions shall be before my eyes as an engraved Precept, I will say to God, 'My Righteousness' and 'Author of my Goodness' to the Most High. (1QS X, 12-13)

If I stagger because of the sin of flesh, my justification [מ שׁ פ טי]35 will be by the righteousness of God which endures for all time. (1QS XI, 12)

As can be from 1QS I, 7-8, there are strict requirements for Jews entering the Community. As previously discussed in Chapter 2, this argues against Sanders' view that all Jews are presumed to be in the Covenant and 'getting in' is by grace.

As can be seen from many of the above quotes, 'staying in' the Community requires strict adherence and penance for misdeeds. Although in principle this does not contradict Sanders' view of 'staying in' by works (not works righteousness in his view), would one not agree that this strictness would tend in works righteousness direction even for one who was committed to Sanders' covenantal nomism?

In 1QS III, 9-12, ritual atonement is connected to doing good deeds. The Qumran Community did not participate in the existing Temple sacrifices. Yes, this could be taken in a metaphorical third-use-of-the-law way, as does the NT (Heb. 13:15-16); however, the strictness of the Community's rules and the lack of a clear avenue of actual atonement, such as Christ's death, argue against this.

---

35. 'My judgment' would be a better translation.

Much is made of the psalm-like ending showing God's grace (1QS X-XI).[36] And it should be. However, this at best gives the document a semi-Pelagian view. Possibly the two parts of the *Rule of the Community* were separate; if so, the first part would indicate the presence of Pelagianism in the community.[37]

Nickelsburg, a pro-covenantal-nomism author, notes that 'we should not presume that Judaism was characterized by a "works righteousness" that excluded the grace integral to the structure of biblical covenantal theology.' He goes on to quote from the ending psalm of the *Rule of the Community*. He further notes the 'corresponding lists of good and evil deeds and their respective rewards and punishments' in the *Rule of the Community*. He concludes by saying, 'In all these respects, these ancient documents defy the consistency of later philosophical speculation about free will and much Christian theology that derives from that speculation.'[38] Nickelsburg solution is to see the documents as simply inconsistent.[39] I prefer to see it as semi-Pelagian.

---

36. Preston M. Sprinkle agrees that 1QS X-XI is gracious to a significant degree, but he notes that the context is the final judgment of those who have demonstrated obedience. He further notes that Paul has a higher view of divine agency because he advocated for the *initial* justification of the *ungodly* (*Paul & Judaism Revisited: A Study of Divine and Human Agency in Salvation* [Downers Grove: IVP Academic, 2013], 167-70).

37. Although not conclusive, supporting the two-separate-documents view is that the *Damascus Document* (CD) is very similar to the *Rule of the Community* excepting the psalm-like ending.

38. George W. E. Nickelsburg, *Ancient Judaism and Christian Origins: Diversity, Continuity, and Transformation* (Minneapolis: Fortress, 2003), 50-51. VanLandingham argues that the psalm is not actually grace-based at all; this is going too far for me (*Judgment & Justification in Early Judaism and the Apostle Paul*, 126-34). See Robert J. Cara, review of *Judgment & Justification in Early Judaism and the Apostle Paul*, by Chris VanLandingham, *WTJ* 70 (2008): 388-92.

39. Markus Bockmuehl similarly concludes that 1QS has an 'unsystematic soteriology.' 'As it stands, salvation is on the one hand "legalistic" both in its individualistic voluntarism and in its closely regimented corporate life; and yet it is the gift of divine grace alone, both objectively in regard to predestination and subjectively in the experience of the believer. The evidence

Sanders admits that there 'may appear to be a significant distinction between the legalistic works righteousness of 1QS I-IX' and the ending psalm. But properly understood, it confirms his view of covenantal nomism in that 'the principal point of the punishment for deeds but reward for mercy theme is that, while man can forfeit salvation by transgression, he can never be sufficiently deserving to earn it by obedience.'[40] I beg to differ and simply note that the ending psalm proves that the *Rule of Community* is not, at least as a total document, Pelagian. However, it appears to be clearly semi-Pelagian.[41]

PESHER HABAKKUK (1QPHAB)

The word 'pesher' translates as 'commentary.' Hence, *Pesher Habakkuk*, is a commentary on Habakkuk. In the DSS, there are approximately eleven different commentaries. This one is the most well known. It is the longest of the pesherim, the best preserved, and it provides useful information about the Teacher of Righteousness.[42]

Pesher Habakkuk expounds the biblical book of Habakkuk half verse by half verse from Hab. 1:1 through 2:20. The author reads

---

itself now confirms that the intrinsically unsystematic soteriology of a central document like 1QS is due at least in some part to textual development over a considerable length of time' ('1QS and Salvation at Qumran,' in *The Complexities of Second Temple Judaism*, vol. 1 of *Justification and Variegated Nomism* [ed. D. A. Carson, Peter T. O'Brien, and Mark A. Seifrid; Grand Rapids: Baker, 2001], 381-414, esp. 413).

40. Sanders, *Paul and Palestinian Judaism*, 291, 293 (second quote, italics in original).

41. Peter Stuhlmacher cites 1QS, along with 4 Ezra, 1QpHab, 4QMMT, and *2 Baruch*, as an example throughout Second Temple Judaism of 'two contrary principles ... a principle of election and a principle of retribution' within the same documents (*Revisiting Paul's Doctrine of Justification: A Challenge to the New Perspective* [Downers Grove: InterVarsity, 2001], 41). Barry D. Smith, an anti-NPP author, evaluates the Qumran literature, including 1QS, and concludes that God is shown as both merciful and as a righteous judge. This produces a synergistic soteriology. See his *What Must I do to be Saved? Paul Parts Company with His Jewish Heritage* (New Testament Monographs 17; Sheffield: Sheffield Phoenix, 2007), 22-34, 47-72.

42. The standard reference work on *Pesher Habakkuk* is W. H. Brownlee, *The Midrash Pesher of Habakkuk* (SBLMS 24; Missoula: Scholars, 1979).

contemporary events into the biblical book (e.g., the Chaldeans are the Romans ['Kittim'], Hab. 1:6 // 1QpHab I, 10). There are three prominent persons, (1) the Teacher of Righteousness, who is the leader of the Qumran community, (2) the Liar, who apparently used to follow the Teacher, but has now rebelled, and (3) the Wicked Priest, who initially followed the truth, but now is a horrible ruler that abuses the poor and desecrates the Temple, and has 'pursued the Teacher of Righteousness to the house of his exile' (1QpH X, 5-6). There is a significant emphasis on the final age and judgment.

The following are quotes related to the question of works righteousness.

> 'If it tarries, wait for it, for it shall surely come and shall not be late' [Hab. 2:3b]. Interpreted, this concerns the men of truth who keep the Law, whose hands shall not slacken in the service of truth when the final age is prolonged. (1QpHab VII, 10-13)

> 'Behold, [his soul] is puffed up and is not upright' [Hab. 2:4a]. Interpreted, this means that [the wicked] shall double their guilt upon themselves [and it shall not be forgiven] when they are judged. (1QpHab VII, 14-16)

> 'But the righteous shall live by his faith' [Hab. 2:4b]. Interpreted, this concerns all those who observe the Law in the house of Judah, whom God will deliver from the House of Judgment because of their suffering and because of their faith in the Teacher of Righteousness. (1QpHab VIII, 1-3)

> [Interpreting Hab. 2:16] For [the Wicked Priest] did not circumcise the foreskin of his heart, and he walked in the ways of drunkenness that he might quench his thirst. (1QpHab XI, 12)

> [Interpreting Hab. 2:17] The 'beasts' are the simple of Judah who keep the Law. (1QpHab XII, 4-5)

The text that receives the most attention is 1QpHab VIII, 1-3 as this is the interpretation of Hab. 2:4, 'the just shall live by faith,' which Paul refers to in Rom. 1:17 and Gal. 3:11 (also see Heb. 10:38). The author of *Pesher Habakkuk* inserts the observance of the Law into this 'faith alone' text. (He interprets 'faith' as faith in the Teacher of

Righteousness.) In several other places, the observance of the Law is also inserted (1QpHab II, 14, VII, 10-13, XII, 4-5). Sprinkle summarizes, 'Faith and works of the law are seen as essential partners in humanity's justification and deliverance.'[43] Although Sprinkle does not like the term semi-Pelagian, this is the substance of his conclusion.[44]

Helyer goes further and concludes that *Pesher Habakkuk* is making the exact opposite point that Paul makes.

> [In *Pesher Habakkuk*,] one gains God's grace and favor by a punctilious observance of all the law, in this case, of course, the halakic interpretation advocated by the Teacher of Righteousness. This pesher on Habakkuk is evidence that Paul's polemic against salvation by works is not a fabrication on his part.[45]

The author of *Pesher Habakkuk* multiple times inserts observance of the Law into his interpretation of Habakkuk, which at that point in Habakkuk, has little to do with the Law. This shows that the author is clearly not using the Law in a 'third use' way. He probably has a Pelagian understanding. Hence, I agree with Helyer.

MIQSAT MA'ASE HA-TORAH (4QMMT)[46]

Miqsat Ma'ase Ha-Torah is an apparent letter that was found in six incomplete manuscripts with the composite text being about 120 lines.[47] The manuscripts are numbered 4Q394-99, and the letter is

---

43. Preston M. Sprinkle, *Paul and Judaism Revisited*, 167. Similarly, Francis Watson, 'Right interpretation, practice, and belief belong together, ensuring that the righteous person will live—that is, be delivered from "the house of judgment"' (*Paul and the Hermeneutics of Faith* [London: T & T Clark, 2004], 523, also see 119-26).

44. Sprinkle prefers to evaluate the relationship between 'divine and human agency' and not use the terms typical of 'Old or New Perspectives on Paul' (*Paul and Judaism Revisited*, 25).

45. Larry R. Helyer, *Exploring Jewish Literature of the Second Temple Period: A Guide for New Testament Students* (Downers Grove: InterVarsity, 2002), 232-33.

46. מקצת מעשי התורה.

47. For a good summary article of 4QMMT, see Elisha Qimron, 'Miqsat Ma'ase

separated by scholars into three major sections (4MMT A, 4MMT B, 4 MMT C). The title is the transliteration of the Hebrew phrase 'some of the works of the Law,' which is near the end of letter (4QMMT C 27).

This letter has garnered much scholarly attention, including articles from both Dunn and Wright, the two leading proponents of the NPP.[48] Two important expressions are similar to those in Paul. The 4QMMT C 27 wording 'works of the law' matches Paul (e.g., Rom. 3:20, Gal. 2:16).[49] Also, 'and it will be reckoned to you as righteousness' in 4QMMT C 31 is very similar to Gen. 15:6, Ps. 106: 31, and various Pauline passages (e.g., Rom. 4:3, Gal. 3:6).[50] In addition, on the surface, 4QMMT appears to have a clear works righteousness theology.

The opening and closing of the apparent letter is missing. The first section that is extant, 4QMMT A, is a 364-day calendar that primarily lists the dates for the sabbath, e.g., 'On the twenty-eighth day of the [twelfth month], sabbath' (4QMMT A 19). The second section, 4QMMT B, lists 20 halakhot (rules) that mostly relate to Temple ceremonies, e.g., 'concerning the skin of the carcass of a clean animal, he who carries their carcass shall not touch the [sacred] purity' (4QMMT B 22-23). In the final extant section, 4QMMT C,

---

Hatorah,' *ABD*, 4:843-45. Also see John Kampen and Moshe J. Bernstein, eds., *Reading 4QMMT: New Perspectives on Qumran Law and History* (SBL Symposium Series 2; Atlanta: Scholars, 1996).

48. James D. G. Dunn, '4QMMT and Galatians,' in *The New Perspective on Paul* (rev. ed.; Grand Rapids: Eerdmans, 2008), 339-45. This article was originally found in *NTS* 43 (1997): 147-53. N. T. Wright, '4QMMT and Paul: Justification, "Works," and Eschatology,' in *History and Exegesis: New Testament Essays in Honor of Dr E. Earle Ellis for His 80th Birthday* (ed. Sand-Won Son; New York: T & T Clark, 2006), 104-32.

49. The Hebrew מעשי התורה includes the definite article before 'Law.' Paul's expression, ἐξ ἔργων νόμου, does not. This can easily be explained—within a Greek prepositional phrase, the definite article is often dropped. For the general rule, see BDF § 255 and Daniel B. Wallace, *Greek Grammar Beyond the Basics: An Exegetical Syntax of the New Testament* (Grand Rapids: Zondervan, 1996), 247.

50. ויחשבה לך לצדקה (4QMMT C 31); ונחשבה לך לצדקה (Gen. 15:6).

the author notes that he and his group have separated themselves from the 'mass of people' and wants the addressee (singular 'you') to follow the author's interpretation of Moses, Prophets, and David as to the halakhot (4QMMT C 7-12). Following these halakhot will be beneficial for Israel (4QMMT C 27).

Although not explicitly stated, the author appears to be the leader of the Qumran community, and it is a reasonable guess that he is the Teacher of Righteousness. The addressee is some type of leader in Israel (4QMMT C 23-25) who has influence at the Temple. There is also references to 'they.' This appears to be a group with competing views for proper Temple ceremonies, maybe the Pharisees or Sadducees.

The following are quotes related to the question of works righteousness.

> These are some of our teachings which are the works which we think all of them concern the purity. (4QMMT B 1-2)

> And he shall not sow his field and vineyard with two kinds. For they are holy and the sons of Aaron are most holy. And you know that some of the priests and the people mingle and they unite and defile the holy seed and also their seed with whores. (4QMMT B 78-82)

> And you know that we have separated from the mass of people and from mingling with them in these matters and from being in contact with them in these matters. And you know that no treachery or lie or evil is found in our hands. (4QMMT C 7-9).

> We recognize that some of the blessings and curses which are written in the Book of Moses have come. (4QMMT C 20-21)

> Remember the kings of Israel and understand their works that each of them who feared the Law was saved from troubles, and to those who were seekers of the Law, their iniquities were pardoned. Remember David, that he was a man of piety, and that he was saved from many troubles and pardoned. (4QMMT C 23-26)

> We have also written to you concerning some of the works[51] of the Law, which we think are beneficial to you and your people. For we

---

51. Vermes translates as 'observances.'

have noticed that prudence and knowledge of the Law are with you. (4QMMT C 26-28)

Understand all these matters and ask Him to straighten out your counsel and put you far away from thought so evil and the counsel of Belial. (4QMMT C 28-29).

You will rejoice at the end of time when you discover that some of our sayings are true. And it will be reckoned for you as righteousness when you perform what is right and good before Him, for your own good and for that of Israel. (4QMMT C 30-32).

First, a side issue is presented. In their discussion of Paul, NPP authors want to connect Paul's use of 'works of the Law' to Jewish boundary markers (food laws, circumcision, sabbath), not to an overarching following of the entire law. Dunn, one of the leading NPP authors, argues that 4QMMT parallels Galatians in that both use 'works of the Law' to 'defin[e] a boundary which marks out those of faith/faithfulness from others.' The Qumran dispute was 'intra-Jewish,' and the Galatians one, 'between Jew and Gentile.'[52] I argue that in 4QMMT the expression 'works of the Law' (4QMMT C 27) is broader than boundary markers and includes the Qumran's community's view of keeping all of the law, which does entail partially their own idiosyncratic views.

Certainly 'works of the Law' does include Sabbath, as the calendar section shows (4QMMT A). Although it is possible that some minor parts of the calendar were in dispute, I assume that all Jewish groups would agree to the basic Sabbath observance. Various Temple ceremonial laws are also stressed, although it is noteworthy that some of these have clear moral/ethical warnings, such as priests interacting improperly with women (4QMMT B 78-82). Deuteronomy 30:1-2 is quoted which is part of the Deut. 27-30 blessings and curses section (4QMMT C 13-16). This biblical section includes many straightforward ethical commands that all Jews would agree with. The piety of the kings of Israel is included as works of the Law (4QMMT 23-26), and these are more than

---

52. Dunn, '4QMMT and Galatians,' 343.

ceremonial works. Finally, the Hebrew word translated as 'works' (מעשי, construct plural) is directly related to the verb 'to do' (עשה). This is the verb that is often used in OT statements to follow the whole law. For example, 'Cursed is anyone who does not confirm the words of this law by doing (עשה) them' (Deut. 27:26, cf. Gal. 3:10, 13). 'Be careful to do (עשה) all the law that my servant Moses commanded you' (Josh. 1:7). These OT texts support that 4QMMT sees 'works of the Law' as referring to all laws, not just those that separated the Qumran community from other Jewish communities.[53]

What about works righteousness? In 4QMMT C 20-21 and 26-28 the benefits/blessings of a return to following the Law relate to the current time. However, in 4QMMT C 30-32, the 'reckoned to you for righteousness' is in an eschatological context. And in that context, it is the 'works of the Law' from 4QMMT C 27 that are the basis for being reckoned righteous and receiving eschatological blessings. Is this not a straightforward works righteousness view? One could argue that the author does believe that (prior?) sins may be pardoned, but the way to obtain that pardon is to do the Law (4QMMT C 23-24). In 4QMMT C 28-29, the author does urge the addressee to ask God for 'counsel' and for God to 'put you far away from thoughts of evil.' This is the only verse with divine agency in 4QMMT. Even though, this would admit at best to a semi-Pelagian view of works righteousness.

How do Dunn and Wright respond? After citing Gen. 15:6 and Ps. 106:31, Dunn confusingly agrees that here justification, righteousness, and works of the law are all related. He notes that this is just another example in Second Temple Judaism of 'covenant faithfulness.'[54] I assume Dunn means by 'covenant faithfulness,' Sanders' covenantal-nomism scheme. Apparently, it is this scheme that allows him to not term this works righteousness.

Wright agrees that 4QMMT C 30-32 is ultimately eschatological, although he wants to stress that it is also covenantal.[55]

---

53. So also Gathercole, *Where is Boasting?*, 92-93.

54. Dunn, '4QMMT and Galatians,' 343-44.

55. Wright, '4QMMT and Paul: Justification, "Works," and Eschatology,' 112.

Fair enough. Wright then sees these emphases as confirming that 4QMMT has the Sanders' scheme and is not works righteous theology. For him, 'righteousness'/'justification' is being designated that one is 'staying in' the community and not about 'getting in.'[56] He argues that 'the language of C 31 is not about entry into the community, but about being demonstrated to be within it.'[57] However, the context of the letter is implicitly asking the addressee and his followers to 'get in' the community. Also, the final judgment is in view which is more that 'staying in.' To prove his point about 'staying in,' Wright paraphrases 4QMMT C 30-32:

> If through prayer and the moral strength that God supplies (C 28-29) *you keep these precepts*, you will rejoice at the end of time, in finding that the advice given, this selection of commands, was on the right track. That is when (C 31) '*it will be reckoned to you as righteousness when you perform* what is right and good before him.'[58]

Based simply on the above paraphrase, Wright attributes a semi-Pelagian view to the author of 4QMMT.[59] I appreciate his emphasis on works being done by the power of God, but the problem is that he attaches these works to justification. Whether one is referencing justification related to 'getting in,' 'staying in,' or the final judgment, if it involves works, it is works righteousness theology.[60]

He goes on to argue that 'Paul's doctrine has exactly the same *shape* as that of MMT' (p. 120, italics his).

56. Wright explicitly refers to Sanders' terms here ('4QMMT and Paul: Justification, "Works," and Eschatology,' 117).

57. Wright, '4QMMT and Paul: Justification, "Works," and Eschatology,' 117, italics in original. In *Paul and the Faithfulness of God*, Wright views the Pharisees as sharing the same 'shape of how eschatology works in relation to election and thus to present justification' as does 4QMMT (Minneapolis: Fortress, 2013, p. 184).

58. Wright, '4QMMT and Paul: Justification, "Works," and Eschatology,' 116, italics mine.

59. Sprinkle complains that Wright will not admit that 'a return to the law in the eschatological age is a means of eliciting the covenant blessing, not merely a way to identify who the righteous really are' (*Paul & Judaism Revisited*, 78).

60. M. G. Abegg Jr. disagrees with me and considers my view a 'knee-jerk

RABBINIC LITERATURE

Rabbinic Judaism is the name given to the religious party after the A.D. 70 fall of Jerusalem that is the continuation of the Pharisee party. For our purposes, the classic Rabbinic literature beginning with the Mishnah and ending with the Babylonian Talmud (A.D. 200–600) will be considered.[61]

Before A.D. 200, there are no extant written documents for Rabbinic Judaism. Not all scholars want to use Rabbinic literature to evaluate Second Temple Judaism. I believe there certainly is some continuity between the Pharisees and the Mishnah and Tosefta. I have my doubts about later Rabbinic literature, including the Talmuds.[62] Sanders bases much of his argument on traditional Tannaitic material (rabbis who lived from 50 B.C.–A.D. 200) in the Rabbinic literature. This would include the Mishnah, major portions of the Tosefta, supposed Tannaitic portions of the Talmuds,[63] and even later midrashim such as the *Midrash Rabbah.*

This section will present various texts that I believe show a works righteousness soteriology. Sanders, of course, does not view these texts this way. I note here that not even all Jewish authors agree with Sanders. Some give an explicit Pelagian view of the rabbis. Epstein argues:

> [Talmudic] Judaism further denies the existence of original sin, needing a superhuman counterweight, and allows only the free choice

---

reaction.' 'The emphasis on the need for repentance and focus on God's grace in this and other Qumran writings should convince that a knee-jerk reaction that suggests that 4QMMT reflects a "works-earn-righteousness" religion is hardly justified.' He goes on to reference Sanders. See 'Miqṣat Maʿaśey Ha-Torah (4QMMT),' *DNTB*, 709-11, esp. 710-11. Also see his article '4QMMT C 27, 31 and "Works Righteousness,"' *DSD* 6 (1999): 139-47.

61. For background on Rabbinic literature, see the discussions in sections 'Include Rabbinic Literature?' and 'Rabbinic Literature' in the Appendix. For a broad critique of Sanders' covenantal nomism related to Rabbinic literature, see 'Halakah Emphasis Tends Toward Legalism' and 'Reliability of the New Testament for Second Temple Judaism Views' in Chapter 2.

62. See the 'Usefulness for First-Century A.D. Judaism?' section of the Appendix.

63. When the Talmuds refer to earlier Tannaitic material that is not in the Mishnah nor Tosefta, this is referred to as 'baraitot.'

to sin, an inevitable concomitant of free will. ... Obedience or return to God after offending carries with it divine favour and reward. ... Judaism makes salvation depend on right conduct.[64]

Neusner, while not explicitly Pelagian, argues that the rabbis' view of an eschatological resurrection and an eschatological judgment by God clearly requires that 'deeds done in this world bear consequences for his situation in the world to come, and the merit attained through this-worldly deeds, for example, generosity, persists.'[65]

MISHNAH[66]

The Mishnah was completed in approximately A.D. 200 and is the foundational document for Rabbinic Judaism. The Mishnah is a large book (about half the size of the Bible) arranged in six major divisions that separates sixty-three topics or 'tractates.' An extended discussion of the Mishnah is included in the Appendix.

M. ABOT

'Abot' translates as 'Fathers.' It is one of the few tractates that does not have an explicit parallel in the Tosefta or the two Talmuds. Of all the tractates in the Mishnah, this one has more theological comments per se and less halakah.[67] Unrelated to works righteousness, this tractate is important in the Mishnah as it presents the view that the oral law, in addition to the written law, came from Moses (*m. Abot* 1:1-2). Also, it includes the concept that the oral law is a fence around the written law (*m. Abot* 1:1, 3:13). Related to works righteousness, *m. Abot* 3:15 is often quoted.

---

64. Isidore Epstein, *Judaism: A Historical Presentation* (New York: Penguin, 1990 [1959]), 142-43.

65. Jacob Neusner, *Judaism When Christianity Began: A Survey of Belief and Practice* (Louisville: Westminster John Knox, 2002), 167.

66. All English translations from the Mishnah are from Jacob Neusner, *The Mishnah: A New Translation* (New Haven: Yale University Press, 1988).

67. Some see this tractate as the latest of those in the Mishnah and added to the Mishnah in A.D. 250. So Jacob Neusner, *Rabbinic Literature: An Essential Guide* (Nashville: Abingdon, 2005), 8.

The following are quotes related to the question of works righteousness.

Be meticulous in a small religious duty as in a large one, for you do not know what sort of reward is coming for any of the various religious duties. ... And keep your eyes on three things, so you will not come into the clutches of transgression: Know what is above you: An eye which sees, an ear which hears, and all your actions are written down in a book. (*m. Abot* 2:1-2)

Rabbi Eliezer says, 'Let the respect owing to your fellow be as precious to you as the respect owing to you yourself. And don't be easy to anger. And repent one day before you die.' (*m. Abot* 2:10)

Rabbi Simeon says, 'Be meticulous in the recitation of the *shema* and the Prayer. ... But let it be a plea for mercy and supplication before the Omnipresent blessed be he.' (*m. Abot* 2:13)

If you have learned much Torah, they will give you a good reward. And our employer can be depended upon to pay your wages for what you do. And know what sort of reward is going to be given to the righteous in the coming time. (*m. Abot* 2:16)

Rabbi Eleazar the Modite says, 'He who treats Holy Things as secular, and he who defiles the appointed times, he who humiliates his fellow in public, he who removes the signs of the covenant of Abraham, our father, may he rest in peace, and he who exposes aspects of the Torah not in accord with the law, even though he has in hand learning in Torah and good deeds, will have no share in the world to come.' (*m. Abot* 3:11)

Rabbi Aqiba says, ... 'Everything is foreseen and free choice is given. In goodness the world is judged. And all is in accord with the abundance of deeds.' (*m. Abot* 3:15)

Rabbi Eliezer son of Jacob says, 'He who does even a single religious duty gets himself a good advocate. He who does even a single transgression gets himself a prosecutor. Penitence and good deeds are like a shield against punishment.' (*m. Abot* 4:11)

Despite your wishes [you are] going to give a full accounting before the King of kings, the Holy One, blessed be he. (*m. Abot* 4:22)

He who brings merit to the community never causes sin. ... Moses attained merit and bestowed merit on the community. So the merit of the community is assigned to his credit. (*m. Abot* 5:18)

Ben He He says, 'In accord with the effort is the reward.' (*m. Abot* 5:23)

As can be seen from the above quotes, there is a large emphasis on performing good deeds and that God will evaluate those deeds now and at the final judgment.[68] In addition to individual merit, there is some aspect of community merit (*m. Abot* 5:18). It appears that one did not have to perfectly fulfill the law to enter heaven as allowance is made for repentance, but it is still true that good deeds in conjunction with repentance are required (*m Abot 4:11*). The somewhat well-known *m. Abot* 3:15 ('all in accordance of the abundance of deeds') implies that the majority of one's deeds need to be positive for eschatological life.

How does Sanders respond? First, Sanders admits that *m. Abot* 3:15, *m. Abot* 4:22, and *t. Qiddushin* (discussed below) at first reading 'may be taken to support the view that weighing fulfillments against transgressions constitutes Rabbinic soteriology.'[69] However, Sanders argues that elsewhere in these texts it is implied that by one good deed (*m. Abot* 2:10) one may get into the afterlife and one evil deed (*m. Abot* 3:11) may prevent it. And if that is true, the weighing-of-good-and-evil-deeds statements must be considered against the one-deed statements. Hence, Sanders concludes that 'it is apparent that the [*m. Abot 3:15*] saying intends to hold judgment by grace and by works in balance. Not being a systematic theologian, Rabbi Akiba did not explain how the two parts of the

---

68. See Philip S. Alexander's discussion of *m. Abot* specifically and the Tannaitic literature in general. He concludes that 'Tannaitic Judaism can be seen as fundamentally a religion of works righteousness, and is none the worse for that.' He does, however, note that the scales of justice for the amount of good works required for entrance into heaven were weighted toward mercy ('Torah and Salvation in Tannaitic Literature,' in *The Complexities of Second Temple Judaism*, vol. 1 of *Justification and Variegated Nomism* [ed. D. A. Carson, Peter T. O'Brien, and Mark A. Seifrid; Grand Rapids: Baker, 2001], 261-301, esp. 283-88, 298-301, quote on 300).

69. Sanders, *Paul and Palestinian Judaism*, 128.

saying fit together.'[70] Sanders also uses the argument that these works-oriented statements are merely 'exhortative' and 'the point is to encourage people to obey and not transgress.'[71]

In response, I note that the one-good-deed argument is suspect in *m. Abot*. Sanders only cites *m. Abot* 2:10, 'repent one day before you die.' It is hard to believe that this comment, which is among two other deeds, is to be taken with the sense that all of life's previous sins are forgiven and only good deeds on the final day of life are required for heaven. (Admittedly, this view may be elsewhere in the Mishnah, e.g., *m. Sanhedrin* 6:2, *t. Qiddushin* 1:16, but not here.) As to the one-evil-deed argument, it seems to me that *m. Abot* 3:11 proves the opposite of Sanders' intention. In *m. Abot* 3:11, Rabbi Eleazar lists five sins that prevent one from entering the afterlife despite having 'learning in Torah and good deeds.' That is, there are sins so heinous that positive deeds cannot overcome these. This, I conclude, implies that there is a scale of judgment that good and evil deeds are weighed upon.

From my perspective, it is not necessary to prove that the rabbis had a scale of good verses evil deeds. Yes, maybe this is a broad metaphor. However, it is clear that works are involved in the final judgment to determine eschatological life, and overwhelmingly so. This is a works righteousness soteriology.

As quoted above, Sanders even agrees that 'grace and works are held in balance,' but this is excused because Rabbi Aqiba is not a 'systematic theologian.' I assume, tongue in cheek, that Sanders means that if Rabbi Aqiba were a systematic theologian, he would have solved the grace and works tension by means of the covenantal-nomism scheme. In any case, Sanders' comment about grace and works is, at least on the surface of it, semi-Pelagian. Also, he excuses some of these works statements based on their being 'exhortative.' That is, the rabbis used a soteriological incentive for good works that violated their actual soteriology. Even if that were true, one's incentive for good works *is* part of one's theology, even

---

70. Sanders, *Paul and Palestinian Judaism*, 132, also see discussion on 138-39.

71. Sanders, *Paul and Palestinian Judaism*, 129.

if it is inconsistent. On the other hand, it appears to me that it is better to say that the rabbis' exhortation was consistent with their view that final judgment is related to works.

M. SOTAH

'Sotah' translates as a wife who has possibly 'turned astray' and in context is a suspected adulterer.[72] This tractate is primarily related to Num. 5:11-31, which is case law for a woman suspected of adultery. A key aspect of the OT ceremony is the suspected woman's drinking of 'bitter' water, whose effects will be physically evident if she is guilty of adultery (Num. 5:18, 26-27).

Concerning the question of works righteousness, two texts are quoted below. The first concerns a woman who is guilty of adultery. She drinks the bitter water, but the curse effects do not immediately show. The second is the final pericope in the tractate. It follows a somewhat sad section that recounts various losses to the Jewish people from the destruction of Jerusalem through the defeat of Bar Kochba (m. Sotah 9:10-14).

> There is the possibility that merit suspends the curse for one year, and there is the possibility that merit suspends the curse for two years, and there is the possibility that merit suspends the curse for three years.
>
> On this basis Ben Azzai says, 'A man is required to teach Torah to his daughter. For if she should drink the water, and she should know that if nothing happens to her, merit is what suspends the curse from taking effect.'
>
> … Rabbi Simeon says, 'Merit does not suspend the effects of the bitter water. And if you say, "Merit does suspend the effects of the bitter water," you will weaken the effect of the water for all the women who drink it who turned out to be pure.' (m. Sotah 3:4-5)

> Upon whom shall we depend? Upon our Father in heaven. Rabbi Pinhas son of Yair says, 'Heedfulness leads to cleanliness, cleanliness leads to cleanness, cleanness leads to abstinence, abstinence leads

---

72. Sotah is from the Hebrew root שׂטה, 'to turn aside, go astray.' In Num. 5:12, 19, 20, 29, it is used to refer to a wife who has 'turned astray,' that is, committed adultery.

to holiness, holiness leads to modesty, modesty leads to the fear of sin, and fear of sin lead to piety, piety leads to the Holy Spirit, the Holy Spirit leads to the resurrection of the dead, and the resurrection of the dead come through Elijah, blessed be his memory, Amen.' (*m. Sotah* 9:15)

In *m. Sotah* 3:4-5, if a guilty women does not immediate show the effects of the bitter water, it is because she has previously accrued 'merit.' Rabbi Simeon objects to this because it confuses the results of the ceremony for those who are pure.

Concerning our purposes related to works righteousness, how does the woman acquire merit? Commonly in Rabbinic literature, studying the Torah is a good deed. Ben Azzai argues that this ceremony teaches that even daughters should learn the Torah because doing so acquires merit. This comment by Ben Azzai prompts a long discussion in the Babylonian Talmud (*b. Sotah* 20b-22b).[73] Part of the discussion relates to whether women should study the Torah and Mishnah with the answer being that women need to know about the Torah and Mishnah in order to encourage their sons to read them (*b. Sotah* 21a). Another part of the discussion is whether transgressions may cancel out merit. That is, does not the adultery cancel out any merit from good deeds? The rabbis answer that 'while a transgression extinguishes the merit of a religious duty one has performed, it does not extinguish the merit of Torah one has studied' (*b. Sotah* 22a).[74] Although the above discussions in the Mishnah and Babylonian Talmud are referring to merit that is applied during this life (the women does not show immediate effects of the bitter water), this still shows a works righteousness system as good and evil deeds are balanced against each other in this life, and presumably would be for eschatological life also (cf. *m. Sotah* 9:15).

Sanders, in an offhanded comment, concedes that *m. Sotah* 3:4 does teach that good deeds 'may suspend the punishment of

---

73. The Tosefta skips *m. Sotah* 3:4-5 in its discussion, see *t. Sotah* 2:3-4.

74. All English translations of the Babylonian Talmud are from Jacob Neusner, *The Babylonian Talmud: A Translation and Commentary* (22 vols.; Peabody, MA: Hendrickson, 2005).

transgressions,' but he will not concede that good deeds are used 'to offset or compensate for transgressions at the judgment.'[75]

m. Sotah 9:15 is written in more of poetical manner than most of the Mishnah.[76] Various good habits lead to 'piety,' which in turn leads to the 'Holy Spirit,' which in turn leads to the 'resurrection of the dead.' The reference to the 'Holy Spirit' is fairly rare in the Mishnah and is probably associated with the Ezek. 37 resurrection. This is a clear eschatological context that includes 'piety' as the rationale for the resurrection. The reference to the Holy Spirit aiding in the resurrection and the comment that one is to depend on the Father implies strongly that God would also aid in piety. If so, this would be a semi-Pelagian view of works righteousness.

TOSEFTA[77]

The Tosefta is very similar to and an expansion of the Mishnah. It is four times as large as the Mishnah, but it has the same six divisions and virtually the same tractate titles. The Tosefta was written approximately A.D 300, one-hundred years after the Mishnah. Two extra generations of rabbis are included in addition to those quoted in the Mishnah. An extended discussion of the Tosefta is included in the Appendix.

T. QIDDUSHIN

'Qiddushin' translates as 'sanctification.' This tractate primarily concerns betrothals of a woman to a man. The title relates to a woman becoming 'sacred' (or 'set apart') to a man upon their betrothal (*t. Qiddushin* 1:1).

Below is a fairly long passage related to the question of works righteousness (*t. Qiddushin* 1:13-16). The passage is not discussing betrothals per se but laws to obey when in the promised land. This

---

75. Sanders, *Paul and Palestinian Judaism*, 146. He goes on to say that 'Transgressions … are atoned for rather than balanced by a corresponding good deed.'

76. These ending comments in *m. Sotah* 9:15 are not discussed in the Tosefta or the Babylonian Talmud.

77. All English translations are from Jacob Neusner, *The Tosefta: Translated from the Hebrew with a New Introduction* (Peabody, MA: Hendrickson, 2002).

passage is often quoted as it includes a balance for weighing good and evil deeds.

> Whoever does a single commandment—they do well for him and lengthen his days and his years and he inherits the Land. And whoever commits a single transgression—they do ill to him and cut off his days, and he does not inherit the Land. And concerning such a person it is said, 'One sinner destroys much good' [Eccles. 9:18]. By a single sin this one destroys many good things. *A person should always see himself as if he is half meritorious and half guilty. If he did a single commandment, happy is he, for he has inclined the balance for himself to the side of merit. If he committed a single transgression, woe is he, for he has inclined the balance to the side of guilt.* Concerning this one it is said, One sinner destroys much good. By a single sin this one has destroyed many good things.
>
> Rabbi Simeon son of Eleazar says in the name of Rabbi Meir, '*Because the individual is judged by his majority of deeds,* the world is judged by its majority. *And if one did one commandment, happy is he, for he has inclined the balance for himself and for the world to the side of merit.* If he has committed one transgression, woe is he, for he has inclined the balance for himself and for the world to the side of guilt. And concerning such a person it is said, One sinner destroys much good [Eccles. 9:18]. By the single sin which this one committed, he destroyed for himself and for the world many good things.'
>
> Rabbi Simeon says, 'If a man was righteous his entire life but at the end rebelled, he loses the whole, since it is said, "The righteousness of the righteous shall not deliver him when he transgresses" [Ezek. 33:12]. If a man was evil his entire life but at the end he repented, the Omnipresent accepts him. As it is said, "And as for the wickedness of the wicked, he shall not fall by it when he turns from his wickedness" [Ezek. 33:12]. Whoever occupies himself with all three of them, with Scripture, Mishnah, and good conduct, concerning such a person it is said, "And a threefold cord is not quickly broken"' [Eccles. 4:12]. (*t. Qiddushin* 1:13-16, italics mine)[78]

In *t. Qiddushin* 1:13-16, three Rabbinic views are presented that do not necessarily contradict each other, although they may. The first view, from the Tosefta editors, focuses on a single good or

---

78. This is an expansion of *m. Qiddushin* 1:10.

evil deed. Every deed is important and could be the one that either gets one into the promised Land or prevents one from entering. This then prompts the recommendation that one should always see themselves on a balance with exactly half good and half evil deeds so that one presumably will have more incentive for the next deed to be a good one.

The second view is from Rabbi Meir communicated by Rabbi Simeon son of Eleazar. Every deed is important because both the individual and the world will be judged by a majority of either their good or evil deeds.

The third view is from Rabbi Simeon and has a different tack than the first two. Based on Ezek. 33:12, it is the end of life just before one dies that counts. If one is righteous his whole life but then rebels at the end, he will not enter the world to come. If one is rebellious his whole life, but repents at the end, he will have eschatological life. Rabbi Simeon then comments that the righteous life is filled with 'Scripture, Mishnah, and good conduct.'

The first and second views on the surface are very works righteousness oriented as the balance of good and evil deeds shows. The third view, with its emphasis on end-of-life repentance, does not seem to present a works righteousness soteriology. Repentance does not appear to be presented as a work, although the following statement about 'Scripture, Mishnah, and good conduct' may contradict this. Whether intentional or not, the editors allowed both a clear works righteousness soteriology and possibly a non-works righteousness soteriology to stand side by side in the Tosefta.

In the Babylonian Talmud, the tension is seen between the first two views and the third view. The question is asked, 'Why not regard the case of the righteous one who rebels at the end as one that is half transgression and half merit?' That is, could it be really true that if one's life is mostly merit but falls at the end, he would not receive eschatological life? Rabbi Simeon son of Laquish answers, 'Yes, it is a case of his regretting his former good deeds.'[79] That is, if one intentionally renounces all of his good deeds, his balance would be

---

79. *b. Qiddushin* 40b.

negative and that explains his not receiving eschatological life. The Babylonian Talmud turns the third view into works righteousness theology. Thus all three views exhibit works righteousness in the Babylonian Talmud.

Sanders' response to *t. Qiddushin* 1:13-16 is included with his response to *m. Abot* 3:15. He explicitly comments about *t. Qiddushin* 1:13 that the balance of good and evil deeds is a 'non-systematic exhortation.'[80] For Sanders, the rabbis' non-systematic character and exhortative contexts mitigate against concluding that passages teach a works righteousness soteriology even though they appear on the surface to do so.[81] See above at *m. Abot* 3:15 for more of his argument and my rebuttal.[82]

T. SANHEDRIN

A 'sanhedrin' in Rabbinic literature refers to a Jewish law court in any city. According to Rabbinic literature, in Jerusalem, there were two courts: the 'great sanhedrin' of 71 members and a lesser sanhedrin of twenty-three members (*m. Sanhedrin* 1:6).[83] There is a large section of *t. Sanhedrin* that deals with capital punishment. The seven exegetical rules of Hillel the Elder, which in context are seven modes of arguing at court, are found in *t. Sanhedrin* 7:11.

In *m. Sanhedrin* 10 is a discussion concerning who will 'have share in the world to come' (*m. Sanhedrin* 10:1). According to Cohen, 'not a single tractate in the Mishnah is devoted to a theological topic' and *m. Sanhedrin* 10 is 'the lone chapter of the Mishnah that treats theological topics.'[84] Cohen is probably overstating the case as to the absolute uniqueness of *m. Sanhedrin* 10, but it is certainly true

---

80. Sanders, *Paul and Palestinian Judaism*, 130.

81. Sanders, *Paul and Palestinian Judaism*, 141-47.

82. For Gathercole's response to Sanders view of *t. Qiddushin* 1:14, see *Where is Boasting?* 153-56. Gathercole's view is similar to mine.

83. Many doubt the historical accuracy of much of Rabbinic literature's comments about the great sanhedrin. So Anthony J. Saldarini, 'Sanhedrin,' *ABD*, 5:975-80.

84. Shaye J. D. Cohen, *From the Maccabees to the Mishnah* (2d ed.; Louisville: Westminster John Knox, 2006), 212.

that *m. Sanhedrin* 10 and its exposition in *t. Sanhedrin* 12:9-14:11 are important for our topic. Also, this section of the Tosefta has many more quotes of the OT than is usual.

As to the question of works righteousness, below are three passages from *t. Sanhedrin*. The first shows an aspect of the gracious character of a judge in an arbitration case (*t. Sanhedrin* 1:3-5). The second and third passages relate to the eschatological question of who will enter the world to come. The second deals with Manasseh (*t. Sanhedrin* 12:11), and the third argues that there are three groups to consider (*t. Sanhedrin* 13:2-4).

> And so it says in the case of David, 'And David acted with judgment and charity to all his people' [2 Sam. 8:15]. Now is it not so that in any case in which there is judgment, there is no charity, and in any case in which there is charity, there is no judgment? So what is the judgment in which there also is charity? You have to say, This is arbitration.
>
> If one has judged a case, declaring the guiltless to be guiltless, and imposing liability on the guilty party, if one then has imposed liability on a poor man, he takes the necessary funds out of his own pocket and gives it to him. That is how he turns out to do charity with this one and true justice with that one.
>
> Rabbi says, 'If one has judged a case, declaring the guiltless to be guiltless and imposing liability on the guilty party, he turns out to do charity with the one who is liable, for he removes the stolen goods from his possession. And he does justice to the innocent party, for he restores to him what belongs to him.' (*t. Sanhedrin* 1:3-5)

> Four kings, Jeroboam, Ahab, Ahaz, and Manasseh have no portion in the world to come.
>
> Rabbi Judah says, 'Manasseh has a portion in the world to come since it is said, "His prayer also, and how God was entreated of him, and all his sin and his trespass, and the place wherein he built high places and set up the asherim and the graven images, before he humbled himself, behold they are written in the book of Hozeh" [2 Chron. 33:19]. This teaches that God accepted his prayer and brought him into the life of the world to come.' (*t. Sanhedrin* 12:11)

> Rabbi Eliezer says, 'None of the gentiles has a portion in the world to come, as it is said, "The wicked shall return to Sheol, all the gentiles

who forget God" [Ps. 9:17]. The wicked shall return to Sheol—these are the wicked Israelites.' [Implied that the 'wicked' in Ps. 9:17 refers to Jews, and Gentiles in Ps. 9:17 are Gentiles.]

Said to him Rabbi Joshua, 'If it had been written, "The wicked shall return to Sheol—all the gentiles" [Ps. 9:17], and then said nothing further, I should have maintained as you do. Now that it is in fact written, "All the gentiles who forget God" [Ps. 9:17], it indicates that there are also righteous people among the nations of the world, who do have a portion in the world to come.'

The House of Shammai says, *'There are three groups, one for eternal life, one 'for shame and everlasting contempt' [Dan. 12:2]—those who are completely evil. An intermediate group [evenly balanced][85] go down Gehenna and scream and come up again and are healed. As it is said, I will bring the third part through fire and will refine them as silver is refined and will test them as gold is tested, and they shall call on my name and I will be their God [Zech. 13:9].* And concerning them did Hannah say, "The Lord kills and brings to life, brings down to Sheol and brings up"' [1 Sam. 2:6].

And the House of Hillel say, '"Great in mercy" [Exod. 34:6]— He inclines the decision toward mercy, and concerning them David said, "I am happy that the Lord has heard the sound of my prayer" [Ps. 116:1], and concerning them is said the entire passage.'

The Israelites who sinned with their bodies and gentiles who sinned with their bodies go down to Gehenna and are judged there for twelve months. And after twelve months their souls perish, their bodies are burned, Gehenna absorbs them, and they are turned to dirt. (*t. Sanhedrin* 13:2-4, italics mine)

The first quote above, *t Sanhedrin* 1:3-4, is about arbitration as opposed to a normal judicial ruling.[86] Second Samuel 8:15 states that David 'administered justice and equity' (ESV). The Hebrew behind 'equity' is צדקה and is often translated in English Bibles as 'righteousness.' However, the rabbis often interpret this as righteous acts, pre-eminently, alms to the poor. Hence, the translation above

---

85. A more mechanical translation for 'intermediate group' is 'evenly balanced.' Sanders agrees to this translation (*Paul and Palestinian Judaism*, 142).

86. This is not discussed in the *m. Sanhedrin*. This section of the Tosefta is quoted in the Babylonian Talmud, but there is no further discussion of it (*b. Sanhedrin* 6b).

that 'David acted with judgment and *charity.*' This then prompts the question as to how could a judge act both with 'judgment and charity' in an arbitration case. Two conflicting answers are given with the first one being more mercy oriented.

An example is given of a case of a poor man who has stolen goods. The first answer is that the judge should declare the poor man guilty and require him to pay restitution, but also, the judge should give the poor man money out of his own pocket. Hence, a merciful way to combine 'judgment and charity.'

The second answer is to take the money from the poor guilty man and give it to the innocent man. Taking money from the poor man is considered true charity. It is implied that charity should not be defined as giving alms to thieves.

I have included *t. Sanhedrin* 1:3-5 because I am assuming the rabbis viewed some sense of continuity between their judgments and God's eschatological judgments. I note that this section includes both a very interesting 'mercy' solution and also a straightforward judgment solution as to how to combine 'judgment and charity.'

The second quote above, *t. Sanhedrin* 12:11, concerns the case of Manasseh. The OT presents Manasseh as a very evil king (2 Kings 21:1-18, 23:26, 24:3, 2 Chron. 33:1-20). However, 2 Chron. 33:12-13, 18-19 records that he repented through prayer.

As can be seen from the above quote, some believed that Manasseh would not have eschatological life and Rabbi Judah believed he would. Rabbi Judah's argument is explicitly based on Manasseh's prayer of repentance that qualified him for eschatological life.

In the Mishnah parallel, *m. Sanhedrin* 10:2, both views of Manasseh are also given. A significant difference is that Rabbi Judah quotes 2 Chron. 33:13, as opposed to 2 Chron. 33:19. Because in 2 Chron. 33:13 God restores Manasseh's 'kingdom,' an explicit rationale is given as to why Manasseh will not have eschatological life—the restoration only relates to his earthly kingdom, not to the world to come.[87]

---

87. Another difference is that the Mishnah parallel only has three kings; Ahaz is left out.

The Babylonian Talmud parallel also acknowledges that the Tannaitic authorities disagree on Manasseh's fate (*b. Sanhedrin* 102b-103b). Additional arguments are included to buttress both sides of the debate. One argument for Manasseh receiving eschatological life is that he did not repent just one time but did so for twenty-three years (*b. Sanhedrin* 103a). This argument is based on supposed Tannaitic authority.

Clearly, some of the rabbis do not accept that Manasseh's repentance made him fit for eschatological life. Possibly they saw repentance as a work and not enough works were done by Manasseh to overcome his evil deeds. Either way, this appears to be a problem for Sanders.

One of Sanders' primary arguments that his covenantal nomism is grace-based is because of the 'staying in' aspect of repentance.

> Repentance was the sovereign means of atonement. … Repentance is not a 'status-achieving' activity by which one initially courts and wins the mercy of God. It is a 'status-maintaining' or 'status-restoring' attitude which indicates that one intends to remain in the covenant. … Obedience is rewarded and disobedience punished. In case of failure to obey, however, man has recourse to divinely ordained means of atonement.[88]

What does Sanders do with these discussions in the Mishnah, Tosefta, and the Babylonian Talmud that at least some rabbis deny eschatological life to the repentant Manasseh? He cannot say that they are Amoraic rabbis (A.D. 225-500) as these sources virtually all refer to Tannaitic rabbis (50 B.C.–A.D. 200). Sanders simply admits this is an 'exception to the rule that repentance atones.'[89] Given the importance of this tractate as one of the few that has a sustained discussion of who will be in the world to come, this response appears inadequate.[90]

---

88. Sanders, *Paul and Palestinian Judaism*, 180, 178.

89. Sanders, *Paul and Palestinian Judaism*, 180. Other exceptions that Sanders notes are *m. Abot* 5:8, *p. Hagigah* 77b, and *Sifre Numbers* 136.

90. For my broad-brush critique of Sanders' view of repentance, see 'Repentance and Works Righteousness' section in Chapter 2.

Now to the third quote above, *t. Sanhedrin* 13:2-4. This concerns the eschatological judgment of the three groups.[91] To give some context, both the Mishnah and Tosefta note many who will *not* have eschatological life. These include Gentiles, various evil Jewish kings, inhabitants of apostate towns, men of Sodom, Balaam, Doeg, Ahithophel, Gehazi, the flood generation, Epicureans, minors of wicked parents (only in Tosefta), those who deny the resurrection of the dead, those who deny the Torah is from heaven, those who pronounce the divine Name as it is spelled out, and the ten tribes who did not return (*m. Sanhedrin* 10:1-4 // *t. Sanhedrin* 12:9-14:3).

Before getting to the three groups, Rabbi Eliezer and Rabbi Joshua disagree. Rabbi Eliezer believes based on Ps. 9:17 that no Gentiles will have eschatological life. Rabbi Joshua disagrees because Ps. 9:17 says 'all gentiles *who forget God*' (italics mine). Therefore, there are some righteous Gentiles who did not forget God.

The House of Shammai argues for three groups related to eschatological judgment: (1) the one with 'eternal life'; (2) the one destined to 'everlasting contempt'; and (3) the intermediate one that is the 'evenly balanced.' The intermediate-evenly-balanced group goes 'down' to Gehenna for a time to be 'refined' (Zech. 13:9). Then the Lord will 'bring up' those in this group to the world to come (1 Sam. 2:6).

The House of Hillel notes that God 'inclines the decision toward mercy.' I assume the House of Hillel is speaking of the evenly balanced group. They are on the 'fence,' but God decides toward eschatological life. Possibly, the difference with the House of Shammai is that this group does not have to go to Gehenna for a while and may go straight to eschatological life.

The quoted passage above ends by describing both Israelites and Gentiles who have 'sinned with their bodies.' They go to Gehenna for twelve months and then after being burned, are and turned into dirt. These are obviously part of the 'everlasting contempt' group.

The above presents two problems for Sanders: (1) Gentiles receiving eschatological life and (2) the three groups. The first

---

91. The three groups are not discussed in *m. Sanhedrin* nor *b. Sanhedrin*.

problem concerns Gentiles who receive eschatological life. They are not in the covenant. Hence, based on what do they 'get in,' 'stay in,' and pass the final judgment? Apparently, it is their righteous deeds. But on the surface of it, Sanders cannot assume that grace comes from their 'getting in' through a gracious election by means of the covenant. Sanders agrees that the righteous Gentiles are a problem for him, especially our passage in *t. Sanhedrin*.[92] For those Rabbinic passages that confirm that Gentiles may receive eschatological life, he admits that it would be on the basis of being 'kind and charitable and who did not transgress any of the principal prohibitions of Judaism.'[93] Since the covenantal nomism is so strong, it shows that the situation of righteous Gentiles 'did not, however, lead to a fundamental re-thinking of the soteriology that applied to the members of the covenant, and the Gentiles are not systematically worked into Rabbinic soteriology.'[94] Again, Sanders reverts to his standard explanation that the rabbis were not systematic to solve this 'Gentile problem.'

The second problem has to do with logic of the three ways. For the House of Shammai and the House of Hillel, eschatological life for the intermediate-evenly-balanced group is based on the weighing of their good and evil deeds. This produces no preponderance in either direction. But God does eventually refine them in Gehenna (House of Shammai option) and does give them eschatological life (both Houses). This evenly-balanced group is reminiscent of *T. Ab. A* 14:1-8 (see above discussion). Once given that the intermediate group gains eschatological life by a weighing of good and evil deeds, it is then further implied that the good group also gains eschatological life by an overwhelming amount of good deeds. This discussion of the intermediate group in *t. Sanhedrin* is a clear example of works righteousness soteriology.

Sanders directly addresses this problem also. He turns my argument on its head. He notes that those in the intermediate group

---

92. Sanders, *Paul and Palestinian Judaism*, 206-12, esp. 209.

93. Sanders, *Paul and Palestinian Judaism*, 211.

94. Sanders, *Paul and Palestinian Judaism*, 212.

do get eschatological life and it is only the 'whole-heartedly wicked' that do not. Hence, 'the righteous are not the sinless, but those who confirm the covenant.'[95] I might respond that the immediately previous verses concern righteous Gentiles whom he admits do not have a covenant. Why bring the covenant in here? Also, how is the intermediate group distinguished from the good group? Is it not by the weighing of good and evil deeds?

From my perspective, *t. Sanhedrin* overall includes a variety of views. It certainly includes works righteousness views. I have presented Sanders' three arguments: (1) rabbis' not allowing for Manasseh's repentance was just an exception to the rule, (2) righteous Gentiles who were not in covenant is another example of non-systematic Rabbinic thought, and (3) the existence of an intermediate somewhat sinful group that receives eschatological life shows that Rabbinic soteriology was gracious. I am not convinced by these arguments.

However, I do find the possibility of some more gracious aspects set alongside the works righteousness. The examples of the judge who shows charity and the rabbis who accept Manasseh's repentance show more of the possibility of a grace system, although not clearly so. Having conflicting soteriological systems existing in Rabbinic literature appears to fit the data better than Sanders' one-size-fits-all supposed grace system. Although I must say, the eschatological sections in the Mishnah and Tosefta for tractate Sanhedrin are significantly oriented toward works righteousness.

BABYLONIAN TALMUD

Rabbinic Judaism produced two large talmuds, the Jerusalem Talmud and the Babylonian Talmud. The Babylonian Talmud is the more well known and is the dominant one. To give a sense of size, my version of the Babylonian Talmud is twenty-two volumes.

The Babylonian Talmud consists primarily of quotes of the Mishnah and then extended commentary about the quotes. This commentary is called the 'Gemera,' which translates as 'completion.'

---

95. Sanders, *Paul and Palestinian Judaism*, 142-43.

Not all of the Mishnah tractates are quoted and commented upon, only thirty-six of the sixty-three. Also, quotes of the Tosefta are often included.

The Gemera portion of the Babylonian Talmud was finalized approximately A.D. 600. Obviously, rabbis living after the Mishnah are responsible for the Gemera. However, they do refer often to the views of 'tannaite authority'—rabbis who lived from 50 B.C. to A.D. 200—in the Gemera. Therefore, taken at face value, we have additional information stretching back to the second temple time-period. An extended discussion of the Babylonian Talmud is included in the Appendix.

As opposed to the Mishnah and Tosefta, I have no confidence in using the Babylonian Talmud to determine views that may have existed during the first-century A.D.[96] Theoretically, it is possible, but I do not want to make an argument based on information from the Talmuds. At a minimum, the Babylonian Talmud may be used to determine what Jews in A.D. 600 thought of the Mishnah and Tosefta. However, Sanders does use the Talmuds to determine Second Temple Judaism views when a Tannaitic authority is mentioned, which is reasonably often.

From my perspective, there are many passages in the Babylonian Talmud in which at least certain rabbis are presented as having a works righteousness soteriology.[97] For purposes of completeness, I will include just one Babylonian Talmud tractate, *b. Rosh Hashanah*, which is well known.

B. ROSH HASHANAH

'Rosh Hashanah' translates as 'new year' and implies a New Year feast. In the Bible, there is a New Year related to the ecclesiastical year, Nisan, and a New Year related to the civil year, Tishri. Tishri is the month that includes the Day of Atonement. This tractate covers ceremonies and the new moons related to both of these new

---

96. See 'Usefulness for First-Century A.D. Judaism?' section in the Appendix.

97. E.g., *b. Berakhot* 28b, *b. Eruvin* 19a, *b. Qiddushin* 39b-40b, *b. Bava Qamma* 38a, *b. Sanhedrin* 97b, 110b-111a, *b. Horayot* 10b. Also see *Genesis Rabbah* 9.5.

years in Jewish tradition, although little is actually said in the Bible beyond there being trumpets and the details of animal sacrifices. In fact, there is no New Year festival in the Bible (see Exod. 12:1-2, Lev. 23:23-25, Num. 29:12-38, Ezek. 40:1).[98] In this tractate, there is a significant discussion of the trumpet or ram's horn (shofar) associated with the Tishri ceremony.

Genesis Rabbah 56.9 (A.D. 425–450) is an exposition of Gen. 22:13 but connects it to Zech. 9:14. In Gen. 22:13, Abraham takes the ram caught by his horns in a thicket and sacrifices him instead of Isaac. In Zech. 9:14, God blows a shofar (ram's horn) and comes and protects Israel. In *Genesis Rabbah* 56.9 the two horns are connected and Abraham's trial parallels Israel's day of judgment and salvation. Rabbi Hannia son of Rabbi Isaac concludes that 'Throughout the year Israel[ites] are in sin's clutches and led astray by their troubles, but on New Year they take the shofar and blow on it, and eventually they will be redeemed by the ram's horn.'[99] With this apparent background, *b. Rosh Hashanah* 16a connects the New Year to the Day of Judgment for Israel.

The parallel Mishnah tractate has only two minor references connecting the New Year to judgment.[100] The Tosefta adds just two short comments.[101] However, *b. Rosh Hashanah* 16a-18b is a long discussion of the Day of Judgment related to the New Year Tishri ceremony. There is a portion that includes three different groups on the Day of Judgment, which is reminiscent of *t. Sanhedrin* 13:2-4 discussed above.

---

98. The expression *rosh hashshanah* (רֹאשׁ הַשָּׁנָה) is only used once in the Bible, Ezek. 40:1. There in Ezekiel's vision it is connected to the Day of Atonement. See discussion in Henkrik L. Bosman, 'רֹאשׁ הַשָּׁנָה', *NIDOTTE*, 3:1022-23.

99. Translation from *Midrash Rabbah Genesis* (trans. H. Freedman; 2 vols.; London: Soncino, 1939), 1:498.

100. 'At the New Year all who enter the world pass before Him like troops, since it is said, "He who fashions the hearts of them all, who considers all their works"' [Ps. 33:15] (*m. Rosh Hashanah* 1:2). 'They do not make mention of verses of Remembrance, Sovereignty, or Shofar, which speak of punishment' (*m. Rosh Hashanah* 4:6).

101. See *t. Rosh Hashanah* 1:11, 1:13, and 2:12.

Below are four quotes that relate to the question of works righteousness. The first gives a variety of ways to 'cancel a negative judgment.' The second and third concern the three groups. The fourth relates to a weighing scale and showing God's mercy.

And said Rabbi Isaac, 'Four things cancel a person's [negative] judgment. And these are they: charity, crying out, change of name, and change of character.'

'Charity—as it is written, "but righteousness delivers from death"' [Prov. 10:2].

'Crying out—as it is written, "And they cried out to the Lord in their trouble, and he delivered them from their distress"' [Ps. 107:6].

'Change of name'—[quote of Gen. 17:15-16 related to Sarai's changing her name].

'Change of character'—[quote of Jonah. 3:10 relating to Ninevites' changing their ways]. (b. Rosh Hashanah 16b)

Said Rabbi Kruspedai said Rabbi Yohanan, 'Three books are opened by God on the New Year: one for the thoroughly wicked, one for the thoroughly righteous, and one for middling people.'

'The thoroughly righteous immediately are inscribed and sealed for continued life.'

'The thoroughly wicked immediately are inscribed and sealed for death.'

'Middling people are left hanging from New Year until the Day of Atonement. If they are found to have merit, they are inscribed for life. If they are found not to have merit, they are inscribed for death.' (b. Rosh Hashanah 16b, italics mine)

It has been taught on Tannait authority: The House of Shammai says, 'There will be three groups on the Day of Judgment: one comprised of the thoroughly righteous, one comprised of the thoroughly wicked, and one of middling people.'

'The thoroughly righteous immediately are inscribed and sealed for eternal life.'

'The thoroughly wicked immediately are inscribed and sealed for Gehenna. As it is written, "And many of those who sleep in the dust of the earth shall awake, some to eternal life and some to shame and everlasting contempt"' [Dan. 12:2].

'Middling people go down to Gehenna, scream in prayer, and rise again. As it is written, "And I will put this third into the fire and refine them as one refines silver and test them as gold is tested. They will call on my name, and I will answer them."' [Zech. 13:9]. (*b. Rosh Hashanah* 16b-17a, italics mine)

The House of Hillel say, 'But God who abounds in mercy leans towards a judgment of mercy.'

How does God act? Rabbi Eleazar says, *'He presses down on the side of the balance-scale representing merit,* as it is said, "He will again have compassion upon us. He will push down our iniquities"' [Micah 7:19].

Rabbi Yose son of Hanina said, *'He lifts the side of the balance-scale representing wrongdoings, as it is said,* "Who is a God like you, raising iniquity and passing over transgression?"' [Micah 7:18].

It is taught on Tannait authority in the house of Rabbi Ishmael: He passes over the first transgression of each type, and this is God's attribute of mercy.

Said Rava, 'The transgression itself is not erased, so that if there turns out to be a majority of transgressions, God considers it with the others.' (*b. Rosh Hashanah* 17a, italics mine)

Concerning the first quote above in *b. Rosh Hashanna* 16b, there are four ways to cancel one's negative judgment. Note the one for 'charity' connects righteous acts to a positive judgment. 'Change of character' could be considered repentance, although most likely it is performing good deeds subsequent to repentance. 'Crying out' is clearly prayer. The logic surrounding 'change of name' is not clear. In any event, at least one of these, if not two, have a works component.

The second (*b. Rosh Hashanna* 16b) and third quotes (*b. Rosh Hashanna* 16b-17a) above refer to the three groups. The difference between the two quotes relates to what happens to the 'middling' group. For Rabbi Kruspedai, those in the middling group only have to wait the ten days between the New Year and the Day of Atonement. For the House of Shammai, those in the middling group go to Gehenna for a while. They are refined in Gehenna before going onto eschatological life. As noted above in the *t. Sanhedrin* discussion, having a 'middling' group, even if they eventually get eschatological life, does imply some level of weighing good and evil deeds. This weighing, even if the rabbis considered as a metaphor, has a works righteousness aspect to it.

The fourth quote concerns how God shows mercy. It assumes a balance-scale with both good and evil deeds. How does God show mercy? Which side does He help? Rabbi Eliazar says that God presses down on the merit side, thereby giving it more weight. On the other hand, Rabbi Yose says that God lifts up on the evil deeds' side, thereby reducing its weight and effectively giving more weight to the merit side. Rabbi Rava says God shows mercy by forgiving the first of each type of transgression, although if there is a significant amount of this one type of transgression, God does consider it negatively. In the fourth quote, God's mercy is highlighted at the final judgment, but it appears to me to be highlighted within a framework that includes some level of works righteousness.

Sanders' general response is to admit that later Amoraic literature (e.g., Babylonian Talmud), as opposed to earlier Tannaitic literature, did go further with the weighing analogy. He explicitly references *b. Rosh Hashanah* 16b-17a in this regard.[102] Although Sanders would not agree, I see the works righteousness aspect of *b. Rosh Hashanah* as a further evidence that the earlier Tannaitic literature also had a works righteousness soteriology.

SUMMARY OF CHAPTER

Sanders argues that despite the variegated nature of Second Temple Judaism, there exists a grace-based covenantal-nomism soteriological-framework across all Jewish groups. As a consequence, he insists that a works righteousness soteriology was not evident in Second Temple Judaism.

---

102. 'We can find in Amoraic literature several statements to the effect that God keeps books on individual's deeds, but such statements are very rare in Tannaitic literature. ... Nor should we suppose (as some of the Amoraim may have done) that the 'wholly wicked' are those who have only one more evil deed than good' (Sanders, *Paul and Palestinian Judaism*, 140, 142).

In the previous chapter, I presented both the broad Reformed framework and Sanders' covenantal-nomism framework so as to compare and contrast the two frameworks' interpretation of various Second Temple Judaism documents. In this chapter, I have considered a variety of documents. For most of these documents, I included Sanders' explanation of how these fit into his framework. I also considered these documents from a Reformed-framework perspective. The documents considered were two works from the Apocrypha (4 Ezra and Sirach), three from the OT Pseudepigrapha (*2 Baruch*, *Testament of Abraham*, and *Psalms of Solomon*), three from the DSS (*Rule of the Community*, *Pesher Habakkuk*, and *Miqsat Ma'ase Ha-Torah*), and five Rabbinic literature tractates (*m. Abot*, *m. Sotah*, *t. Qiddushin*, *t. Sanhedrin*, and *b. Rosh Hashanah*).

I have concluded that all of these documents have a works righteousness soteriology, whether Pelagian or semi-Pelagian. To be clear, I am not saying that all documents in Second Temple Judaism have a works righteousness soteriology; however, I am insisting that many do. Hence, I conclude that Sanders' conclusion that works righteousness did not exist in Second Temple Judaism is completely wrong.

NPP authors base their new views of Pauline justification on the supposed 'new perspective on Judaism,' which is Sanders' covenantal nomism. The NPP authors do not see Paul arguing against works righteousness because in their view, it did not exist in Second Temple Judaism. Further, they conclude that some aspect of our works contribute to the supposed Pauline justification. *Once given my conclusion that there is an abundance of works righteousness soteriology in Second Temple Judaism documents, the NPP foundation of covenantal nomism has crumbled. And with it, their new view of Pauline justification also crumbles as it is built upon that faulty foundation.*

The only sure foundation for justification is the work of Christ, and Him alone.

CHAPTER 4

WORKS RIGHTEOUSNESS IN 'DEUTERO-PAUL'?

Every year at my seminary I teach a course entitled 'Acts and Romans.' Part of this course involves a description and critique of the NPP. As opposed to this book, most of the critique concentrates on Pauline passages. I present my final point of critique with some rhetorical flair—or at least I think so. I ask the students to turn to Eph. 2:8-9:

> For by grace you have been saved through faith. And this is not your own doing; it is the gift of God, not a result of works, so that no one may boast. (Eph. 2:8-9)

I then ask if they could guess how Dunn will justify his view that Paul does *not* use 'works' as a works righteousness soteriological-principle that is contrasted to a grace soteriological-principle. 'How can one read this text and *not* conclude that two principles of soteriology are presented—and one is works righteousness?'

As soon as the first student begins to answer, I interrupt and exclaim, 'trick question.' I then read Dunn's comments on Eph. 2:8-9 from his *The Theology of Paul the Apostle*. He admits that the 'issue does seem to have moved from one of works of the law to one of human effort.' I then rhetorically opine as if I am Dunn, 'But that just proves that Paul was not the author of Ephesians!' Yes, Dunn believes that Eph. 2:8-9 indicates a works righteousness principle, but he uses this 'shift in the debate' as part of an argument that Paul did not write Ephesians.[1] (I will give more nuances to Dunn's view below.)

For my students, who all believe that Paul wrote Ephesians, this makes a significant impact upon them as they consider whether Paul uses 'works' and 'works of the law' to mean works righteousness.

INTRODUCTION

Clearly, the emphasis of this book is the questioning of the foundation of the NPP, the works righteousness assumptions about Second Temple Judaism. I have not included sustained discussions of Pauline texts because this is not the focus of this book and many other anti-NPP authors have done this. However, I want to concentrate on three Pauline texts for this chapter. Below is my rationale.

DEUTERO-PAUL

Ephesians 2:8-10, Titus 3:4-7, and 2 Tim. 1:8-10 are three texts that on the surface appear to contrast works righteousness with grace. However, they receive surprisingly little or no discussion compared to Romans, Galatians, and Philippians 3. Even when the subject is 'works of the law'—does it mean Jewish boundary markers or works righteousness?— these three texts are often ignored even though all three use the term 'works.' Why? Because for many all three of these texts are from 'Deutero-Paul.'

Most scholars in the critical/liberal world believe Paul only wrote seven letters. These are designated as the 'authentic' or 'undisputed' letters of Paul: Romans, First and Second Corinthians, Galatians, Philippians, First Thessalonians, and Philemon. The remaining six

---

1. James D. G. Dunn, *The Theology of Paul the Apostle* (Grand Rapids: Eerdmans, 1998), 370-71, 371 n 150, 13 n. 39.

are designated as 'Deutero-Pauline' or the 'disputed' letters: Second Thessalonians, Ephesians, Colossians, First and Second Timothy, and Titus. These scholars do not believe that the same person wrote all six of these letters, only that it was not Paul. To be clear, my view is that Paul is the author of all thirteen letters.

NPP authors have differing views as to how many letters Paul wrote. However, often their discussion of works righteousness does not include Eph. 2:8-10, Titus 3:4-7, and 2 Tim. 1:8-10 because of one and/or two reasons. (1) A NPP author does not believe Paul is the author,[2] or (2) A NPP author is arguing in the critical arena and believes his appeal to Deutero-Paul would be moot. For example, Wright states in his very influencial book, *What Saint Paul Really Said*:

> Most of what I say in this book focuses on material in the uundisputed letters, particularly Romans, the two Corinthian letters, Galatians, and Philippians. I regard Colossians as certainly by Paul, and Ephesians as far more likely to be by him than by an imitator. But nothing in my present argument hinges on this one way or the other.[3]

Of course, not all anti-NPP authors agree that Paul wrote all thirteen letters, although many do. For even those that do, there is an understandable tendency by anti-NPP authors to highlight

---

2. For example, the following two scholars agree with Sanders' covenantal nomism and they self-identify as NPP, or 'radical NPP,' but their views about Paul are *not* the more mainstream Dunn/Wright type. There is not one mention of Eph. 2:8-10, Titus 3:4-7, 2 Tim. 1:8-10 in these books. See Magnus Zetterholm, *Approaches to Paul: A Student's Guide to Recent Scholarship* (Minneapolis: Fortress, 2009); and Troels Engberg-Pedersen, *Paul and the Stoics* (Louisville: Westminster, 2000). For a long critique of Engberg-Pedersen by N. T. Wright, see *Paul and the Faithfulness of God* (Minneapolis: Fortress, 2013), 1386-1407.

3. N. T. Wright, *What Saint Paul Really Said: Was Paul of Tarsus the Real Founder of Christianity?* (Grand Rapids: Eerdmans, 1997), 8. In his chapter on 'Justification and the Church,' Wright does not discuss Eph. 2:8-10, 2 Tim. 1:8-10, nor Titus 3:4-7 (pp. 113-33). Similarly, there is not one reference to any of these three texts in Wright's *The Climax of the Covenant: Christ and the Law in Pauline Theology* (Minneapolis: Fortress, 1991). His minimal use of three texts in his large work, *Paul and Faithfulness of God*, will be discussed below.

Romans, Galatians, and Philippians 3 because these are the books/ texts that the NPP authors are directly discussing (many times 2 Cor. 5:21 is also included). Although, to their credit, many of these anti-NPP authors do include some discussion of Eph. 2:8-10, Titus 3:4-7, and 2 Tim. 1:8-10.[4]

To confirm the above, I quote Yinger, who is a *pro*-NPP author, from a section entitled, 'Ephesians 2:8-10; 2 Timothy 1:9; Titus 3:5-6':

> Several passages from the disputed letters of Paul seem to point unmistakably to precisely the grace-verses-works contrast that the NPP says was not in Paul's mind. … In spite of the clear challenge to the NPP posed by these verses, writers aligned with this perspective have been 'strangely silent' in some cases because these passages are not considered Pauline.[5]

Similarly, Westerholm, an *anti*-NPP author, notes that Sanders' *Paul and Palestinian Judaism* and Wright's *The Climax of the Covenant* do not discuss these three texts. He then opines:

> No study that took Ephesians and the Pastorals into account could conclude, what proponents of the new perspective have sometimes claimed, that the Pelagian crisis or the sixteenth-century controversies are the source of the 'misreading' of Paul that sees him excluding human works from salvation rather than particular works from the terms for Gentile admission to the people of God.[6]

---

4. Frank Thielman, *Paul and the Law: A Contextual Approach* (Downers Grove: InterVarsity, 1994), 225-37; Guy Prentiss Waters, *Justification and the New Perspective on Paul: A Review and Response* (Phillipsburg: P&R, 2004), 167; Mark A. Seifrid, *Christ, Our Righteousness: Paul's Theology of Justification* (NSBT 9; Downers Grove; InterVarsity, 2000), 90-93; Thomas R. Schreiner, *Paul Apostle of God's Glory in Christ: A Pauline Theology* (Downers Grove: InterVarsity, 2001), 123-25 and his *Faith Alone: The Doctrine of Justification* (The Five Solas; Grand Rapids: Zondervan, 2015), 109-11.

5. Kent L. Yinger, *The New Perspective on Paul: An Introduction* (Eugene, OR: Cascade, 2011), 67-68.

6. Stephen Westerholm, *Perspectives Old and New on Paul: The 'Lutheran' Paul and His Critics* (Grand Rapids: Eerdmans, 2004), 406. Interestingly, Westerholm has virtually no discussion of Eph. 2:8-10, Titus 3:4-7, and 2 Tim. 2:8-10 except here.

In sum, because there is surprisingly little discussion of these three texts, in this book it is useful to include more of a sustained discussion. Also, if one concedes that these texts are contrasting a works righteousness soteriology with grace, then one would also have to concede works righteousness existed in Second Temple Judaism.

FIVE SCENARIOS

These three texts, Eph. 2:8-10, Titus 3:4-7, and 2 Tim. 1:8-10, create difficulties, at least on the surface, for the NPP. There is not a standard NPP answer to them because the exegetical conclusions are not uniform. Allow me to give five possible scenarios of specific exegetical conclusions and then *my* assumed implications for NPP authors once given those exegetical conclusions. These are not the only five scenarios, but hopefully, these will aid the reader in seeing some of the difficulties that the three texts create for the NPP. Later we will see some of the actual NPP responses as opposed to my assumptions as to what they should say.

(1) Assuming the exegetical conclusion of *Pauline* authorship, one needs at least to incorporate Eph. 2:8-10, Titus 3:4-7, and 2 Tim. 1:8-10 into one's view of Romans, Galatians, and Philippians 3. NPP authors ought more clearly to do this, although as we will see, some have.

(2) Assuming the exegetical conclusions of (a) *Pauline* authorship, (b) Eph. 2:8-10, Titus 3:4-7, and 2 Tim. 1:8-10 *do* contrast a works righteousness soteriology with a grace one, and (c) Romans, Galatians, and Philippians 3 do *not* contrast a works righteousness soteriology with a grace one; it would be difficult for the NPP's view to stand. They would have to argue that the 'later' Paul 'developed' toward this view, and it had nothing to do with Romans, Galatians, and Philippians 3. Also, NPP authors would have to concede that 'a significant number of Christians within the Pauline circle [were] preoccupied with the problem of "works righteousness."'[7] Finally,

---

7. Moisés Silva, 'Faith Versus Works of Law in Galatians,' in *The Paradoxes of Paul*, vol. 2 of *Justification and Variegated Nomism* (ed. D. A. Carson, Peter T. O'Brien, and Mark A. Seifrid; Grand Rapids: Baker, 2004), 217-48, esp. 245.

Sanders' uniformity of covenantal nomism would be challenged as at least Paul, a Jew, had this category.

(3) Assuming the exegetical conclusions of (a) *Deutero-Pauline* authorship and (b) Eph. 2:8-10, Titus 3:4-7, and 2 Tim. 1:8-10 *do* contrast a works righteousness soteriology with a grace one; this conclusion would be another example that a works righteousness soteriology existed in the Second Temple period. At a minimum, one would have to admit that Deutero-Paul, at least posing as a Jew, was aware of this works righteousness category. Even if his chacterization of works righteousness was aimed at Gentiles or Gentile Christians, it would prove that works righteousness was 'in the air.'[8] It is just a small step from there to admitting that portions of Judaism were not immune. Hence, Sanders' claim of uniformity of covenantal nomism would not be taking into account all of the evidence.

(4) Assuming the exegetical conclusions of (a) *Deutero-Pauline* authorship, (b) Eph. 2:8-10, Titus 3:4-7, and 2 Tim. 1:8-10 *do* contrast a works righteousness soteriology with a grace one, and (c) Romans, Galatians, and Philippians 3 do *not* contrast a work-righteousness soteriology with a grace one; an argument is needed to explain why Deutero-Paul so quickly misunderstood one of Paul's main thrusts.[9] Also, the modern exegete, who is living 2,000 years after Paul, would have to conclude that he understands Paul better than Deutero-Paul, who lived within a few decades of Paul.

(5) Assuming the exegetical conclusions of (a) either Pauline or Deutero-Pauline authorship, (b) Eph. 2:8-10, Titus 3:4-7, and 2 Tim. 1:8-10 do *not* contrast a works righteousness soteriology

---

8. Although not exactly against my point, Richard N. Longenecker has another option. He agrees to Sanders' covenantal nomism. However, in Galatians, he believes that the Jewish Christians, whether 'consciously' or 'inadvertently' moved toward 'legalism.' So Paul uses works of the law in Gal. 2:16 as a 'catch phrase to signal the whole legalistic complex of ideas having to do with winning God's favor by a merit-amassing observance of Torah' (*Galatians* [WBC 41; Dallas: Waco, 1990], 86). That is, Judaism was not legalistic, but some Christians turned the Torah into legalistic law.

9. So asks Waters, *Justification and the New Perspective on Paul*, 167.

with a grace one, and (c) Romans, Galatians, and Philippians 3 do *not* contrast a works righteousness soteriology with a grace one; this would be consistent with a NPP view.

BRIEF REMINDER OF NPP VIEWS

Before getting into the exegetical details below related to Eph. 2:8-10, Titus 1:4-7, and 2 Tim. 1:8-10, a reminder of pertinent NPP issues is advantageous.

The NPP argues against Reformed theology that Paul is not contrasting two soteriological systems when he contrasts grace/faith against works. That is, he is not contrasting grace against works righteousness. Instead, he is contrasting grace against those who trust in their Jewish identity associated with the Torah, or as Wright initially coined it, they trust in a 'national righteousness.'[10] This Jewish identity is summarized in the expression 'works of the law' or sometimes just 'works' when it is implied 'works of the law.' Hence, 'works of the law,' although technically inferring all of the Torah, really get down to three Jewish boundary/identity markers, circumcision, food laws, and Sabbath.[11] These three boundary markers separated Jews and Gentiles in the first-century A.D. Since Paul was a missionary and the Jew/Gentile conflict existed in the early Christian church, Paul's doctrine of justification by faith and *not* following boundary markers was a key theme for him.

---

10. N. T. Wright, 'The Paul of History and the Apostle of Faith,' *TynBul* 29 (1978): 61-88, esp. 65, 71, 83. '[Israel] is guilty not of "legalism" or "works righteousness" but of what I call "national righteousness," the belief that fleshly Jewish descent guarantees membership of God's true covenant people' (65).

11. James D. G. Dunn admits that he initially gave the impression that 'works of the law' only meant the three boundary markers and nothing more. See his adjusted discussion in 'The New Perspective: whence, what and whither?' in *The New Perspective on Paul* (rev. ed.; Grand Rapids: Eerdmans, 2008), 1-97, esp. 23-28. Also see his 'New Perspective View' in *Justification: Five Views* (eds. James K. Beilby and Paul Rhodes Eddy; Downers Grove: IVP Academic, 2011), 176-201, esp. 193-95; and *The Theology of Paul the Apostle*, 354-59. According to Dunn, '"works of the law" is the Pauline term for "covenantal nomism"' (*The Theology of Paul the Apostle*, 355).

In addition, NPP authors emphasize that Paul's doctrine of justification is more about who is in the church. How does one define the people of God? Are you defined by Jewish boundary markers or by faith in Christ? Justification is not about how one enters salvation. Wright says,

> Justification in this setting [Paul's Jewish context], is not a matter of *how someone enters the community of the true people of God*, but of *how you tell who belongs to that community...* In standard Christian theological language, it wasn't so much about soteriology as about ecclesiology; not so much about salvation as about the church.[12]

As to the technicalities of the NPP definition and logic of justification, I will not pursue this here as there are many different views.[13] (I give more details on Dunn and Wright below.) I will simply say that the definition of justification, usually final justification, includes an aspect of a human's works, albeit works inspired by the Spirit.[14] Also, justification does not include the imputed righteousness of Christ.[15]

---

12. N. T. Wright, *What Saint Paul Really Said*, 119, italics his.

13. For one standard NPP view of justification, see Richard B. Hays, 'Justification,' *ABD*, 3:1129-33.

14. N. T. Wright comments, 'Justification, at the last, will be on the basis of performance, not possession,' 'The Letter to the Romans: Introduction, Commentary, and Reflections,' in *The New Interpreter's Bible* (vol. 10; Nashville: Abingdon, 2002), 440. Similarly, 'Future justification, acquittal at the last great Assize, always take place on the basis of the totality of the life lived' ('The Law in Romans 2,' in *Paul and the Mosaic Law* [ed. James D. G. Dunn; Tübingen: Mohr Siebeck: 1996], 131-50, esp. 144). Also see Wright's *Justification: God's Plan & Paul's Vision* (Downers Grove: IVP Academic, 2009), 186, 260 n. 11. To be clear, Wright sees these works done in the power of the Spirit. Similarly, Dunn, 'Paul's theology of justification by faith alone has to be qualified as final justification by faith *and* works accomplished by the believer in the power of the Spirit' ('The New Perspective: whence, what and whither?,' 88, italics his).

15. Kent L. Yinger disagrees with me and says that 'some do and some don't' deny imputation. His only positive example is Don Garlington; however, Garlington gets to Christ's righteousness through union with Christ, not traditional imputation (*The New Perspective on Paul: An Introduction*), 75-77; also see the 'Afterword by Don Garlington' in the same book, 101-5, esp.

How were people justified in the OT? As I understand the NPP view, OT saints were finally justified based on faith in God *and* works done out of grace. Similarly, the NT saints are finally justified based on faith in Christ *and* works done out of grace. The difference is that in the OT, one was to follow the Torah. In the NT, one does not have to follow the Torah (especially boundary markers) and needs faith in Christ.

So that the reader can better contrast the exegetical conclusions of NPP with a Reformed view while reading the below, a very brief response to the above is presented. The Reformed view is that one can have an unhealthy interest in Jewish boundary markers *which is also* part of a works righteousness soteriology.[16] In fact, the works righteousness soteriology is a more basic problem. In Galatians at least, Paul was confronted with two problems. (1) Some did not understand that aspects of the ceremonial law (including boundary

---

104. I have read widely, and I do not know one NPP author who has the traditional view of imputation. For a vigorous defense of 'incorporated righteousness' similar to Garlington's, see Michael Bird, *The Saving Righteousness of God: Studies on Paul, Justification, and the New Perspective* (Paternoster Biblical Monographs; Eugene, OR: Wipf & Stock, 2007), 71-87. For Wright's comments on imputation, see *Paul and His Recent Interpreters: Some Contemporary Debates* (Minneapolis: Fortress, 2015), 120-21. For a defense of the traditional view of imputation that is purposely interacting with NPP, see John Piper, *Counted Righteous in Christ: Should We Abandon the Imputation of Christ's Righteousness?* (Wheaton: Crossway, 2002); D. A. Carson, 'The Vindication of Imputation: On Fields of Discourse and Semantic Fields,' in *Justification: What's at Stake in the Current Debates* (ed. Mark Husbands and Daniel J. Treier; Downers Grove: InterVarsity, 2004), 46-78; Brian Vickers, *Jesus' Blood and Righteousness: Paul's Theology of Imputation* (Wheaton: Crossway, 2006); Schreiner, *Faith Alone*, 179-90; and R. Scott Clark, 'Do This and Live: Christ's Active Obedience as the Ground of Justification,' in *Covenant, Justification, and Pastoral Ministry* (ed. R. Scott Clark; Phillipsburg: P&R, 2007), 229-65.

16. Moisés Silva noted this point early in his excellent and often quoted article against Sanders and Dunn, 'The Law and Christianity: Dunn's New Synthesis,' *WTJ* 53 (1991) 339-53. Silva complained about Dunn's false antitheses. One example was 'the particular point emphasized by Dunn, namely that Paul's concern was *not* with self-righteousness *but rather* with national markers—as though these were mutually exclusive concepts' (p. 351, italics his).

markers) were ending—this was a minor problem. (2) Some thought that doing works would gain righteousness and did not understand that all mankind, whether Jew or Gentile, were under the curse of the Covenant of Works (moral law) and could not obtain salvation by doing works—this was a major problem. Note, Reformers have long known that Paul was fighting two related problems in Galatians. The NPP is not the first to point out that circumcision was a problem.[17]

In Romans, Paul's use of 'works' sometimes includes the Mosaic legislation, but at other times the Mosaic legislation is clearly not the issue. His discussions of Abraham and Isaac clearly show this as they lived before the Mosaic legislation (Rom. 4, 9:10-12). Also, his discussion of David does not appear to focus on the Mosaic legislation (Rom. 4:6-8). Since Paul uses 'works' in situations that include and do not include Mosaic legislation, it is evident that works righteousness soteriology is more basic than national boundary markers. Similarly in Galatians, Paul indicates that both Christ and NT Christians were 'under the law' (Gal. 4:4-5). Since the NT Christians were not under the Jewish-markers aspect of the law, then 'under the law' must have a works righteousness component that is more basic.

Is the OT always brought up in the midst of a Jew/Gentile problem? Since Christ was the Messiah and God's redemptive purposes started with Adam and then through Israel, it would be

---

17. John Calvin is well aware of these two issues in Galatians. In fact, he notes Origen and Jerome's view that the 'works of the law' only refer to 'ceremonies'—which at one level is very similar to the NPP view! See *The Epistles of Paul the Apostle to the Galatians, Ephesians, Philippians and Colossians* (trans. T. H. L. Parker; eds. David W. and Thomas F Torrance; Calvin's Commentaries 11; Grand Rapids: Eerdmans, 1965 [1556]), 38. Similarly, William Perkins and Peter Martyr Vermigli distinguish between the ceremonial question and the works righteousness question, see William Perkins, *A Commentary on Galatians* (ed. Gerald T. Shephard; Pilgrim Classic Commentaries; New York: Pilgrim, 1989 [1617]), 102, 187; Peter Martyr Vermigli, *Predestination and Justification* (trans. and ed. with introduction and notes Frank A. James III; Peter Martyr Library 8; Sixteenth Century Essays & Studies 68; Kirksville: MO, 2003 [1558]), 115-17.

natural for a church that treasured the OT to be interested in OT Israel. That is, there does not necessarily have to be a first-century A.D. Jew/Gentile problem for a biblical writer to discuss the OT, although many times there was.

Answering Wright's comments about justification not being soteriology but ecclesiology, I agree it makes sense in the context of his system. Since the Reformed view sees justification as strongly related to preaching the Gospel and 'getting in' for individuals; justification is clearly connected to soteriology. Of course, once given this conclusion, there will be many implications for ecclesiology. All that to say, the debate about whether to term justification as soteriology or ecclesiology is simply an implication of the logically prior debate about the definition of justification. And the debate about justification, at least according to the NPP, is dependent upon a prior proper understanding of Second Temple Judaism.

THREE NON-NPP VIEWS

How do scholars relate their views of Eph. 2:8-10, Titus 3:4-7, and 2 Tim. 1:8-10 to the undisputed Pauline letters? In this section, I will present three scholars who are not either fully NPP or Reformed. All three are/were 'heavy hitters' in the field of NT scholarship. The first, I. Howard Marshall, is included because his article is the most often quoted on this topic.[18] The latter two, Michael Wolter and John M. G. Barclay, have each recently published a major book on Paul. Their focus is not at all on Deutero-Paul, but they do touch on 'him/them' in ways that relate to this chapter's topic. Again, none of these three scholars is a NPP author, although the latter two have some affinity for NPP. The discussion of these three will hopefully establish the difficulty that these verses in my view cause for the NPP.

---

18. A close second is Andrew T. Lincoln's article, 'Ephesians 2:8-10: A Summary of Paul's Gospel?,' *CBQ* 45 (1983): 617-30. Also see his 'The Theology of Ephesians,' in *The Theology of the Later Pauline Letters* (NTT; Cambridge: CUP, 1993), 75-166, esp. 131-32.

Following the discussion of these three non-NPP authors, I will give my exegesis of the three texts. Subsequent to that, I will present some responses from NPP authors along with my critique of those responses.

I. HOWARD MARSHALL

Marshall was a well-known British evangelical professor. He was definitely an anti-NPP author and wanted to uphold the traditional Protestant view. Paul saw Judaism as a mixture of grace and works. Paul's justification matches the traditional Protestant view, although Marshall's Paul would be close to a Wesleyan Arminian.[19]

Marshall's 1996 article 'Salvation, Grace and Works in the Later Writings in the Pauline Corpus' is quoted in virtually every discussion on our topic.[20] As to authorship, in this article, Marshall is coy as to whether Paul wrote Ephesians, but he clearly sees the Pastorals as written by Deutero-Paul.[21] In a later book, Marshall argues for Pauline authorship of Ephesians and an 'allonymous' Deutero-Pauline authorship of the Pastorals.[22] Marshall prefers a distinction between earlier and later letters rather than Paul and Deutero-Paul because he sees a close connection between the two groups of letters.[23]

In the article, Marshall compares the Paul *Hauptbriefe* letters (Romans, First and Second Corinthians, and Galatians) to Eph. 2:8-10, Titus 3:4-7, and 2 Tim. 1:8-10. He concludes that use of 'salvation' in Eph. 2 is an understandable development from

---

19. For his critique of NPP, see I. Howard Marshall, *New Testament Theology: Many Witnesses, One Gospel* (Downers Grove: InterVarsity, 2004), 445-50.

20. I. Howard Marshall, 'Salvation, Grace and Works in the Later Writings in the Pauline Corpus,' *NTS* 42 (1996): 339-58.

21. Marshall, 'Salvation, Grace and Works in the Later Writings in the Pauline Corpus,' 347-48.

22. Marshall, *New Testament Theology*, 379, 398. 'Allonymous' for Marshall means a document composed in someone else's name but *not* intended to deceive (398 n. 4).

23. Marshall, *New Testament Theology*, 420.

'justification' in Romans and Galatians. The use of grace-versus-works in Titus and Second Timothy is compared to the more common faith-versus-works of the law in Romans and Galatians, although Paul does use grace-versus-works in Rom. 11:6 (cf. Rom. 3:27, 4:4, 9:11-12). Hence, this difference is just an emphasis difference. Marshall sees both 'works of the law' and 'works' referring to works righteousness. He concludes his exegesis by noting that Eph. 2:8-10, Titus 3:4-7, and 2 Tim. 1:8-10 have broadened the more Jewish 'works of the law' of Romans and Galatians to general human works.[24]

How does Marshall relate his exegetical conclusions to NPP? He notes that the NPP only sees 'works of the law' related to Jewish 'national righteousness' that created a barrier between Jews and Gentiles. One should instead see 'works of the law' as *both* (1) a barrier between Jews and Gentiles and (2) a works righteousness soteriology.[25] This is the proper exegesis of Romans and Galatians which is confirmed by the later Pauline texts.[26]

To summarize Marshall in terms of the scenarios above, he concludes: (a) *Pauline* authorship for Ephesians and *Deutero-Pauline* authorship for Pastorals, (b) Eph. 2:8-10, Titus 3:4-7, and 2 Tim 1:8-10 *do* contrast a works righteousness soteriology with a grace one, (c) Romans, Galatians, and Philippians 3 *do* contrast a Mosaic law work righteousness soteriology with a grace one, and (d) Ephesians and Deutero-Pauline texts *should* affect and confirm the interpretation of earlier Pauline texts.

MICHAEL WOLTER

Michael Wolter is a German NT professor. His 2011 German publication has just been translated into English *Paul: An Outline*

---

24. Marshall, 'Salvation, Grace and Works in the Later Writings in the Pauline Corpus,' 348-54.

25. 'By the time we get to Ephesians and Pastoral Epistles there is a tendency to include any kind of human endeavors to win God's favor and not just obedience to the Mosaic law (Eph. 2:9, 2 Tim. 1:9, Titus 3:5)' (Marshall, *New Testament Theology*, 444 n. 34).

26. Marshall, 'Salvation, Grace and Works in the Later Writings in the Pauline Corpus,' 355-58.

of His Theology (2015).[27] He believes that Paul only wrote the seven 'undisputed' letters, and he is aware of the NPP.[28]

Wolter has similarities to the NPP. He sees Paul's doctrine of justification as arising out of his Jew/Gentile missions context in Galatians, and then continuing into Romans and Philippians 3. Paul's use of 'works of the law' means the whole Torah, but due to the social environment, this functioned as promoting the three boundary markers.[29] Israel's error is that they did not want 'to give up the exclusivity of their relationship to God,' which was what the Jews boasted about (Rom. 2:17 with Rom. 3:27).[30] Justification 'presupposes *Christian* addressees, and for this reason one should not speak either of a "*message* of justification," or of a "*proclamation* of justification."'[31] This message is not a missionary message; it is to those converted. Wolter has a strong emphasis that Paul wants Christians to do ethical commands and complains about the Lutheran view of Paul in this regard.[32]

On the other hand, Wolter has views that do not match NPP. Wolter pushes to distinguish between Paul's 'context of discovery' of justification (Jew/Gentile problem) and the doctrine per se.[33] Paul does believe that 'God pronounces people righteous on the basis of

27. Michael Wolter, *Paul: An Outline of His Theology* (trans. Robert L. Brawley; Waco: Baylor University Press, 2015). Yes, this is the same title as Ridderbos' work.

28. Wolter, *Paul: An Outline of His Theology*, 6, 332-33.

29. Wolter, *Paul: An Outline of His Theology*, 337, 346, 395.

30. Wolter, *Paul: An Outline of His Theology*, 351.

31. Wolter, *Paul: An Outline of His Theology*, 394, italics his. Wolter complains that Acts 13:38-39 wrongly presents Paul as preaching a missionary message of justification.

32. Wolter, *Paul: An Outline of His Theology*, 365-66. 'One ought not to endorse the Lutheran understanding of the law and assume that Paul's proclamation of the gospel of Jesus Christ could have been understood as a summons to liberation from moral conventions and ethical norms.' This is not a correct understanding of Lutherans! Read Luther's Small Catechism and Large Catechism.

33. Wolter, *Paul: An Outline of His Theology*, 393.

their faith' in Christ, and there is no final justification related to works because no one can perform the full Torah due to sin.[34] That is, the Torah has a works righteousness aspect to it in addition to a separating (of Jew and Gentile) function. Sin has made the Jew and the Gentile equal even though the Jew had the initial advantage of the Torah. Wolter interprets the judgment by works in Rom 2 as referring to a historical situation where Christ has not come yet.[35]

Here is my summary of Wolter: Paul begins with an ecclesiological problem (Jew/Gentile). This then moves him toward an anthropological insight—sin has made the Jew and Gentile equal because the Jew's Torah (both ceremonial and moral demands) could not be relied upon to produce (works) righteousness. This anthropological insight moves him toward a soteriological solution— all need justification by faith in Christ. This then solves his initial ecclesiastical problem.[36]

In the summary section of his justification chapter, Wolter notes that the NPP wanted to 'liberate the interpretation of the Pauline doctrine of justification from the hermeneutical grasp of Luther and Luther's theology.'[37] And he agrees in principle. Wolter complains that Luther did not understand that 'law' for Paul is the Torah, which always must include its ceremonies to distinguish Jews from Gentiles. Luther improperly moved Paul's Torah to generalized ethical and moral requirements which denuded important aspects of Torah. (Apparently, Wolter would agree that both Luther and Paul's Torah had works righteousness aspects, but Wolter believes that for Paul the works righteousness portion of the Torah cannot be properly separated from the national Jewish identity.[38])

And now let us get to the point. *Wolter notes that Deutero-Paul in Eph. 2:8-9, Titus 3:5, and 2 Tim. 1:9 has done the same thing as Luther;*

---

34. Wolter, *Paul: An Outline of His Theology*, 336, 355-57, 370, 379. Quote is on p. 336 and original in italics.

35. Wolter, *Paul: An Outline of His Theology*, 367.

36. Wolter, *Paul: An Outline of His Theology*, 331-92.

37. Wolter, *Paul: An Outline of His Theology*, 397.

38. Wolter, *Paul: An Outline of His Theology*, 16-17, 312-13, 398.

Deutero-Paul changed Torah into general ethical actions required for works righteousness.

> The same kind [as Luther] of moralizing of 'works' and with it the detachment from the question of Israel exists as early as the reception of the Pauline doctrine of justification, as it is present in the Deutero-Pauline Epistles of the New Testament. ... Pauline 'works of the law' have become generally ethical actions. ... without establishing a relationship with Torah.[39]

As a consequence, Deutero-Paul has also changed the negative boasting. The real Paul complained that Israel was boasting about their special relationship with God (same view as NPP). Deutero-Paul universalized it to a boasting in general works righteousness.[40]

Wolter then exonerates Luther to a degree. Luther is doing the same thing that Deutero-Paul did. Yes, argues Wolters, Luther altered Paul's message when he separated it from its historical Jew/Gentile context; however, 'in so doing [Luther] preserves crucial components of its context of justification.' On the other hand, Wolter wants to be clear, let us not bring Deutero-Paul or Luther into our interpretation of the real Paul.[41]

To summarize Wolter in terms of the scenarios above, he concludes: (a) *Deutero-Pauline* authorship, (b) Eph. 2:8-10, Titus 3:4-7, and 2 Tim. 1:8-10 *do* contrast a works righteousness soteriology with a grace one, (c) Romans, Galatians, and Philippians 3 *do* contrast a fully-Jewish Torah works righteousness soteriology with a grace one, and (d) the change in theology is a consequence of the change away from the Jew/Gentile problem, and (e) Deutero-Pauline texts should *not* affect the interpretation of Pauline texts.

---

39. Wolter, *Paul: An Outline of His Theology*, 398.

40. Wolter, 'The Development of Pauline Christianity from a "Religion of Conversion" to a "Religion of Tradition,"' trans. J. M. McConnell and D. P. Moessner, in *Paul and the Heritage of Israel* (eds. D. P. Moessner, D. Marguerat, and M. Wolter; LNTS 452; London: T&T Clark, 2012), 49-69, esp. 66.

41. Wolter, *Paul: An Outline of His Theology*, 399.

JOHN M. G. BARCLAY

John Barclay is a well-known British professor. He has just published a major work, *Paul & the Gift* (2015).[42] In general, he is known for critiquing N. T. Wright and various aspects of the NPP.[43] But also he has affinities with the NPP. In *Paul & the Gift*, Barclay considers himself either doing a 're-contextualization of the Augustinian-Lutheran tradition' or doing a 'reconfiguration of the "new perspective."'[44] Concerning Pauline authorship of Eph. 2:8-10, Titus 3:4-7, and 2 Tim. 1:8-10, Barclay sees these texts as Deutero-Pauline.[45] These three texts are barely mentioned in the majority of the book; however, they are discussed in the final section of the book, 'New Contexts and New Meanings of Grace.'[46]

Somewhat paralleling my complaint that Sanders has not adequately defined 'works righteousness,' Barclay complains that terms like 'grace' and 'gift' have not been well defined. This partially explains the confusion about grace in Judaism. As he says several times in the book, 'Grace is everywhere in Second Temple Judaism, but not everywhere the same.'[47] He proposes to evaluate Paul on the concept level, not simply the word level, for the category of 'gift.'

Using anthropological studies as to how gifts operate between giver and receiver, Barclay first concludes that in the Greco-Roman world gifts operated in 'reciprocal relations, and entail the expectation and obligation of return, whether the parties are equal or unequal in status.'[48] That is, the default position is to assume

---

42. John M. G. Barclay, *Paul & the Gift* (Grand Rapids: Eerdmans, 2015).

43. For example, see his response to Wright's view of Paul's critique of the Roman Empire, 'Why the Roman Empire Was Insignificant to Paul,' in *Pauline Churches and Diaspora Jews* (WUNT 275; Tübingen: Mohr Siebeck, 2011), 363-87; and see his review of *Paul and the Faithfulness of God*, by N. T. Wright, *SJT* 68 (2015): 235-46.

44. Barclay, *Paul & the Gift*, 573.

45. Barclay, *Paul & the Gift*, 546 n. 57, 571.

46. Barclay, *Paul & the Gift*, 569-74.

47. Barclay, *Paul & the Gift*, 565, also 2, 6.

48. Barclay, *Paul & the Gift*, 63.

that the giver of a gift gives to someone who is deserving and expects something in return. The receiver of a gift feels obligated to give something to the giver. Barclay then goes beyond the default position. He notes that a gift could be 'perfected' beyond an implied reciprocal gift (an analogy to a *perfect* storm). He proposes six 'perfections.' For example, a gift with 'superabundance' would be one that the scale or extravagance of the gift is so overwhelming relative to the situation. Another example, a gift with 'incongruity' is one that does not take into account the worth of the recipient; this is as opposed to the assumed practice of normally only giving gifts to those who deserve them.[49] These six do not necessarily go together; they are not a 'package deal.'[50] Barclay uses these six perfections to evaluate nuances of 'grace' in various Christian theologians and Second Temple documents. Then he looks in detail at Galatians and Romans.

Barclay evaluates Sanders' covenantal nomism. He agrees with Sanders that grace is everywhere in Second Temple Judaism and Sanders has destroyed the caricatures of Judaism as a works righteousness religion. 'Nonetheless, at the heart of [Sanders'] project is a lack of clarity concerning the very definition of grace.' Sanders emphasized the temporal 'priority' aspect of a gift—a gift is perfected because it is given before the recipient asked for it (election). However, the concept of the 'incongruity' aspect of a gift (the recipient did not deserve the gift at all) is assumed by Sanders to always be present if the 'priority' aspect is present. And this is not the case.[51] Hence, Sanders cannot explain the merit of the Patriarchs as a basis for election. Also, this flattening of grace to 'priority' allowed Sanders to 'unwittingly create a spurious uniformity within Judaism, and [explains] why interpreters have been variously satisfied or dissatisfied with his conclusions.'[52]

---

49. Barclay, *Paul & the Gift*, 70-75.

50. Barclay, *Paul & the Gift*, 563.

51. Barclay, *Paul & the Gift*, 154-58, esp. 157.

52. Barclay, *Paul & the Gift*, 564.

Barclay does discuss Wright and Dunn.[53] Barclay notes that both are against seeing Judaism as having a works righteousness soteriology and both emphasize the group and not the individual. Also, he notes that both see Paul's grace as including both 'priority' and 'incongruity' aspects, as opposed to Sanders. Barclay distinguishes Wright and Dunn based on the degree to which grace is an important concept in Paul. Wright so emphasizes the universality of Paul's mission, that, according to Barclay, Wright has *not* made grace the 'core feature in Paul's understanding of faith or in his definition of membership in the people of God in Christ.'[54] Dunn, on the other hand, does see grace as 'significant.'[55]

Barclay's Paul highlights the gift of the Christ-event. This gift emphasizes the 'incongruity' aspect—that is, the unworthiness of the recipient. Paul connects this incongruous grace of the Christ-event to his Gentile mission to form 'innovative communities' that break the divide between Jew and Gentile and break the value systems of any non-Christian community. By 'works of the law,' Paul is attacking the 'value-system of the Torah' that gave supreme worth to following the Torah and other cultural aspects associated with the Torah. He is *not* attacking the 'subjective motivation of the worker.' He is critiquing the '*criteria* of worth being applied in the formation of a community.' Although the emphasis is communal, this Christ-event gift will produce communal practices and individual ethical lives. This downplaying of the Torah is 'no denigration of Judaism,' but a reclassification of the 'ultimate authority of the Torah.'[56]

Barclay evaluates the different historic answers to Rom. 2 and its justification by works (Rom. 2:13). He explains the standard Reformed answer that this is a 'hypothetical' situation (Covenant of Works option) based on Rom. 2 being within the larger

---

53. Barclay, *Paul & the Gift*, 162-65, 342-44.

54. Barclay (Barclay, *Paul & the Gift*, 163 n. 246) cites Wright's discussion of Rom. 4 as evidence of his assertion (N. T. Wright, 'Romans,' 497, cf. 485).

55. Barclay, *Paul & the Gift*, 164.

56. Barclay, *Paul & the Gift*, 443-45, 546 n. 57, italics his.

Rom. 1:18-3:20 everyone-has-sinned section.[57] However, he dis-agrees. He proposes to solve the 'conundrum' by his idea of multi-faceted aspects of grace. The Pauline incongruous grace, although Paul's primary emphasis, does not necessarily involve eliminating the 'circularity' aspect of grace (the recipient will present a reciprocal gift). That is, the believer will do good works by the power of God as a natural response to the incongruous gift. These 'transformative results [good works] are finally *congruous* with the just judgment of God.'[58] At least as I interpret Barclay, there will be a final justification by works, but again, as in Dunn and Wright, the works will be Spirit-empowed works.

Finally, let us get to Eph. 2:8-10, Titus 3:4-7, and 2 Tim. 1:8-10. With these Deutero-Pauline letters, the context has shifted away from the Jew/Gentile problem. '"Works" are refocused as moral achievements and "boasting" indicates not the cultural confidence of the Jew in the Torah (or of the Greek in wisdom), but pride in achievement.' No longer was the Christ-gift undermining the Christian's 'criteria of worth but their pride or purpose in achieving Christian worth.' 'Paul's critique of the *criteria* of worth [for a] community becomes a critique of the *achievement* of worth.' Similarly, Luther 'translate[d] Paul's missionary theology of grace into an urgent and perpetual *inward mission*, directed to the church, but especially to the heart of each believer.'[59]

---

57. More accurately, this is a 'principles of justice' view. For a classic Reformed defense of this view, see Charles Hodge, *A Commentary on Romans* (Geneva Commentary; Carlisle: Banner of Truth, 1972 [1864], 54). For a modern Lutheran view that is very similar to the Reformed, see Stephen Westerholm, *Perspectives Old and New on Paul: The 'Lutheran' Paul and His Critics*, 267-73. Francis Watson, an author who has moved away from NPP, used to see Rom. 2 as referring to Gentile Christians, but now advocates the 'hypothetical' view (*Paul and the Hermeneutics of Faith* [London: T&T Clark, 2004], 351-53, esp. 352 n. 57).

58. Barclay, *Paul & the Gift*, 464-67, esp. 467, italics his. 'That the wholly incongruous divine gift ("without works") forms the foundation and frame for human works that fit God's judgment ([Rom.] 2:6-10) is contradictory only if the unconditioned gift is taken to be also unconditional (in the sense of seeking no return)' (486 n. 101).

59. Barclay, *Paul & the Gift*, 546 n. 57, 570-71, italics his.

To summarize Barclay in terms of the scenarios above, he concludes: (a) *Deutero-Pauline* authorship, (b) Eph. 2:8-10, Titus 3:4-7, and 2 Tim. 1:8-10 *do* contrast a works righteousness soteriology with a grace one, (c) Romans, Galatians, and Philippians 3 do *not* contrast works righteousness soteriology with a grace one, but *do* include a critique of Torah 'community criteria,' (d) the change in theology is a consequence of the change away from the Jew/Gentile problem, (e) implied that Deutero-Pauline texts should *not* affect the interpretation of Pauline texts, and (f) Second Temple Judaism has various levels of grace.

SUMMARY OF THREE NON-NPP VIEWS

A key point is that the three authors surveyed agree that Eph. 2:8-10, Titus 3:4-7, and 2 Tim. 1:8-10 do use 'works' in the sense of works righteousness. How do they relate this conclusion to Galatians, Romans, and Philippians 3?

Marshall sees significant *continuity* despite his view that he believes that the Pastorals are Deutero-Pauline (Ephesians is Pauline). This is not a surprise because he also believes that Paul also argues against works righteousness in Galatians, Romans, and Philippians 3.

Wolters and Barclay see significant *discontinutiy* between the Deutero-Pauline Eph. 2:8-10, Titus 3:4-7, and 2 Tim. 1:8-10 and Paul. Their logic is not as straightforward as Marshall's. They interpret 'works of the law' in Paul as so closely tied to Torah and a missionary Jew/Gentile problem, that it is inappropriate to use this category anywhere but in a similar situation. (Note, they assume that Ephesians is not truly addressing the Jew/Gentile problem despite the possible implication from Eph. 2:11-22.) Wolters acknowledges that 'works of the law' does have works righteousness aspects, and Barclay less so, although Barclay does see the Torah as setting up commnuity 'criteria' that function to some degree as works righteousness. However, both see the boasting in Paul as related to boasting in Jewish nationalism and not in one's personal works. Both Wolters and Barclay complain that Luther misused Paul; and both admit that Luther's misuse was similar to what Deutero-Paul did.

EXEGESIS OF EPHESIANS 2:8-10, TITUS 3:4-7, SECOND TIMOTHY 1:8-10

The following is my exegesis of Eph. 2:8-10, Titus 3:4-7, and 2 Tim. 1:8-10 and some conclusions as to their relationship to other Pauline texts.[60] Following this section, I will present various NPP explanations and also my response to them.

EPHESIANS 2:8-10

I affirm that Ephesians was written by Paul.[61] Given that, I conclude that the provenance is Paul's first Roman imprisonment (house arrest) in A.D. 60–62 (Eph. 3:1, 4:1, 6:20). From Rome, Tychicus and Onesimus carried the Ephesians, Colossians, and Philemon letters. They delivered the Ephesians letter to the Ephesian church on their way to Colossae to deliver the letters to Colossians and Philemon (Eph. 6:21, Col. 4:7-9, Philem. 10).[62]

Concerning the composition of the Ephesian church, Paul founds the church during his third missionary journey.[63] Acts indicates

---

60. Although I will not discuss it, another similar early text is *1 Clement* 32:4, 'And therefore, we who having been called by his will in Christ Jesus, *are not justified by ourselves*, neither by our wisdom nor understanding nor piety *nor works* (ἔργων) *which we worked in holiness of heart, but by faith, by which [faith] almighty God justified all [men]* from the age [past], to him be glory for ever and ever' (translation and italics mine).

61. For a long defense of Pauline authorship, see Harold W. Hoehner, *Ephesians: An Exegetical Commentary* (Grand Rapids: Baker, 2002), 2-61. For the standard critical Duetero-Pauline position, see Werner Georg Kümmel, *Introduction to the New Testament* (trans. Howard Clark Kee; rev. ed.; Nashville: Abingdon, 1975), 357-63.

62. My explanation assumes that ἐν Ἐφέσῳ (Eph. 1:1) is part of the autographa. If Ephesians later became a circular letter to Asian churches, this might explain the absence of ἐν Ἐφέσῳ in some manuscripts.

63. Although Paul previously visited Ephesus briefly at the end of his second journey (Acts 18:19–21) and Apollos was there before Paul's arrival (18:24-26), it is during the third missionary journey that the Ephesian church is founded. Acts 18:10 implies that other areas in Asia are also evangelized during his stay at Ephesus. Probably, during this time, the

that the church included both Jewish and Gentile Christians (Acts 19:1-10, 20:21). Ephesians itself more directly addresses Gentile Christians (2:11, 19, 3:1, 4:17; debateable 1:12-13). My view is that the Ephesian church has grown to be more and more Gentile-dominated, although Jewish Christians certainly are still part of the church.

As to the purpose of the letter, as with most scholars, I conclude that there is no obvious, major problem that Paul is addressing. Paul had previously spent three years at the Ephesian church and taught them many things (Acts 19:8-10). Why then the letter? Because when Paul was addressing a heresy problem with his Colossian letter, why not also include a letter to the Ephesians as Tychicus and Onesimus were passing by Ephesus on their way to Colossae? Hence, most of the issues discussed are more generic concerns that typical Gentile Christians would have in the Greco-Roman culture, or maybe more specifically, in the Greco-Roman culture in the Ephesian area.

Going slightly beyond me, Arnold reasonably proposes to do a 'mirror reading' of Ephesians. He finds four themes/issues that Paul addresses. (1) Supposed Greco-Roman spiritual powers are not above God. (2) Christ's united church should overcome the cultural pressure of Gentile animosity toward Jews. (3) Gentile Christians need encouragement to cease from immoral practices. (4) Christians' identity in Christ positively affects their spirtual life, their relationship to other Christians, and ability to follow moral imperatives.[64] Note that Arnold's second theme/issue is pertinent for this book as some will base their exegesis on Jew/Gentile-relationship assumptions.[65]

---

relatively nearby churches in Colossae, Laodicea, and Hierapolis are evangelized by Paul's companions (cf. Acts 20:4; Eph. 6:21; Col. 1:7–8; 2:1; 4:7, 12–13; 2 Tim. 4:12).

64. Clinton E. Arnold, *Ephesians* (ZECNT; Grand Rapids: Zondervan, 2010), 43-45.

65. E.g., how does one explain the alternating 'we' and 'you' in Eph. 1:11-13 and 2:1-10? Is the 'we' Paul and the Ephesian church; or is the 'we' Jewish Christians, and the 'you' Gentile Christians?

Ephesians 2:8-10 is within the larger unit of Eph. 2:1-10. This unit is easily outlined as: (1) All are spiritually dead and under God's wrath (Eph. 2:1-3), (2) God made us alive with Christ to show His immeasurable grace toward us (Eph. 2:4-7), and (3) Explanation and emphasis of immeasureable grace that is toward us (Eph. 2:8-10). This unit is tied together linguistically by περιπατέω ('to walk') in Eph. 2:2 and 2:10—before being in Christ, one walked in 'trespasses and sins'; but after being in Christ, one walks in 'good works.' Also, in the middle of Eph. 2:5, Paul breaks the flow of thought and parenthetically exclaims 'by grace you have been saved.' This phrase is then used again and is the lead topic in Eph. 2:8-10.

Union with Christ is emphasized in Eph. 2:5-6 with the language of 'made us alive *with* Christ,' 'raised us up *with* him,' and 'seated us *with* him.'[66] This is coordinated with the salvation/justification theme in Eph. 2:8-10.[67] There are several union with Christ and justification parallels to Col. 2:11-15.

Ephesians 1:2-23 is the unit before Eph. 2:1-10. These two units have significant conceptual and linguistic connections, including an emphasis on being in/with Christ and grace.[68] The unit following

---

66. All three of the verbs use the prefix σύν ('with'), meaning 'with Christ.'

67. For an excellent historical study of the relationship of union with Christ and justification in the ordo salutis, see J. V. Fesko, *Beyond Calvin: Union with Christ and Justification in Early Modern Reformed Theology (1517-1700)* (Reformed Historical Theology 20; Bristol: CT; Vandenhoeck & Ruprecht, 2012). Fesko concludes, among other things, that virtually all theologians had both a doctrine of union with Christ and a doctrine of ordo salutis. Further, justification was always assigned priority (logical or theological, not temporal) over sanctification (pp. 380-82). For a discussion of union with Christ and justification in the context of NPP concerns, see Lane G. Tipton, 'Union with Christ and Justification,' in *Justified in Christ: God's plan for us in Justification* (ed. K. Scott Oliphint; Ross-shire, Scotland: Mentor, 2007), 23-49. See my discussion of union with Christ related to the WLC in Robert J. Cara, 'Redemptive-Historical Themes in the Westminster Larger Catechism,' in *The Westminster Confession into the 21st Century: Essays in Rememberance of the 350th Anniversary of the Westminster Assembly* (ed. J. Ligon Duncan III; 3 vols.; Ross-Shire, Scotland: Mentor, 2003-2009), 3:55-76.

68. Some less obvious linguistic connections include ὑπερβάλλον ('immeasurable') in Eph. 1:19 and 2:7; ἐξουσία ('authority') in Eph. 1:21 and 2:2; αἰών ('age') in Eph. 1:21, 2:2, 2:7.

Eph. 2:1-10 is Eph. 2:11-22. This unit encourages the Gentile Christians to remember that even though they were 'strangers to the covenants of promise' (Eph. 2:12), now in Christ they are part of one, unified church, both Jewish and Gentile Christians. Best sees Eph. 2:1-10 as providing the logic as to why the church should be unified—all enter the church by grace.[69]

Here is my mechancial translation of Eph. 2:8-10 with the Greek text.

8a   For by grace you have been saved through faith
      τῇ[70] γὰρ χάριτί ἐστε σεσῳσμένοι διὰ[71] πίστεως·

8b   And this is not from you, [it is] the gift of God
      καὶ τοῦτο οὐκ ἐξ ὑμῶν, θεοῦ τὸ δῶρον·

9   Not from works so anyone may not boast.
      οὐκ ἐξ ἔργων, ἵνα μή τις καυχήσηται.

10a   For we are his product,[72] created in Christ Jesus for good works
      αὐτοῦ γάρ ἐσμεν ποίημα, κτισθέντες ἐν Χριστῷ Ἰησοῦ ἐπὶ ἔργοις ἀγαθοῖς

---

69. Ernest Best, *A Critical and Exegetical Commentary on Ephesians* (ICC; Edinburgh: T&T Clark, 1998), 199.

70. As all agree, the article τῇ is anaphoric and points back to χάριτί in χάριτί ἐστε σεσῳσμένοι in Eph. 2:5 (cf. 2:7) which does not have the article; e.g., Hoehner, *Ephesians*, 340. For explanation of anaphoric articles, see Daniel B. Wallace, *Greek Grammar Beyond the Baics: An Exegetical Syntax of the New Testament* (Grand Rapids: Zondervan, 1996), 217-20.

71. Paul sometimes uses διὰ πίστεως (Rom. 3:25, Gal. 2:16) and sometimes ἐκ πίστεως (Rom. 3:26, 30, Gal. 3:11, 22). There is no difference in meaning. So also Andrew T. Lincoln, *Ephesians* (WBC; Dallas: Waco, 1990), 111 and Peter T. O'Brien, *The Letter to the Ephesians* (PNTC; Grand Rapids: Eerdmans, 1999), 174.

72. The predominant translation is 'workmanship,' with which I agree conceptually. However, I prefer not to use this because it includes the English word 'work,' which is not included at the Greek level. The translation 'workmanship' has a historic pedigree; it is included in Tyndale's initial 1526 NT edition, the Geneva Bible (1560), and the KJV (1611).

10b   which [works] God made-beforehand so we may
walk in them [works]
οἷς[73] προητοίμασεν ὁ θεὸς, ἵνα ἐν αὐτοῖς
περιπατήσωμεν.

The main emphasis of Eph. 2:8-10 is 'for by grace you have been saved through faith' (8a above). The 'for' connects back to the previous verse and explains further and emphasizes the 'immeasurable riches of [God's] grace in kindness toward us in Christ Jesus.' Paul here as elsewhere couples his common terms 'grace' and 'faith' (e.g., Rom. 3:22-24, 4:16, 5:2, Gal. 2:20-21, 1 Tim. 1:14). The expression 'you have been saved' (ἐστε σεσῳσμένοι) is a perfect-passive periphrastic construction. Here and Eph. 2:5 are the only occurences of the perfect for σῴζω in Paul.[74] The perfect alludes to the past point of salvation which thus emphasizes its present state. As is well known, Paul varies his use of σῴζω, sometimes he refers to past/present salvation (e.g., Rom. 8:24, 1 Cor. 15:2, 2 Thess. 2:10) and more often to future salvation (Rom. 5:9-10, 1 Cor. 3:15, 1 Tim. 4:16). Since Paul alludes back to the initial salvation, this concept is what he terms elsewhere, justification.[75] Romans 10:9-10 is the classic verse where Paul equates justification and salvation at the word level. From a Reformed theology perspective, Paul uses the term 'salvation' sometimes to mean justification, or sanctification, or glorification, or all three.[76] Context determines his meaning. Here, Paul's use of salvation refers to justification.

---

73. One would expect the *accusative* neuter plural ἅ; however, the *dative* neuter plural οἷς is used due to 'attraction' to ἔργοις ἀγαθοῖς.

74. For some this is a major evidence for Deutro-Pauline authorship. See discussion in Lincoln, who although he holds to Deutero-Pauline authorship, believes this point 'should not be exaggerated' ('Ephesians 2:8-10: A Summary of Paul's Gospel,' 620).

75. John Owen sees justification as 'principally' intended in 'by grace you have saved,' but 'conversion to God and sanctification are also included therein, as is evident from vv. 5-6' (*The Doctrine of Justification by Faith through Imputation of the Righteousness of Christ: Explained, Confirmed, and Vindicated* [Grand Rapids: Reformation Heritage Books, 2006 {1677}], 402). For his extended discussion of Eph. 2:8-10, see pp. 399-407.

76. More accurately, 'salvation' would include all aspects of the ordo salutis,

Following verse 8a, Paul rhetorically adds two 'not' clauses, verses 8b and 9 to emphasize that one is saved by grace through faith. Hence, I understand 'this' (τοῦτο) in 8b to refer to the whole 8a clause, although the exegesis is not substantially different if 'this' only refers to 'faith.'[77] The first 'not' clause (8b) emphasizes that one's salvation, including your faith, is not ultimately from 'you.' It is the opposite of *your* merit; it is a 'gift' from *God* (see Rom. 4:4). The second 'not' clause (9) makes a related point. One's salvation is not from 'works,' because if it was, someone would be able to 'boast.' Again, here, 'works' are taken as *your* works that would produce something to boast about. That is, 'works' are taken as potential merit (see Rom. 4:2, 1 Cor. 1:26-31). Clearly, there are two systems of soteriology, one by God/Christ/grace/faith/gift and the other by you/works/boasting. In fact, they are so clearly opposites, that to prove the one, Paul simply says that it is *not* the other.

'Works' in Eph. 2:9 is obviously used negatively as a soteriological system.[78] Although Jew/Gentile concerns are not totally absent from Ephesians,[79] the emphasis on Gentiles (Eph. 2:11) and their 'works' surely means general moral works as opposed to Jewish nationality markers. As seen above with the 'three non-NPP

---

including calling, regeneration, adoption, and perseverance.

77. τοῦτο is a neuter singular relative pronoun that would normally refer back to a neuter singular noun or a whole phrase/clause. πίστεως is femine singular. Hence, most likely grammatically, τοῦτο is referring back to the whole clause, which does include πίστεως. So also most commentators, e.g., Best, *Ephesians*, 226; and Hoehner, *Ephesians*, 343. On the other hand, one could argue that τοῦτο could refer back to the closest noun regardless of gender, that is, back to πίστεως. Chrysostom seems to assume this grammatically, and he is a Greek-speaker ('Homily IV' in 'Homilies on Ephesians,' *NPNF*[1], 8:67). For the best arguments for τοῦτο referring to only πίστεως, see Charles Hodge, *A Commentary on Ephesians* (Geneva; Carlisle: Banner of Truth, 1964 [1856]), 77-78; and William Hendricksen, *Exposition of Ephesians* (NTC; Grand Rapids: Baker, 1967) 120-23.

78. Why negatively?—Paul assumes that no one can perfectly perform the requirements of the works system (Gal. 3:10-14). Or to say it in Reformed theology terms, once Adam sinned, no one can fulfill the Covenant of Works except for Christ.

79. The word 'law' is only used once in this letter, Eph. 2:15.

views' and in many commentaries, the vast majority of scholars, but not all, believe that 'works' here are general moral works done for soteriological reasons.[80] Depending on one's starting point in Galatians and Romans, 'works' is ultimately not a change from Galatians and Romans (my view[81]) or it is a broadening from Galatians and Romans (Wolters and Barclay above). Either way, here the overwhelming consensus is that 'works' is general moral effort done within a works righteousness system.[82]

What does 'for' in Eph. 2:10 refer back to? Some opt for 'gift' in 8b, or 'not works' in 9, or to the whole of 8a.[83] There is not much difference in these options as they are all magnifying grace as opposed to the work we do. Using God's creation of the physical world as a backdrop, the emphasis in Eph. 2:10 is on God's re-creating Christians. This would conceptually dovetail with the wording of 'dead' (Eph. 2:1) and 'make alive' (Eph. 2:5). If God is our spiritual creator, then again it is pressed home that salvation is not from us.

---

80. Stephen E. Fowl is typical. '[Paul] does not mean works of the law as in Gal. 2:16 or Rom. 3:27... Rather, Paul is referring to human striving and performance in hopes of winning God's approval (cf. 2 Tim. 1:9; Titus 3:5)' (*Ephesians: A Commentary* [NTL; Louisville: Westminster John Knox, 2012], 79). To the contrary, Thomas B. Slater sees Eph. 2:10 as evidence that Sanders' scheme is correct—entry into the community by grace and good works are the means to stay in it (*Ephesians* [SHBC; Macon: Smyth & Helwys, 2012], 64-65).

81. Romans 3:27-28 connects 'boasting' and 'works of the law,' and Eph. 2:9 connects 'boast' and 'works.' Hence, 'works of the law' and 'works' are parallel.

82. Pheme Perkins sees Deutero-Paul expanding upon Paul's language related to Jewish works of the law to 'a more general reading audience ... An audience familiar with the conversion language of popular philosophical teachers might conclude that turning away from sin, the powers of the cosmos, can be accomplished by human efforts or human teaching' ('The Letter to the Ephesians: Introduction, Commentary, and Reflections,' in *The New Interpreter's Bible Commentary: Volume Ten* [Nashville: Abingdon, 2015], 1-104, esp. 37).

83. For example, Frank Thielman opts for 'gift' (*Ephesians* [BECNT; Grand Rapids: Baker, 2010], 144). Hoehner opts for 'not works' (*Ephesians*, 346). Lincoln opts for either 8a or all of 8-9 (*Ephesians*, 229).

Further, if God is our spiritual creator, then He must have had a predestinating plan for us to perform good works (Eph. 1:4).

As Paul sometimes does elsewhere, in Eph. 2:10 he uses 'works' in a good sense.[84] This good sense of works continues the contrast that 'works' in Eph. 2:9 must be soteriological works righteousness. That is, any truly good work that one does is because of God's power and origin, and thus is not to be considered as works righteousness. These good works in Eph. 2:10 are part of our sanctification and are clearly disinguished from the soteriological 'works' option in Eph. 2:9.

TITUS 3:4-7

The vast majority of critical scholarship sees Deutero-Paul as the author of Titus.[85] However, I affirm that it was written by Paul.[86] Following the traditional view, the letter was written after Paul's

---

84. Intriguingly, Paul combines work and faith in 1 Thess. 1:3, 'your work of [coming from] faith.' See my discussion in Robert J. Cara, *A Study Commentary on 1 and 2 Thessalonians* (EP Study Commentary; Webster: NY: EP, 2009), 36-37. Other examples of Paul using works positively include Rom. 15:18, Col. 1:10, 3:17, 1 Thess. 5:13, 2 Thess. 1:11, 2:17, 1 Tim. 2:10, Titus 2:7, 3:8.

85. Those against Pauline authorship include, for example, Kümmel, *Introduction to the New Testament*, 384; Bart D. Ehrman, *The New Testament: A Historical Introduction to the Early Christian Writings* (New York: OUP, 2008), 393-96; and Raymond F. Collins, *1 & 2 Timothy: A Commentary* (NTL; Louisville: Westminster John Knox, 2002), 3-9. Although these statistics are debatable, Raymond E. Brown believes that '80 to 90 percent of modern scholars' opt for Deutero-Paul (*An Introduction to the New Testament* [ABRL; New York: Doubleday, 1997], 668).

86. Those in favor of Pauline authorship include George W. Knight III, who primarily explains the differences between the Pastorals and the other ten Pauline letters as related to one comprehensive difference: 'The [Pastorals] were written to different recipients—colleagues not churches' (*The Pastoral Epistles: A Commentary on the Greek Text* [NIGNT; Grand Rapids: 1992], 51). He secondarily notes that Luke may have been an amanuensis due to linguistic similarities of the Pastorals to Luke-Acts (pp. 50-52). William D. Mounce sees Paul as the author of the Pastorals, but with Paul using an amanuensis with more freedom than normal to partially explain the linguistic differences from the other ten Pauline letters (*Pastoral Epistles* [WBC 46; Nashville: Thomas Nelson, 2000], lxxxii-cxxix). My view is that Paul used a word-for-word amanuensis.

first Roman imprisonment (A.D. 63–64) while Paul was in Nicopolis (Titus 3:12). The letter is addressed to Titus who is on the island of Crete (Titus 1:5). In addition to being addressed to Titus, the ending benediction is directed to a plural 'you' indicating that Paul expects this letter to be read to the church at Crete (Titus 3:15).[87] The purpose of the letter is to give encouragment and instruction to Titus on church polity and church life and warn him about false teachers. Secondarily, the church as a whole is being instructed also.

All three of the Pastorals are partially directed against false teachings that appear to be similar.[88] This teaching is a not-too-well-defined combination of proto-gnostic (maybe just generic Hellenistic ideas) and Jewish-Christian elements.[89] Maybe the false teaching was not a combination of views into one group, but false teachings of several groups, or maybe, a continuum of views. Titus 1:10 implies a distinction between 'circumcision party' and others.[90] Of the three Pastorals, Titus is considered more Jewish. Jewish elements in Titus include 'circumcision party' (Titus 1:10), 'Jewish myths' (Titus 1:14), 'genealogies' (Titus 3:9), and 'quarrels about the law' (Titus 3:9).

---

87. Ἡ χάρις μετὰ πάντων ὑμῶν ('Grace [be] with all of you').

88. Luke Timothy Johnson disagrees. See his list of false-teaching differences between First Timothy and the two other Pastorals (*The First and Second Letters to Timothy: A New Translation with Introduction and Commentary* [AB 35A; New York: Doubleday, 2001], 146).

89. Frances Young places these 'Jewish gnostic ideas' into the second century (*The Theology of the Pastoral Letters* [NTT; Cambridge: CUP, 1994], 11-20, esp. 11). D. A. Carson and Douglas J. Moo comment, 'It is usually assumed that the same false teaching is opposed in all three letters. This may or may not be the case, but some of it, at any rate, certainly included a strong Jewish element' (*An Introduction to the New Testament* [2d ed.; Grand Rapids: Zondervan, 2005], 563). Carson and Moo affirm the same date as I do (p. 578). Mounce sees the heresy as closer to the 'errors at Colossae and Corinth, mixed with portions of aberrant Judaism, speculative superstition, and possibly magic' (*Pastoral Epistles*, lxxv). Philip H. Towner argues for an 'over-realized eschatology' similar to the one combated in First Corinthians (*The Goal of Our Instruction: The Structure of Theology and Ethics in the Pastoral Epistles* [JSNTSup 34; Sheffield: JSOT Press, 1989], 43).

90. Knight comments, 'The false teachers were primarily but not exclusively Jewish (Titus 1:10)' (*Pastoral Epistles*, 12).

There is a parallel between Titus 2 and Titus 3. Titus 2:1-10 includes practical instructions to different categories of Christians followed by a wonderful theological motivation to do those good works (Titus 2:11-15). Similarly, Titus 3:1-2 includes practical instructions for Christians who interact with those outside the church followed by a wonderful theological motivation to do those good works (Titus 3:3-8a). Also, the same verb 'appeared' is in both Titus 2:11 and 3:4. Also, 'good works' is in both Titus 2:14 and 3:8.

Titus 3:4-7 is within the larger unit of Titus 3:1-11. This unit may be outlined as follows: (1) Practical instructions for Christians who interact with non-Christians (Titus 3:1-2), (2) Theological motivation and basis for interacting with non-Christians (Titus 3:3-8a), (3) Given the theological motivaton, I insist—do good works and avoid foolish ones (Titus 3:8b-11).

In Titus 3:8a is the comment, 'This is a faithful saying' (πιστὸς ὁ λόγος), which is one of the five 'faithful sayings' in the Pastorals.[91] This faithful saying is referring back to Titus 3:4-7.[92] Because of the core Christian language of Titus 3:4-7 plus the faithful saying comment in verse 8a, various scholars view Titus 3:4-7 as some type of creed, hymn, or baptismal catechism.[93] For some of these scholars, seeing Titus 3:4-7 as a pre-existing saying is connected with their view of Deutero-Pauline authorship. I consider all of Paul's faithful sayings as 'standard mini-speeches' he used often in his ministry. He probably adjusted them slightly when they were

---

91. The others are 1 Tim. 1:15, 3:1, 4:9, 2 Tim. 2:11. For the classic study, see George W. Knight III, *The Faithful Sayings in the Pastoral Epistles* (Grand Rapids: Baker, 1979).

92. Virtually all scholars agree that the 'faithful saying' points backwards with options including verses 4-7, or 5-7, or end of 7. For example, verses 4-7, see William Hendriksen, *Exposition of the Pastoral Epistles* (Grand Rapids: Baker, 1957), 393; verses 5-7, see Mounce, *Pastoral Epistles*, 451; end of verse 7, see John Chrysostom, 'Homily V' in 'Homilies on Titus,' *NPNF*[1], 8:539.

93. For example, Mounce views Titus 3:4-7 as more of a creed than a hymn due to the 'highly condensed theological structure,' which could have been by Paul himself (*Pastoral Epistles*, 440-41). Collins views Titus 3:4-7 as a 'baptismal hymn' that reminds the reader of his 'baptismal catechesis' (*1 & 2 Timothy and Titus*, 358-60).

inserted to one of his letters to fit the context. Whether Paul was the absolute originator of the sayings or not, he still used them.

Here is my mechancial translation of Titus 3:4-7 with the Greek text.

4   But when the kindness and love-of-man of God our
       Savior appeared
       ὅτε δὲ ἡ χρηστότης καὶ ἡ φιλανθρωπία ἐπεφάνη τοῦ
       σωτῆρος ἡμῶν θεοῦ,

5a   not from works, those in righteousness, which
       [works] we did
       οὐκ ἐξ ἔργων τῶν ἐν δικαιοσύνῃ ἃ ἐποιήσαμεν ἡμεῖς

5b   but according to his mercy
       ἀλλὰ κατὰ τὸ αὐτοῦ ἔλεος

5c   he [God the Father] saved us
       ἔσωσεν ἡμᾶς

5d   through the washing of regeneration
       διὰ λουτροῦ παλιγγενεσίας

5e   and [through] the renewing of the Holy Spirit
       καὶ ἀνακαινώσεως πνεύματος ἁγίου,

6   whom [Holy Spirit] he poured out on us through
       Jesus Christ our savior
       οὗ[94] ἐξέχεεν ἐφ᾽ ἡμᾶς πλουσίως διὰ Ἰησοῦ Χριστοῦ
       τοῦ σωτῆρος ἡμῶν,

7a   in order that having been justified by his [God the
       Father] grace
       ἵνα δικαιωθέντες τῇ ἐκείνου[95] χάριτι

---

94. One would expect the *accusative* neuter singular ὅ; however, the *genitive* neuter singular οὗ is used due to 'attraction' to πνεύματος ἁγίου.

95. Why ἐκείνου instead of αὐτου? Probably the far demonstrative aspect ('that') encourages the reader to go back to God the Father in the middle of verse 5 as opposed to Jesus Christ in the immediately preceding clause. So also Knight, *Pastoral Epistles*, 346. ἐκείνου is in the attributive position instead

7b   we might become heirs according to the hope of
      eternal life.
      κληρονόμοι γενηθῶμεν κατ᾽ ἐλπίδα ζωῆς αἰωνίου.

As can be seen from the above, the main grammatical structure
of Titus 3:4-7 is: When the kindness and love-of-man of God our
savior appeared, he saved us in order that we might become heirs.
The primary subject-verb-object is 'he [God the Father] saved us'
(v. 5c). Wonderfully so, this text includes the three persons of the
Trinity participating in our salvation (vv. 5c, 6).[96]

The main focus of Titus 3:4-7 is to stress that God, not man, is
the one who accomplishes salvation.[97] This is stressed in three ways.
The first is Titus 3:3, which emphasizes that 'we' before Christ were
evil. In context, recognizing our past should encourage us to interact
graciously with the non-Christians mentioned in Titus 3:1-2 and
also highlights that we are not able to save ourselves.

The second way that *God's* salvation is stressed relates more
directly to this study. Note that before Paul gives the reader the main
finite verb ('he saved,' v. 5c), he first gives two antithetical parallel
statements. These are (1) 'not from *works*, those in righteousness,
which *we* did' (v. 5a) and (2) 'but according to *his mercy*' (v. 5b).
Grammatically, putting these two statements before the main verb
brings attention to them.[98] The antithetical nature of them does
even more so. First, notice 'we' versus 'his.'[99] Second, notice 'works'
versus 'mercy.'

---

of the normal predicate position because it is being used as a possessive
pronoun (similarly in 2 Tim. 2:26) (BDF § 284.2).

96. Many have noted this wonderful truth, e.g., Patrick Fairbairn, *A Commentary on 1 & 2 Timothy and Titus* (Geneva; Carlisle: Banner of Truth,
2002 [1874]), 298.

97. We are justified 'not for any thing wrought in them [justified believers], or
done by them' (WLC 70). Titus 3:5, 7 and Eph. 1:7 are the footnotes.

98. So also I. Howard Marshall with Philip H. Towner, *A Critical and Exegetical
Commentary on the Pastoral Epistles* (ICC; Edinburgh: T&T Clark, 1999),
313-14.

99. J. N. D. Kelly comments, 'The contrast between *we ... ourselves* and *his*

The third way that God's salvation is stressed is that God washed us. I view the washing and renewing as related at least by analogy to baptism.[100] This is an indication that God through Christ and through the Holy Spirit has to provide the regeneration/faith and subsequent ability for our sanctification.[101]

The phrase 'not from works, those in righteousness, which we did' (v. 5a) is the crux of the issue. As most do, I take 'works' as human actions within a works righteousness soteriology. 'In righteousness' confirms this, as 'righteousness' is the God-ordained standard required by moral law.[102] The use of ποιέω ('do/did') is often used in works righteousness contexts (Rom. 2:14, 10:5, Gal. 3:10, 5:3). Typical of Paul, one reason that the works righteouness soteriological option is not truely available is that all are sinners, as he points out in Titus 3:3.

Given that part of the context of the letter is some type of Jewish-Christian false teaching, what points away from considering 'works' as *primarily* focused on Jewish nationality markers *and not* works righteousness? First, even if 'works' were related primarily here to Jewish nationality markers, the context of Titus 3:3-7 makes clear that nationality markers would still be within the works righteousness framework. Second, Titus 3:4-7 (and Titus 2:11-15)

---

own is emphatic and intentional' (*The Pastoral Epistles* [BNTC 14; Peabody: Hendrickson, 1960], 251, italics his).

100. So also Ridderbos, *Paul: An Outline of His Theology* [trans. John Richard DeWitt; Grand Rapids: Eerdmans, 1975], 223-28; and John Calvin, *The Second Epistle of Paul the Apostle to the Corinthians and the Epistles to Timothy, Titus and Philemon* (trans. T. A. Smail; eds. David W. and Thomas F. Torrance; Calvin's Commentaries 10; Grand Rapids: Eerdmans, 1964), 382.

101. Knight especially stresses that 'renewing' relates to our sanctification and connects it to 1 Cor. 6:11 (*Pastoral Epistles*, 344).

102. Marshall with Towner note, 'Righteousness is the quality required by God in human action and represents conformity to his norms, doing what the law requires' (*Pastoral Epistles*, 314). Although he does not include this verse, see Charles Lee Irons' devastating critique of 'righteousness' as a relational concept (*The Righteousness of God: A Lexical Examination of the Covenant-Faithfulness Interpretation* [WUNT II/386; Tübingen: Mohr Siebeck, 2015]).

is a grand theological statement that is not focused on a particular Jewish-Christian problem but is being used to motivate Christians to be kind to non-Christians (Titus 3:1-2). Third, the 'faithful saying' comment in verse 8a confirms that Titus 3:4-7 is a theological 'mini-speech' that has been applied in many diverse circumstances. Fourth, the sins enumerated in Titus 3:3 are not specific to Jewish nationality markers, although some could apply. The sins listed in Titus 3:9 do include Jewish issues. It is certainly possible that a *part* of the broad 'works' in context included Jewish nationality markers and Jewish works righteousness.

The *exact* meaning of 'saved' (v. 5c) in this context is unclear. It is obviously a past tense. Some see 'he saved' in a big-picture redemptive-historical sense—God accomplished our entire salvation (justification, sanctification, glorification) in the completed work of Christ. This would dovetail with God's kindness appearing in the work of Christ during His first coming and beyond (Titus 3:4).[103] Others have an existential view—God's kindness appeared to an individual.[104] Some have a combination. Of course, both the redemptive-historical and existential views are related—if one is referred to, they both are logically involved. I take God's kindness appearing as primarily related to Christ's first coming; however, I view 'he saved' as primarily existential. Since 'saved' is past tense, I connect it to justification as Titus 3:7 will emphasize. Of course, anyone who is justified, will also be sanctified and glorified.

'We might become heirs' in Titus 3:7b is the main purpose clause related to 'he saved' in Titus 3:5c. However, before getting to the purpose clause, Titus 3:7a restates the previous argument with 'having been justified by his grace.'[105] The use of 'justified' ($\delta\iota\kappa\alpha\iota\acute{o}\omega$)

---

103. Mounce strongly argues for this (*Pastoral Epistles*, 438, 450). Herman Ridderbos sees Titus 3:4 as refering to Christ's coming on earth (*Paul: An Outline of His Theology*, 226).

104. So Calvin, *The Second Epistle of Paul the Apostle to the Corinthians and the Epistles to Timothy, Titus and Philemon*, 380.

105. Mounce well says, 'Before moving on to the goal of God's salvific endeavors (v. 7b), Paul summarizes [v. 7a] the discussion so far (vv. 4-6)' (*Pastoral Epistles*, 450). So also Geerhardus Vos, *Soteriology: The Application of the*

cannot help but be contrasted by the reader with 'righteousness' (δικαιοσύνη) in 'works, done in righteousness.' Hence, by his summary, Paul sees the center of God's past salvation as— not works but mercy/grace. This is termed 'justification,' which is a sinner declared to be righteous based on the work of Christ. Collins notes well the contrast.[106] 'The hymn's double reference to righteousness (vv. 5, 7) captures and emphasizes, by means of its inherent contrast, the apostle's conviction that we are not justified by our own works; rather, we are justified by the saving grace of God.'[107] This justification based on God's saving will result in our fully obtaining the inheritance, which is eternal life in the New Heavens and New Earth.

In sum, Paul first *contrasts* human 'works' and 'mercy' (vv. 5a and 5b). He then *connects* '[God] saved us' (v. 5c) to 'mercy' (v. 5b) and to 'having been justified by grace' (v. 7a). Hence, human works are the soteriological opposite of God's salvation-mercy-justification-grace, that is, human effort is here considered works righteousness. The contrast of works and mercy/grace matches to Rom. 11:6.[108]

SECOND TIMOTHY 1:8-10

As with all of the Pastorals, the majority of critical scholarship sees Deutero-Paul as the author of Second Timothy.[109] Again,

---

Merits of the Mediator by the Holy Spirit, vol. 4 of *Reformed Dogmatics* (trans. and ed. Richard B. Gaffin, Jr.; Bellingham, WA: Lexham, 2015), 136.

106. Not all agree to the definition of justification here. Jerome D. Quinn translates v. 7a as 'God's grace that made us upright' (*The Letter to Titus: A New Translation with Notes and Commentary and An Introduction to Titus, I and II Timothy, The Pastoral Epistles* [AB 35; New York: Doubleday, 1990], 226). J. L. Houlden surmises that Deutero-Paul, in contrast to Paul, uses justification to mean 'to be made morally upright' (*The Pastoral Epistles: I and II Timothy, Titus* (TPINTC; Philadelphia: Trinity Press International, 1989), 154.

107. Collins, *1 & 2 Timothy and Titus*, 363.

108. Faith is not explicitly included in Titus 3:4-7, although it is ('those who have believed') in 3:8. See Marshall with Towner for discussion properly downplaying the absence of faith here as significant (*Pastoral Epistles*, 324).

109. See footnote above related to authorship of Titus. Johnson is a major exception in critical scholarship in that he affirms Pauline authorship (*The*

I affirm Pauline authorship and follow the traditional view that Second Timothy was written while Paul was in a Roman prison (2 Tim. 1:8, 16-17) for the second time (2 Tim. 4:16) in A.D. 65. Timothy was in Ephesus (1 Tim. 1:3, 2 Tim. 1:18, 4:12). As with Titus and First Timothy, Second Timothy is addressed secondarily to the church at Ephesus as the plural 'you' in the final benediction indicates (2 Tim. 4:22).[110] The purpose of Second Timothy is for Paul to encourage Timothy in the multi-faceted aspects of Gospel ministry, including noting the difficulties. Paul especially uses himself as an example.

As mentioned above in the discussion of Titus, the false teaching appears to be similar in all of the Pastorals and is some combination of proto-gnostic (maybe just generic Hellenistic ideas) and Jewish-Christian elements. In Second Timothy per se, there is no explicit mention of Jewish elements; however, 'myths' (2 Tim. 4:4) are probably related to 'Jewish myths' in Titus 1:14. Second Timothy 2:18 explicitly indicates that the false teachers believe that the resurrection has already happened (over-realized eschatology).[111]

Second Timothy 1:8-10 is within the larger unit of 1:6-14. In 2 Tim. 1:6-7, Paul encourages Timothy by reminding him of his ordination and the power of God. Then in 2 Tim. 1:8-12, Paul tells Timothy not to be ashamed of the Gospel nor Paul, as Paul is not ashamed either. Within this section, Paul digresses to speak about the Gospel. Finally, in 2 Tim. 1:13-14, Paul gives two commands to Timothy, follow Paul's words and guard the deposit given to him.

More specifically concerning 2 Tim. 1:8-12, at the end of verse 8, Paul mentions the 'gospel according to the power of God.' This sends Paul on a wonderful digression about our salvation in verses 9-10. In 2 Tim. 1:11, Paul notes that he was appointed for

---

First and Second Letters to Timothy, 48-64).

110. ἡ χάρις μεθ᾽ ὑμῶν ('Grace [be] with you').

111. William Bayless Barcley well notes that this aspect of the false teaching may be a development of what the false teachers were saying in First Timothy and Titus (*A Study Commentary on 1 & 2 Timothy* [EP Study Commentary; Webster, NY: EP, 2005], 17).

ministry as he picks up again on the 'gospel' at the end of verse 10 (cf. 1 Tim. 2:7). Second Timothy 1:12 gets back to the point of verse 8 related to not being ashamed of the Gospel.[112]

As I will show below, in the wonderful digression, there are three two-part contrasting-parallel phrases/clauses that add to the rhetorical flair of these verses. I will label each of them '(1)' and '(2).'

Here is my mechanical translation of 2 Tim. 1:8-10 with the Greek text.

8a   Therefore do not be ashamed of the testimony of our Lord

μὴ οὖν ἐπαισχυνθῇς[113] τὸ μαρτύριον τοῦ κυρίου ἡμῶν

8b   nor of me his prisoner,

μηδὲ ἐμὲ τὸν δέσμιον αὐτοῦ,

8c   but suffer with [me] in the gospel according to the power of God

ἀλλὰ συγκακοπάθησον τῷ εὐαγγελίῳ κατὰ δύναμιν θεοῦ,

9a   who [God the Father] saved us and called [us] with[114] a holy calling

τοῦ σώσαντος ἡμᾶς καὶ καλέσαντος κλήσει ἁγίᾳ,

9b   (1) not according to our works

οὐ κατὰ τὰ ἔργα ἡμῶν

9c   (2) but according his own purpose and grace

ἀλλὰ κατὰ ἰδίαν[115] πρόθεσιν καὶ χάριν,

---

112. Parallel words in 2 Tim. 1:8 and 12 are 'suffer,' 'ashamed,' and 'power.'

113. ἐπαισχυνθῇς is a prohibitive aorist subjunctive, that is, it functions as a negative imperative. This grammatical use is common in the NT, see Wallace, *Greek Grammar Beyond the Basics*, 469; and BDF § 364.

114. Commentators are split as to whether the dative of κλήσει ἁγίᾳ should be taken as 'with' implying that God's calling is holy or should it be 'to' implying that we are called to live holy lives. For an example of 'with,' see Marshall with Towner, *Pastoral Epistles*, 704-5. For 'to,' see Collins, *I and II Timothy and Titus*, 200. I chose 'with' based on Eph. 4:1.

115. ἰδίαν governs only πρόθεσιν and not χάριν. So also Mounce, *Pastoral Epistles*, 483.

9d (1) which [grace] was given to us in Christ Jesus before times eternal

τὴν δοθεῖσαν[116] ἡμῖν ἐν Χριστῷ Ἰησοῦ πρὸ χρόνων αἰωνίων,

10a (2) but which [grace] was manifested now through the appearance of our savior Christ Jesus

φανερωθεῖσαν δὲ νῦν διὰ τῆς ἐπιφανείας τοῦ σωτῆ-ρος ἡμῶν Χριστοῦ Ἰησοῦ,

10b (1) who [Christ], on-the-one-hand, abolished death

καταργήσαντος μὲν τὸν θάνατον

10c (2) who [Christ], on-the-other-hand, made-clear life and immortality through the gospel

φωτίσαντος δὲ ζωὴν καὶ ἀφθαρσίαν διὰ τοῦ εὐαγγελίου

In 2 Tim. 1:8, Paul gives two commands to Timothy related to the Gospel ministry, do not be ashamed and share in the sufferings with Paul. The 'therefore' that is the encouragement for these commands is Timothy's ordination and the power of God (2 Tim. 1:6-7). Timothy is not to be ashamed of two things in context, 'the testimony of the Lord' (v. 8a) and 'me his prisoner' (v. 8b). 'Lord' refers to Christ and is an objective genitive (testimony *about* Christ, not the testimony that Christ gave).[117] The 'testimony' about Christ refers to the gospel message, with maybe an emphasis on the scandal of the cross (cf. 1 Cor. 1:23, Gal. 6:14, 1 Tim. 2:6) paralleling Paul's being a prisoner. With some rhetorical flair, Paul terms himself as 'his' prisoner, which refers to Christ. Yes, Paul is the prisoner of the Roman authorities, but ultimately, he is Christ's

---

116. τὴν δοθεῖσαν is a feminine participle that could refer back to either πρόθεσιν or χάριν, or to both if considered a hendiadys. I opt for χάριν because of the many times Paul says that grace was given (Rom. 12:3, 6, 15:15, 1 Cor. 1:4, 3:10, 15:57, 2 Cor. 8:1, Gal. 2:9, Eph. 3:8, 4:7, 2 Thess. 2:16).

117. Virtually all commentators agree, e.g., C. Spicq, *Saint Paul: Les Épitres Pastorales* (EBib; Paris: Gabalda, 1947), 313.

prisoner and right where Christ wants him to be (cf. Eph. 3:1, 4:1, Philem. 1, 9).

Second Timothy 1:8 ends with 'the gospel according to the power of God.' Based on this phrase, more specifically based on 'God,' Paul begins his wonderful digression in 2 Tim. 1:9-10. It is not unusual for Paul to have a digression praising some aspect of God and/or our salvation (e.g., Rom. 11:33-36, 2 Cor. 2:14-7:4, Eph. 3:8-13, 1 Thess. 3:11-13, and 1 Tim. 1:17). Within this digression are many of Paul's favorite terms, including 'saved,' 'calling,' 'not works,' 'purpose,' 'grace,' 'in Christ,' 'savior,' 'appearance,' 'abolished,' 'death,' 'life,' and 'gospel.' For some critical scholars who deny Pauline authorship, this digression does not match Deutero-Paul's true theology and is considered a 'kerygmatic formulation,'[118] or a 'manifesto'[119] or a 'liturgical source'[120] or a 'theological hymn'[121] coming from remembrances of the real Paul. I see 2 Tim. 1:9-10 as fully Pauline and typical of one of his digressions. Of course, Paul may have often used this type of 'mini-speech' previously in his ministry.

Second Timothy 1:9a begins the digression with God the Father as the one who saved and called us.[122] 'Saved' is in the aorist (past) tense and probably refers to the current situations of Christians as they were saved by Christ the 'savior' (v. 10a) from 'death' (v. 10b) and are now enjoying the benefits of eternal 'life' (v. 10c).[123] 'Called' is also in the aorist (past) tense and emphasizes God's effectual calling that results in our turning to God and leading a holy life.[124]

---

118. Martin Dibelius and Hans Conzelmann, *A Commentary on the Pastoral Epistles* (Hermeneia; Philadelphia: Fortress, 1972), 99.

119. Houlden, *The Pastoral Epistles*, 112.

120. Jerome D. Quinn and William C. Wacker, *The First and Second Letters to Timothy: A New Translation with Notes and Commentary* (ECC; Grand Rapids: Eerdmans, 2000), 597.

121. Collins, *1 & 2 Timothy and Titus*, 201.

122. Note that the one article τοῦ governs both substantival participles.

123. So also Knight, *The Pastoral Epistles*, 373.

124. Virtually always in the NT, God's 'call,' when used to refer to an aspect of salvation, produces the intended effect and thus is known in Reformed

In context, the past tense of these two aspects of God's work relates to justification and current sanctification. Later, in 2 Tim. 4:18, Paul uses σῴζω ('save') referring to future salvation.[125]

The first of the three contrasting parallels is 'not according to our works' (v. 9b) and 'but according to his own purpose and grace' (v. 9c). This parallel is further explaining God's salvation of us. Again, as in Eph. 2:9 and Titus 3:5, there is a soteriological contrast between the works righteousness option and the grace option. As most commentators agree, here 'works' are used in a broad sense of any human effort.[126] In verse 9c, Paul ties 'purpose' and 'grace' together.[127] God's 'purpose' is related to his predestinating will (Eph. 1:4, 11),[128] and elsewhere Paul connects 'call' and 'purpose' (Rom. 8:28, 9:11). The addition of God's 'purpose' further emphasizes the contrast between man's being responsible for his salvation and God's initiative and accomplishment of man's salvation.

The second contrasting parallel brings Christ into the salvific equation and contrasts 'before times eternal' (v. 9d) with the 'now' of Christ's first coming (v. 10a). Both clauses begin with an aorist (past) substantival participle, and both refer back to 'grace.'[129] The

---

theology as the 'effectual call.' The NT often uses the 'call' to emphasize the initial act of bringing a believer to Christ (e.g., 1 Cor. 1:23-24; Gal. 1:6; 1 Thess. 1:4; 2 Pet. 1:10). However, 'call' is also used to show that this initial act includes progressive sanctification and eventually being with Christ in glory (e.g., 1 Thess. 4:7, 5:23; Eph. 1:18; 2 Thess. 2:14). Matthew 22:14 ('Many are called, but few are chosen') is a rare example of the general/universal call. See John Murray's classic study *Redemption: Accomplished and Applied* (Grand Rapids: Eerdmans, 1955) 88-94. WCF 10:2 footnotes 2 Tim. 1:9 as a proof text for the 'effectual call.'

125. So also Marshall with Towner, *The Pastoral Epistles*, 825-26.

126. For example, Johnson, *The First and Second Letters to Timothy*, 348; Dibelius and Conzelmann, *The Pastoral Epistles*, 99; and Marshall and Towner, *The Pastoral Epistles*, 705.

127. Several see this as a hendiadys, 'gracious purpose,' e.g., Quinn and Wacker, *The First and Second Letters to Timothy*, 598.

128. The Second Helvetic Confession 10 quotes both Eph. 1:4 and 2 Tim. 1:9-10 in the text to prove election.

129. τὴν governs both δοθεῖσαν and φανερωθεῖσαν.

grace that effected our salvation was 'given to us in Christ Jesus before times eternal' (v. 9d).[130] In addition to extolling Christ in our salvation, this clause again emphasizes that we did not initiate and had nothing to do with our salvation as it was part of a predestinating plan in eternity past. Also, this grace was 'manifested now through the appearance of our savior Christ Jesus' (v. 10a). Clearly Paul is referring to Christ's first coming (cf. Rom. 16:25-26). Christ is here 'our savior.' This is another emphasis that we did not save ourselves, but that God through Christ did.

The third contrasting parallel gives more detail as to the salvific benefits that Christ accomplished for us. Again, two more aorist (past) substantival particles are used that both refer back to 'Christ Jesus' (or 'savior') at the end of verse 10a. The results of Christ's work for us are summarized both negatively and positively. He 'abolished death' (v. 10b) for us and 'made-clear life and immortality' (v. 10c) for us. 'Death' and 'life' are to be taken in their full-orbed eschatological senses. Although Paul does not explicitly say so here, it is implied that Christ's own death and life provide for our absence of death and obtaining of life. This third contrasting parallel further reinforces that it was not our work by which we defeated death and obtained life.

In sum for our topic, Paul comments upon God the Father's saving us by *contrasting* our 'works' (v. 9b) with God's 'purpose and grace' (v. 9c). Paul further reinforces that God saved us by explicating 'grace' as having been 'given to us in Christ Jesus before times began' (v. 9d) and 'manifested now through the appearance of our savior Christ Jesus' (v. 10a). Finally, Christ Jesus is further defined as the one who 'abolished death' (v. 10b) and 'made-clear life and immortality' (v. 10c). All of this emphasis on what God did for us in salvation shows that 'works' as a *contrast* must be considered works righteousness soteriology.

SUMMARY OF EXEGESIS

The above exegesis of Eph. 2:8-10, Titus 3:4-7, and 2 Tim. 1:8-10 concludes that (1) 'works' is to be taken as works righteousness

---

130. In this phrase, Paul affirms Christ's pre-existence.

soteriology contrasted with God's saving activity, and (2) 'works' in all three texts refer to broad human effort that would be in conformity to God's moral law. Concerning (2), there is an outside possibility that 'works' may have intentionally included Jewish boundary markers in Titus in addition to the broad human effort.

The vast majority of commentators, although not all, agree with the above two conclusions. This was true whether or not a commentator affirmed Pauline authorship. However, a commentator's view of authorship did partially affect his rationale for his conclusions.

As a result of the above two conclusions, I further conclude (3) that works righteousness existed in the Second Temple period, and (4) that the works righteousness aspect of 'works' should be included in 'works,' 'works of the law,' and 'law' in Galatians, Romans, and Philippians 3 when these are contrasted conceptually with salvation/justification.

To put my conclusions in the form of the scenarios above, I conclude: (a) *Pauline* authorship, (b) Eph. 2:8-10, Titus 3:4-7, and 2 Tim. 1:8-10 *do* contrast a works righteousness soteriology with a grace one, (c) Romans, Galatians, and Philippians 3 *do* contrast a works righteousness soteriology with a grace one, and (d) works righteousness existed within the Second Temple period.

If one could step back from all this technical language, it is breathtaking to consider God's gracious saving of the ungodly, not by works, but by grace alone, Christ alone, and faith alone. Of course this saving has both forensic (justification) aspects and existential (sanctification and glorification) aspects all connected to our union with Christ. This grand salvation highlights the glorious grace of the triune God!

SANDERS, DUNN, WRIGHT

As noted above in the 'Five Scenarios' section, NPP authors are not consistent in how they deal with Eph. 2:8-10, Titus 3:4-7, and 2 Tim. 1:8-10, including those who do not consider these texts at all. At one level, one might complain that it is unfair for me to expect the NPP authors to comment in print on every verse in the NT that might affect their view. Fair enough; however, these three texts are so potentially damaging to the NPP argument that an analysis of them should be included within their argument no matter their view of authorship. Or to make a slightly different point, if one accepts Pauline authorship of all thirteen letters and/ or has a high view of the inerrancy of God's Word, one needs to consider these texts when arguing either for or against NPP.

For purposes of this book, I will only consider E. P. Sanders, James D. G. Dunn, and N. T. Wright, the three stars of the NPP. As will be seen below, Sanders only mentions one of the three texts, and he is included here simply for completeness. Dunn has a fairly substantive treatment developed later in his writings. Surprisingly, Wright has virtually nothing to say about Titus 3:4-7 and 2 Tim. 1:8-10 concerning our topic, or at least, what I could find in print. He does comment more substantially on Eph. 2:8-10. Following the presentation of each view, I will offer my critique.

E. P. SANDERS

I will briefly discuss three of E. P. Sanders' books from the mid-70s to mid-80s. Clearly, his 1977 *Paul and Palestinian Judaism* was by far the most influential of the three.[131]

In these three books, Sanders deals minimally with Eph. 2:8-10, Titus 3:4-7, and 2 Tim. 1:8-10. This is apparently a direct implication of his decision to only include the undisputed Pauline letters in his analysis of Paul.[132] In *Paul and Palestinian Judaism*, Sanders does not reference Titus 3:4-7 and 2 Tim. 1:8-10 at all.[133] He includes one mention of Eph. 2:8. In context he is discussing Paul's use of

---

131. Much later E. P. Sanders published *Paul: The Apostle's Life, Letters, and Thought* in 2015 (Minneapolis: Fortress). Sanders notes that this book is not as well footnoted as his other works (p. xiv). He does not reference Titus 3:4-7 and 2 Tim. 1:8-10. Ephesians 2 is referenced once regarding Deutero-Pauline authorship (152 n. 5) and once regarding Luther's interpretation (455-56).

132. E. P. Sanders, *Paul and Palestinian Judaism: A Comparison of Patterns of Religion* (Minneapolis: Fortress, 1977), 431.

133. Sanders, *Paul and Palestinian Judaism*, 588.

the aorist tense for 'save' in Rom. 8:24. In a footnote, he comments, 'The perfect tense of Eph. 2:5, 8 thus represents a distinct theological development.'[134] Given his views of authorship, this confirms that the author of Ephesians is not Paul and has moved beyond Paul.

In his subsequent book (1983), *Paul, the Law and the Jewish People*, he does not reference any of the three texts.[135] In his *Jesus and Judaism* (1985), again he also does not reference any of the three texts.[136] However, he does comment on some Gospel texts that relate Pharisees and 'sinners.' He believes that the early church significantly expanded Jesus' association with 'sinners,' and this negatively affected the presentation of the Pharisees in the Gospels. For example, Sanders sees as inauthentic Jesus' Luke 15 'lost' parables and the Pharisee and the Tax Collector parable (Luke 18:9-14). The early church later added these parables. Hence, the presentation of the Pharisees is not historical.[137]

To put Sanders' conclusions in the form of the scenarios, he concludes: (a) *Deutero-Pauline* authorship, (b) Eph. 2:8-10 and some Gospel texts *do* contrast a works righteousness soteriology with a grace one (I am not absolutely sure this is Sanders' view), (c) Romans, Galatians, and Philippians 3 do *not* contrast works righteousness soteriology with a grace one, and (d) Second Temple Judaism does *not* have a works righteousness soteriology.

Critique of E. P. Sanders

Although not clearly stated, one has the sense that Sanders does believe that some of the early church's texts do present at least aspects of Judaism as having a works righteousness soteriology. He just does not believe that this is historically correct or widespread. Waters, a student of Sanders, notes that 'Sanders has conceded to

---

134. Sanders, *Paul and Palestinian Judaism*, 449 n. 9.

135. E. P. Sanders, *Paul, the Law, and the Jewish People* (Minneapolis: Fortress, 1983), 223-24.

136. E. P. Sanders, *Jesus and Judaism* (Philadelphia: Fortress, 1985), 424-25.

137. Sanders, *Jesus and Judaism*, 175, also see 209-11.

me that Ephesians 2:9 teaches the traditional view [that grace was opposed to works righteousness].'[138]

Even within Sanders' historical assumptions, does he not have to agree that some Jews and Jewish Christians (and even Gentile Christians) in Second Temple Judaism were at least perceived as advocating works righteousness by the early church? And was this not a church that was also reading the OT to justify their views? If so, then is it not likely that there was some truth behind this perception of works righteousness, at least in part? Once that is admitted, then Sanders' uniformity of covenantal nomism among all Jewish-related groups is in jeopardy.

Possibly, Sanders has worked-out answers to my inquiry, but they were not presented in his initial books.[139] (Previously, I have discussed his explanation of Matt. 23.[140]) In any event, Sanders does not deal with Eph. 2:8-10, Titus 3:4-7, 2 Tim. 1:8-10. This was not perceived by many as a problem for his view. Consequently, his presentation of covenantal nomism became the foundation of the NPP.

JAMES D. G. DUNN

Dunn does not believe that Paul wrote Ephesians, Titus, or Second Timothy.[141] Generally, he sees Ephesians closer to Paul than Titus and Second Timothy.[142]

In Dunn's early publications, he rarely discussed Eph. 2:8-10, Titus 3:4-7, and 2 Tim. 1:8-10, even though 'works of the law' and

---

138. Waters, *Justification and the New Perspective on Paul*, 167.

139. Or in his latest book, *Paul: The Apostle's Life, Letters, and Thought*.

140. See Chapter 2, section 'Sanders' Various Explanations of Conflicting Data.'

141. J. D. G. Dunn, 'Pseudepigraphy,' *DLNT*, 977-84; and Dunn, *The Theology of Paul the Apostle*, 13 n. 39. Dunn surmises that even if Paul did write Ephesians, he had so modified his views that one would have to conceive of a '"the late Paul" [who] is little different from "the disciple of Paul"' (J. D. G. Dunn, 'Ephesians,' in *The Oxford Bible Commentary*, ed. John Barton and John Muddiman [Oxford: OUP, 2001], 1165-79, esp. 1166).

142. J. D. G. Dunn, 'Pauline Legacy and School,' *DLNT*, 887-93.

the question of works righteousness were very prominent issues.[143] He was taken to task for this in Silva's often quoted article.[144] In fact, Dunn later admits this omission.[145]

In Dunn's major work on Paul, *The Theology of Paul the Apostle* (1998), he at least mentions Eph. 2:8-10, Titus 3:4-7, and 2 Tim. 1:10. He includes a section entitled, 'Self-achieved righteousness?'[146] Here he discusses Rom. 4:4-5, 10:2-4, and Phil. 3:7-9 and concludes in a confusing way that Paul was *not* 'polemicizing against "self-achieved righteousness"'[147] However, he does admit in this same section that in Eph. 2:8-9 the 'issue does seem to have moved from one of works of the law to one of human effort.' This 'shift in the debate' is then used as another proof that Deutero-Paul wrote Ephesians.[148] Earlier in his book, he notes that Eph. 2:8-9, Titus 3:5, and 2 Tim. 1:9 do seem to confirm that Rom. 4:4-5 envisions works righteousness. This interpretation of Rom. 4:4-5, although wrong, 'is wholly understandable' if one is not aware of 'the new perspective.'[149]

---

143. E.g., the three texts are not discussed in his famous article 'The New Perspective on Paul,' (*BJRL* 65 [1983]: 95-122), nor in his collected essays in *Jesus, Paul, and the Law: Studies in Mark and Galatians* (Louisville, KY: Westminster/Knox, 1990). His commentaries on Galatians and Romans have no substantive discussion (*The Epistle to Galatians* [BNTC 9; Peabody, MA; Hendrickson, 1993]; and *Romans* [WBC 38A, 38B; Dallas: Word, 1988]).

144. Silva, 'The Law and Christianity: Dunn's New Synthesis,' 350-53. In context, Silva is critiquing Dunn's *Jesus, Paul, and the Law: Studies in Mark and Galatians*. He notes 'forgotten verses' that Dunn did not deal with including 'Rom. 4:4-5, 11:6, Eph. 2:8-10, and Phil. 3:9.'

145. Dunn, 'The New Perspective: whence, what and whither?,' in *The New Perspective on Paul* (rev. ed.; Grand Rapids: Eerdmans, 2008), 1-97, esp. 55.

146. Dunn, *The Theology of Paul the Apostle*, 366-71.

147. Dunn, *The Theology of Paul the Apostle*, 366-71. Seyoon Kim calls Dunn's argument here 'quite hazy' (*Paul and the New Perspective: Second Thoughts on the Origin of Paul's Gospel* [Grand Rapids: Eerdmans, 2002], 59).

148. Dunn, *The Theology of Paul the Apostle*, 371, 371 n. 150. For more of his arguments against Pauline authorship of Ephesians, see his *Beginning from Jerusalem*, vol. 2 of *Christianity in the Making* (Grand Rapids: Eerdmans, 2009), 1106-9.

149. Dunn, *The Theology of Paul the Apostle*, 354. John Ziesler, a pro-NPP author, admits that Rom. 4:2 and possibly 9:11 may 'hint' of boasting in works

Dunn addresses the problem more straightforwardly in his 1988 article, 'Whatever Happened to "Works of the Law"?'[150] He notes that the expression 'works of the law' seems to disappear after Romans and Galatians, but then 'works' reappear in Eph. 2:8-9, 2 Tim. 1:9, Titus 3:5-7, and *1 Clement* 32:4. He muses that the easiest solution is simply to assume that for 'works of the law' in Romans and Galatians, Paul simply meant what 'works' meant elsewhere, 'works which we have done.' However, he rejects this simple and traditional Protestant solution.[151] He reiterates that in Romans and Galatians Paul is not attacking works righteousness because Jewish soteriology was covenantal nomism. Deutero-Paul 'expressed a different perspective.' 'The Pastorals seem to go behind Paul's more polemically formulated critique of "works of the law" to the more fundamental insight that all human acceptability before God is dependent not on human activity but on divine grace from start to finish.' The Pastorals are not against Judaism, but they 'appeal to Israel's most fundamental insight into divine grace' (Deut. 9:5).[152] Here, Dunn's view of 'works' in the Pastorals seems close to works righteousness (which is positive from my perspective). However, he and I are going to disagree on the implications of this insight.

In 2000 and 2001, Dunn produced quasi-popular commentaries on Ephesians and the Pastorals. In his Ephesians commentary, he again admits that in Eph. 2:8-10 'the language is very Pauline but the thought has shifted somewhat.' It 'is broadened, or deepened. By "works" the author here seems to mean any product of human

---

righteousness, but this is not what Paul 'focusses on.' 'The boasting Paul opposes is that of Jews over Gentiles.' See *Paul's Letter to the Romans* (TPINTC; Philadelphia: Trinity Press International, 1989), 42-46.

150. 'Whatever Happened to "Works of the Law"?,' in *The New Perspective on Paul* (rev. ed.; Grand Rapids: Eerdmans, 2008), 381-94. This was originally published in *Epitoayto: P. Pokorny FS* (ed. J. Kerkovsky et. al.; Praha: Mlyn, 1988), 107-20.

151. Dunn, 'Whatever Happened to "Works of the Law"?,' 282.

152. Dunn, 'Whatever Happened to "Works of the Law"?,' 392.

effort.' 'Salvation is given by grace, through faith, the very opposite of human contriving or manipulation.'[153]

In his Titus commentary, he affirms that Titus 3:1-8a teaches that 'God's saving purpose is wholly at the initiative of God.' This is not an anti-Jewish statement as it matches to Deut. 9:5.[154] Paul's argument that 'Gentile believers would not be required to take on a Jewish life-style/works is *broadened out* into a restatement of the original purpose behind God's saving act.' Good works are not negative, rather, they are a 'reminder that neither human actions nor human goodness can provide an adequate basis for relationship with God.'[155]

Concerning 'not according our works' in 2 Tim. 1:9, Dunn again views this as an expansion of Paul. It is a 'strong echo of a central Pauline statement of the gospel (Rom. 3:20, 28, Gal. 2:16), but there is a significant shift of emphasis. ... The concept of "works" seems to have broadened out ... to "our works," anything we have done.'[156]

Dunn's most mature discussion of NPP is his ninety-seven-page 2008 article, 'The New Perspective on Paul: whence, what and whither?'[157] Part of his emphasis, certainly a change from his early writings, is to claim that the NPP's view of justification by faith is compatible with and complementary to traditional Protestantism; however, he takes exception to the traditional view 'that Paul

---

153. Dunn, 'Ephesians,' 1170.

154. James D. G. Dunn, 'The First and Second Letters to Timothy and the Letter of Titus: Introduction, Commentary, and Reflections,' in *The New Interpreter's Bible Commentary: Volume Ten* [Nashville: Abingdon, 2015 {2000}], 371-460, esp. 456. Note this commentary is in vol. 11 of the 2000 version.

155. Dunn, 'The First and Second Letters to Timothy and the Letter of Titus,' 457, italics mine.

156. Dunn, 'The First and Second Letters to Timothy and the Letter of Titus,' 422.

157. Dunn's later 2011 article, 'New Perspective View,' concentrates on the undisputed Pauline texts and does not mention Deutero-Pauline texts (in *Justification: Five Views*, 176-201).

affirmed his doctrine against a degenerate Jewish legalism' and that 'neglected important aspects of Paul's original formulation in the context of his mission.'[158]

In this long article, he has a short section on Eph. 2:8-10, 2 Tim. 1:9-10, and Titus 3:5-7, which is similar to his 'Whatever Happened to "Works of the Law"?' discussed above.[159] These texts have a 'different or shifting perspective' than Paul and have 'broadened out to refer to human effort in general as inadequate to the demands of salvation.' Dunn makes the surprising concession that 'at the very least this implies that the Reformation understanding of Paul's theology of justification was already shared by the first Christian commentator of that theology.'[160] Also, confusingly to me, Dunn states that this was already asserted in Rom. 4:4-5 and matches to the Jewish soteriology in covenantal nomism.[161] Because these three texts, including Ephesians, do not have in context Jewish boundary markers, they should not be used to understand Paul's 'works of the law' language.[162]

Finally, in Dunn's 2009 *Beginning from Jerusalem*, he has a section on Ephesians (nothing on Pastorals). More or less, he rehearses the same arguments as above.[163] He adds that in addition to the 'broadening out' of 'works' (Eph. 2:8), the 'boasting' in Eph. 2:9 is a 'more fundamental critique of boasting' and is not to be 'confused with the more distinctively Jewish boasting in the privilege of election.' He again notes that the denial of effort 'was

---

158. Dunn, 'The New Perspective on Paul: whence, what and whither?,' 20-21. Dunn admits that in the past he has provocatively attacked the Lutheran theology of justification 'of which I regret' (p. 21 n. 85).

159. Dunn notes that his discussion follows that of 'Whatever Happened to "Works of the Law"?,' although he 'partly takes [the argument] further' ('The New Perspective on Paul: whence, what and whither?,' 55 n. 222).

160. Dunn, 'The New Perspective: whence, what and whither?,' 56.

161. Dunn, 'Whatever Happened to "Works of the Law"?,' 56. As usual, Dunn wants to separate Rom. 4:4-5 from 'works of the law' and 'should not be taken as a description of the Judaism of Paul's day' (*Romans*, 204).

162. Dunn, 'Whatever Happened to "Works of the Law"?,' 58.

163. Dunn, *Beginning from Jerusalem*, 1106-22.

the theological reasoning which underpinned Paul's more specific assertion that "works of the law" should not be required as essential for justification.' Dunn argues that the author of Ephesians 'pull[ed] apart what had been the two central entwined themes of Paul's gospel' by separating Eph. 2:1-10 from Eph. 2:11-22.[164] Dunn interprets Eph. 2:11-22 as assuming a 'Jewish perspective on Gentile disqualification.' The author of Ephesians properly captured that 'at the heart of Paul's gospel (himself a Jew) was the claim that God in Christ had resolved both alienations [Gentiles need grace; Gentiles need to follow food laws] and that *the one could not be reconciled in isolation from the other.*'[165]

To put Dunn's conclusions in the form of the scenarios, he concludes: (a) *Deutero-Pauline* authorship, (b) Eph. 2:8-10, Titus 3:4-7, and 2 Tim. 1:8-10 *do* contrast a works righteousness soteriology with a grace one, (c) Romans, Galatians, and Philippians 3 do *not* contrast works righteousness soteriology with a grace one, (d) the change in theology is a conseqeunce of the change away from the Jew/Gentile problem and is compatible with covenantal nomism, (e) the Deutero-Pauline texts should *not* affect the interpretation of Pauline texts, and (f) Second Temple Judaism does *not* have a works righteousness soteriology.

Critique of James D. G. Dunn

Allow me to summarize what I think is Dunn's mature view. Dunn argues that Deutero-Paul took the 'works of the law' language and broadened it out to include all human effort, and if I understand Dunn correctly, also turned it into works righteousness. Hence, the real Paul did not contrast works righteousness with justification by faith, but Deutero-Paul did. However, even though Deutero-Paul used 'works' to mean works righteousness, he was not arguing against Jewish works righteousness because of the gracious character of covenantal nomism. In fact, Deutero-Paul's denouncing of works righteousness was always a proper implication of Paul as Rom. 4:4-5

---

164. Dunn, *Beginning from Jerusalem*, 1111-12.

165. Dunn, *Beginning from Jerusalem*, 1113, italics his.

shows.[166] It just happens that Paul was not fighting against works righteousness.

I am still not sure if Dunn is saying that Deutero-Paul intentionally expanded Paul's meaning of 'works of the law,' or that by unintentially doing so, he came to an expanded meaning that is a proper implication of Paul. I think it is the latter. And if it is the latter, Dunn is arguing that his analysis 2000 years later better understands the nuances of Paul than Deutero-Paul does. Of course, this is theoretically possible. If it is the former, then Dunn is admitting that the author of Ephesians was very sophisticated, a better thinker than Paul to separate these two issues. Again, this is theoretically possible.

Given Dunn's view that Deutero-Paul was contrasting works righteousness with grace, against whom was this directed? I could not find where Dunn answers this question. Similar to my questions posed above to Sanders, if it was directed at 'somebody,' then 'somebody' had a works righteousness soteriology during the Second Temple period. I get the impression that Dunn's answer would be that Deut. 9:5, covenantal nomism, Paul, and Deutero-Paul would all affirm that works righteousness is bad, so it is just a theological statement with no intended reference. I might respond, when Paul uses 'works of the law,' Dunn strongly argues that it is against an opponent; however, when Deutero-Paul uses 'works,' it is not against an opponent. The Reformed view would be that all classes of people throughout redemptive-history (post-Adam) have improperly attempted to earn salvation by works righteousness (Covenant of Works). Also, many Jews in redemptive-history properly laid claim on the Covenant of Grace through faith, while others, both Jews and Gentiles, continued under the Covenant of Works. Hence, Paul would have used the category of works righteousness in both Jew and Gentile contexts.

Given Dunn's view that Deutero-Paul used the category of works righteousness, why could not Paul have been using 'works

---

166. Dunn's discussion of Rom. 4:4-5 in several contexts is confusing, at least to me.

of the law' to include boundary markers, but within a broader framework of works righteousness? Dunn's answer, as always, is that Paul's Jewish and Jewish-Christian opponents had a gracious covenantal-nomism structure. There was no need in context to bring up a theoretical works righteousness soteriology against those who were grace oriented.[167]

However, Paul connects both the sins and triumphs of God's people in the past (Rom. 4-5, 9-11, Gal. 3) to the current situation. Would not the sins be related to the Covenant of Works and the triumphs to the Covenant of Grace? Would not both of these be in the past and both be in Paul's current situation? Is this not a better answer than seeing the sin as related to boundary markers and Jewish particularism— which is hard to connect to the past? The boundary-marker/Jewish-particularism sin does not make sense in most of the OT contexts that Paul uses as past examples—that is, who, for example, was Adam, Abraham, and David supposedly wanting to be separated from by 'works of the law'? Again, it is Dunn's assumption of covenantal nomism that is the foundation of his exegesis that will not allow him to see 'works of the law' as works righteousness.

Although this book has not pursued the details of NPP's various views of justification, allow me a few comments. One of the foundational assumptions of Dunn and other NPP authors is that once it is seen that Paul is not contrasting works righteousness with justification by faith, then the traditional Protestant doctrine of justification needs to be adjusted. It can*not* be the traditional my-righteous-works versus Christ's-imputed-works-on-my-behalf. Dunn argues that for Paul, 'justification is not a once-for-all act of God. It is rather the initial acceptance by God into restored relationship.'[168] Final justification will relate at least in part to our

---

167. Zetterholm, a pro-Sanders and radical NPP author, wants Dunn to move even more toward a Jewish Paul that Dunn does. He complains that 'in Dunn's reconstruction, the Protestant opposition between law and the gospel is certainly done away with, but only replaced by a new one—between Jewish particularism and Christian identity' (*Approaches to Paul*, 117).

168. Dunn, *The Theology of Paul the Apostle*, 386. Dunn continues, 'But thereafter

works done through the Spirit.[169] So be it. However, from Dunn's perspective, what is Deutero-Paul's view of justification given that he *does* contrast works righteousness and justification (Titus 3:7)? Because of this absolute contrast, does Deutero-Paul affirm that our works will *not* be involved in justification? And if Deutero-Paul does, why could that not have been Paul's view?[170]

Above I noted that Dunn makes the claim that NPP's view of justification is compatible with and complementary to traditional Protestantism.[171] I wish that were the case, but I just do not see it. Admittedly, there is a fair-sized kernel of truth here. Dunn sees that God's initial acceptance of us to a restored covenantal relationship (his definition of initial justification) is by 'grace alone and through faith alone.'[172] However, given Dunn's view of final justification that includes our Spirit-wrought works,[173] a confusing discussion of 'synergy,'[174] a justification that is *not* 'entirely extrinsic

---

the relationship could not be sustained without God continuing to exercise his justifying righteousness with a view to the final act of judgment and acquittal' (p. 386).

169. For Dunn's extended discussion on final justification, see 'The New Perspective: whence, what and whither?,' 71-89.

170. Part of this answer will depend on one's exegesis of Rom. 2.

171. In addition to individual salvation concerns, Dunn argues that the traditional view of justification is truncated. It does not include 'a social and corporate dimension which is integral to it.' This deficiency is primarily due to not interpreting justification in the 'context of [Paul's] Gentile mission.' It does not matter which race, class, culture, country that one comes from as far as God's acceptance is concerned. 'Super-power, chosen-nation, Western "civilization" presumption needs to hear that aspect of Paul's doctrine as clearly today as ever before' ('The New Perspective: whence, what and whither?,' 96).

172. Dunn, 'The New Perspective: whence, what and whither?,' 23. Note, it is not by 'Christ alone.'

173. Dunn, 'The New Perspective: whence, what and whither?,' 71-77, 88, 95. 'Paul's theology of justification by faith alone has to be qualified as final justification by faith *and* works accomplished by the believer in the power of the Spirit' (p. 88).

174. Dunn argues that if we characterize Jewish soteriology as synergistic (semi-Pelagian), should we not also charge Paul with the same ('The New

and forensic,'[175] and no imputed righteousness of Christ; it is hard to say that this is compatible with traditional Lutheran and Reformed creeds. Possibly, the 'slippage' is that when Dunn says NPP is compatible with the traditional view, he is not giving Paul's view, although I think he is, but he is giving his overall view of the Bible that includes Deutero-Paul or maybe second-level implications from the Bible.

Dunn makes another claim, surprising to me, that directly goes against much in NPP literature, including his own. He admits that the Reformation understanding of Paul's justification was present in Deutero-Paul. This seems to contradict Dunn's previous complaints about the Reformers reading Roman Catholic adversaries into Paul's opponents.[176] Maybe the distinction is Deutero-Paul's opponents, not Paul's. To prove his point in context, Dunn notes that Deutero-Paul has broadened out 'works' and has a grace alone and faith alone perspective.[177] Well, so far so good, but this does not yet get us to a Reformational view of justification.

In sum of Dunn's view, he matches the fourth scenario above, that is (a) *Deutero-Pauline* authorship, (b) Eph. 2:8-10, Titus 3:4-7, and 2 Tim. 1:8-10 *do* contrast a works righteousness soteriology with a grace one, and (c) Romans, Galatians, and Philippians 3 do *not* contrast a work righteousness soteriology with a grace one. Positively, he does not see Paul and Deutero-Paul as ultimately contradictory; however, for me, his explanations within his own

---

Perspective: whence, what and whither?,' 79, 88)?

175. Dunn, 'The New Perspective: whence, what and whither?,' 85.

176. Dunn is quite critical of Luther in his 1992 article 'The Justice of God: A renewed perspective on justification by faith,' *JTS* 43 (1992):1-22. Also, in his famous 1983 article, he notes, 'Since Paul's teaching on justification by faith seems to speak so directly to Luther's subjective wrestlings, it was a natural corollary to see Paul's opponents in terms of the unreformed Catholicism, which opposed Luther, with first century Judaism read through the "grid" of the early 16th century Catholic system of merit' ('The New Perspective on Paul,' 98).

177. Dunn, 'The New Perspective: whence, what and whither?,' 56. Again, no Christ alone, is this intentional?

historical assumptions for why Paul and Deutero-Paul differ on works righteousness are not convincing. These explanations are even less convincing if one assumes Pauline authorship for all thirteen letters and/or has a traditional view of Scriptural inspiration. Finally, these explanations are not compatible with traditional Reformed theology, even though Dunn asserts they are.

N. T. WRIGHT

Wright's mature views of authorship are presented in his massive *Paul and the Faithfulness of God* (2013).[178] As with many other issues, he wants to challenge the prevailing critical views.

After noting that all agree to the seven undisputed letters, Wright proposes to add Colossians as definitely Pauline. Ephesians and 2 Thessalonians are 'highly likely to be Pauline.'[179] To accommodate others who do not agree with Wright here, in *Paul and the Faithfulness of God* he will use these two as 'evidence though perhaps not made to bear an entire load by themselves.'[180]

As to the Pastorals and how Wright will use them in his massive work, Second Timothy 'may well be by Paul, writing in a different mood and context, and may be drawn on similarly [to Ephesians and Second Thessalonians], though again with due caution. 1 Timothy and Titus come in a different category, and will be used ... for illumination rather than support.'[181]

---

178. Wright, *Paul and the Faithfulness of God*, 56–63.

179. Wright, *Paul and the Faithfulness of God*, 61. He suspects that the rejection of Ephesians and Colossians was due to the liberal Protestant paradigm that Paul was against church organization and the egalitarian problem with the 'awkward *Haustafeln*' (Eph. 5:22–6:9, Col. 3:18–4:1). In addition, there is professional pressure, especially in North America, to agree to the standard Deutero-Pauline conclusions. Wright suspects that Second Thessalonians has been rejected for being too apocalyptic (pp. 56–61). In *Paul for Everyone: The Prison Letters: Ephesians, Philippians, Colossians and Philemon*, Wright affirms Pauline authorship for all four letters (2d ed.; London: SPCK, 2004), x.

180. Wright, *Paul and the Faithfulness of God*, 61. He takes the same tack with Acts (p. 63).

181. Wright, *Paul and the Faithfulness of God*, 61. In *Paul for Everyone: The*

These authorship views reasonably match Wright's comment mentioned above in his *What Saint Paul Really Said* (1997). Note that Ephesians is included in the below quote, but nothing is said of Titus and Second Timothy.

> Most of what I say in this book focuses on material in the undisputed letters, particularly Romans, the two Corinthian letters, Galatians and Philippians. In addition, I regard Colossians as certainly by Paul, and Ephesians as far more likely to be by him than by an imitator. But nothing in my present argument hinges on this one way or the other.[182]

To summarize Wright's views of authorship as to Ephesians, Titus, and Second Timothy, Ephesians is 'highly likely' to be Pauline as is Second Timothy. Both of these may be used as 'evidence though perhaps not made to bear an entire load by themselves.' Wright implies, but never exactly says, that Titus is not Pauline. In any event, Titus will be used only 'for illumination rather than support.'

Given Wright's views of authorship, especially for Ephesians and Second Timothy, one is surprised to find that he rarely discusses Eph. 2:8-10, Titus 3:4-7, and 2 Tim. 1:8-10 in his scholarly articles/ books. I assume this is due to the scholarly consensus against using these three letters, even though that is not Wright's view.[183] For example, his early major work, *The Climax of the Covenant: Christ and the Law in Pauline Theology* (1991), he does not reference any of the three texts. His very well-known quasi-popular work, *What Saint Paul Really Said* (1997), does not mention the three texts in the important chapter, 'Justification and the Church.'[184] In Wright's

---

Pastoral Letters: 1 and 2 Timothy and Titus, Wright in a coy way seems to affirm Pauline authorship of the Pastorals, but it is not completely clear (2d ed.; London: SPCK, 2004), x.

182. Wright, *What Saint Paul Really Said*, 8.

183. At an Evangelical Theological Society lecture about his *The Resurrection of the Son of God* book that I attended, Wright commented that he purposely did not quote fellow evangelicals in the book so that critics would have less excuse to dismiss his arguments (London: SPCK, 2003).

184. Wright, *What Saint Paul Really Said*, 113-33.

620-page collection of thirty-three essays on Paul, there are only two references to Eph. 2:8-10 and none to Titus and Second Timothy. Both of the Ephesians references do not relate to this chapter's topic.[185]

Even in contexts that one would expect more than the seven undisputed Pauline letters to be discussed, Wright does not include Eph. 2:8-10, Titus 3:4-7, and 2 Tim. 1:8-10. For example, in 'Justification: The Biblical Basis and its Relevance for Contemporary Evangelicalism,' he has a section on 'Biblical Material.'[186] He includes the OT, Gospels and Acts, Paul: Galatians, Philippians, Romans, and 'Other New Testament Books.' There is no mention of Ephesians, Titus, and Second Timothy. Similarly, the three texts are not mentioned in Wright's dictionary article on 'Justification,' which includes both Paul and James.[187]

Wright has authored a series ('Paul for Everyone') of very nontechnical commentaries that include Ephesians, Titus, and Second Timothy. For Ephesians 2:8-10, Wright's discussion is somewhat confusing. Hence, below is a longer quote:

> In these three [Eph 2:8-10] little verses [God] has summed up his entire view of how this grace works and what it does. This is very close to what [Paul] says about justification in Romans and Galatians. … Paul speaks in Romans, Galatians and Philippians of being 'justified' by faith; here, in verse 8, he speaks of being 'saved' by grace. 'Justification' and 'salvation' are not the same thing. 'Justification' has to do with people belonging to God's family. It answers the question as to how they are marked out as members of it. 'Salvation' has to do with people being rescued from the fate they would have otherwise have

---

185. N. T. Wright, *Pauline Perspectives: Essays on Paul, 1978-2013* (Minneapolis: Fortress, 2013). The two references to Eph. 2:8-10 are on pp. 312 and 347 n. 43.

186. Tom Wright, 'Justification: The Biblical Basis and its Relevance for Contemporary Evangelicalism,' in *The Great Acquittal: Justification by Faith and Current Christian Thought* (ed. Gavin Reid; Glasgow: Fount, 1980), 13-37, 109-19. 'The Biblical Material' section is on pp. 19-29.

187. N. T. Wright, 'Justification,' in *New Dictionary of Theology* (ed Sinclair B. Ferguson and David F. Wright; Downers Grove: InterVarsity, 1988), 359-61.

incurred. ... Faith is not something humans 'do' to make themselves acceptable to God. ... When Paul speaks of justification by faith, not works of the law, the point he is making is that the community of God's people is marked out by their faith in Jesus as the risen Lord, not by various things (sabbath, food laws, circumcision) which were badges of membership in the ethnic people of Israel. This concern is closely related to the present passage. He is going at once to speak in verses 11-22 of the coming together of Jew and Gentile in the Messiah. But the emphasis throughout these verses is on the contrast between the state of the human race as described in verses 1-3 and the state of the human race as God in his generous love has decided to remake it.[188]

What does Wright say in *Paul for Everyone* series about Titus 3:1-8a? Not much as to our topic. He notes that 'God's action in Jesus Christ is not a reward for good work already done. It's an act of free kindness and loving goodness (verse 4).' He says nothing about 'justification' in Titus 3:7.[189] On the surface, Wright is affirming that 'works' are more than boundary markers; however, this could be a modern implication from Titus, not 'Paul's' view per se.

Now let us move to 2 Tim. 1:8-14 in the *Paul for Everyone* series. Here Wright contrasts Christ's 'appearing' with Caesar's.[190] 'The new life ... is a gift of God in sheer grace and power ... this happens not because we're special, or because we've behaved in a particular way up to now, but simply by God's goodness and love.'[191] Again, on the surface, Wright is affirming that 'works' are more than boundary markers; however, this could be a modern implication from Second Timothy, not Paul's view per se.

In Wright's *Paul: In Fresh Perspective* (2005), there is only one mention of any substance concerning Eph. 2:8-10, Titus 3:4-7, and

---

188. Wright, *Paul for Everyone: The Prison Epistles*, 22-23.

189. Wright, *Paul for Everyone: The Pastoral Letters*, 159-62, esp. 160.

190. Wright is known for emphasizing more of Paul's subtle 'counter-imperial theology' than others do. This emphasis came somewhat later in his works. See *Paul: In Fresh Perspective* (Minneapolis: Fortress, 2005), 59-79, esp. 69.

191. Wright, *Paul for Everyone: The Pastoral Letters*, 90.

2 Tim. 1:8-10, and that has to do with Eph. 2:8-10. The larger context of Wright's discussion is his view of election, the Messiah, and the full inclusion of both Jews and Gentiles in God's family by faith. Wright makes somewhat of a side comment that interests us in his discussion of Eph. 2:11-3:13.

> It is one of the telling features of current debate that some within the new perspective have, as it were, highlighted Ephesians 2:11-22, while most of the let's-go-back-to-the-old-perspective brigade have, as it were, highlighted 2:1-10. Clearly for either Paul or one of his first readers this was not an either/or, but a both/and.[192]

In Wright's *Justification: God's Plan & Paul's Vision* (2009), there is no mention of 2 Tim. 1:8-10 and Titus 3:4-7, even though Titus 3:7 includes the participle 'having been justified' and 'justification' is in the title of the book. Wright, however, does discuss Eph. 2:1-10. He makes similar points as he did above in *Paul: In Fresh Perspective*. 'Ephesians 2:1-10 is the old perspective: sinners saved by grace through faith. Ephesians 2:11-22 is the new perspective: Jews and Gentiles coming together in Christ.'[193] The cross 'not only rescued sinful human beings from their eternal fate but also rescued fractured humanity from its eternal antagonism.' Wright notes that 'justification' in Romans and Galatians is slightly different than 'saved' in Ephesians. Wright connects 'law of commandments' in Eph. 2:15 with 'works of the law' in Romans/Galatians (Jewish identity markers)—and commends Dunn for this historic insight. Wright also makes his plea that his reading of Eph. 2:1-22 shows that 'ecclesiology' is very important and should not be a secondary topic to justification.[194] Frustratingly,

---

192. Wright, *Paul: In Fresh Perspective*, 116-17. Of course, I am one of the 'let's-go-back-to-the-old-perspective brigade.'

193. Wright, *Justification: God's Plan & Paul's Vision*, 168. Similarly, Bird, who 'would go so far as to say that confronting legalistic opponents was not the most explosive issue that Paul dealt with. Rather, the most pressing issue of Paul's ministry was trying to get Gentiles accepted *as* Gentiles into fellowship *by* Jewish Christians' (*The Saving Righteousness of God*, 108, his italics).

194. Wright, *Justification: God's Plan & Paul's Vision*, 170-74. Concerning Wright's musings on why old-perspective types do not agree with him on the importance of ecclesiology, 'It cannot be, can it, that part of the old

Wright does not give his definition of 'works' and the specifics of 'boast' from Eph. 2:9.

Now let us consider Wright's massive 1658-page *Paul and the Faithfulness of God* (2013). After I have looked up every reference related to Eph. 2:8-10, Titus 3:4-7, and 2 Tim. 1:8-10, I find he does present a very short overview of Ephesians, which includes 'the soteriological statement of 2:1-10 and the carefully matching ecclesiological statement of 2:11-22.' Other than this, the three texts are not used relative to any discussion of 'works,' 'works of the law,' or 'justification.'

Finally, Wright's latest book is to be considered, *Paul and His Recent Interpreters: Some Contemporary Debates* (2015).[195] There is no mention of Titus 3:4-7 and 2 Tim. 1:8-10. There is only one brief mention of Eph. 2:1-10, and it is similar to his point above concerning the compatibility of Eph. 2:1-10 and 2:11-22. In context, Wright is citing Westerholm's comment that Eph. 2:1-10 shows that the author of Ephesians was pro-Luther.[196] Wright complains that 'Westerholm, like many others, does not point out that Ephesians 2:8-10 is followed at once by the emphatic, indeed climactic, 2:11-22, ... one might suggest that Ephesians 2:1-10 represents the old perspective, and 2:11-22 the new.'[197]

To put Wright's conclusions in the form of the scenarios above, he concludes: (a) *Pauline* authorship for Ephesians and Second Timothy and *maybe Deutero-Pauline* for Titus, (b) Eph. 2:8-10 *does in some way* reflect the 'old perspective' soteriology, (c) Romans, Galatians, and Philippians 3 do *not* contrast works righteousness soteriology with a grace one, (d) the change in theology is slight and is due to 'saved' (and not 'justification') in Eph. 2:8, (e)

---

perspective's reaction to the new is the tacit sense that once we associate ecclesiology with the very center of the gospel we will have to go all the way and rethink the political role and task of the church?' (p. 174).

195. N. T. Wright, *Paul and His Recent Interpreters: Some Contemporary Debates* (Minneapolis: Fortress, 2015).

196. Westerholm, *Perspectives Old and New on Paul*, 406. I have also referenced this above.

197. Wright, *Paul and His Recent Interpreters*, 128.

Eph. 2:11-22 shows that NPP concerns were related to Eph. 2:1-10, and (f) Second Temple Judaism does *not* have a works righteousness soteriology.

Critique of N. T. Wright

Allow me to quickly summarize Wright's views as best as I understand them. Compared to his extraordinary output, Wright has little to say about Eph. 2:8-10, Titus 3:4-7, and 2 Tim. 1:8-10. But what does he say? As to authorship, Wright is fairly strong on Pauline authorship of Ephesians and Second Timothy. He has less confidence that Titus is Pauline. In his *Paul for Everyone* series, he *seems* to affirm that Titus and Second Timothy use 'works' as works righteousness. He says nothing about 'having been justified' in Titus 3:7. Wright has more discussion of Eph. 2:8-10. He affirms the 'old perspective' (traditional Protestant, soteriology) of Eph. 2:1-10 but wants to emphasize that also in this context is 2:11-22 (Jew and Gentile unity, ecclesiology), which shows the 'new perspective.' Thus in Eph. 2:1-22, both old and new must be joined together. Also, he wants to ensure that 'justification' (Romans, Galatians, Philippians 3, anti-boundary markers) is acknowledged as different from 'salvation' in Eph. 2:8-10, although the two concepts are related.

To begin my critique, excepting the brief discussions in his *Paul for Everyone* series, there is virtually no discussion of Titus 3:7 and 2 Tim. 1:8-10. This may be a calculated move due to the scholarly audience Wright is normally addressing. However, similar to my critiques above, when one is claiming that works righteousness, at least a Jewish version of it, does not exist, one needs to provide an answer to these verses whether they are written by Paul or not.

Concerning two commentaries in the *Paul for Everyone* series, Wright implies that 'works' are general works and not specifically related to Jewish boundary markers. If I am reading him correctly here, this begs for more explanation of how 'works' in Titus 3:5 and 2 Tim. 1:9 got expanded from 'works of the law' that supposedly highlight the sin of Jewish ethnocentrism. This is especially true for Titus 3:5 because Titus 3:7 uses 'having been justified' and not only 'salvation' language. That is, Wright cannot use the slippage between justification and salvation language as his answer for Titus.

Let us move to Eph. 2:8-10. Wright does discuss Eph. 2:1-10 several times but not with any sustained exegesis as he normally does for many other Pauline passages. He states that Eph. 2:1-10 does confirm the 'old perspective,' although he never defines exactly what he means in this context by 'old perspective.' Elsewhere he gives sustained critiques of the 'old perspective.'[198] I assume that 'old perspective' here means at least that Paul was arguing against some level of works righteousness and it was broader than boundary markers. (I am not sure of my assumption because Wright does not explicitly indicate his view of 'works' and 'boast' in Eph. 2:9.)

Wright emphasizes that the 'old perspective' in Eph. 2:1-10 is in the context of the 'new perspective' as shown by Eph. 2:11-22. In fact, he interprets 'law' in Eph. 2:15 as referring primarily to boundary markers in the Torah.[199] Fair enough. Is he implying that there are Jewish Christians at the Ephesian church to which 'works' in Eph. 2:9 applied? That is, are there Jewish-Christians who were works righteousness oriented? If yes, this contradicts statements Wright makes elsewhere that Jewish Christians did not attempt to '*earn* covenant membership though keeping the law (such people do not seem to exist in the 1st century).'[200] Further, if Eph. 2:1-22 is both 'old' and 'new,' why does not Wright conclude that both are also in Galatians and Romans? Or to say it another way, within Wright's own logic, the more Wright pushes that 'salvation' in Eph. 2:1-10 is connected to 'ecclesiology' in Eph. 2:11-22, the more he pushes that

---

198. Wright, *Paul and His Recent Interpreters*, 106-31.

199. The interpretation of Eph. 2:15 is notoriously difficult, and Wright's view is not unusual here. For a good listing of a variety of views, see O'Brien, *The Letter to the Ephesians*, 196-99.

200. Wright, 'Justification,' in *New Dictionary of Theology*, 360, italics his. The full quote is, '[Paul's] polemic against "works of the law" is not directed against those who attempted to *earn* covenant membership through keeping the Jewish law (such people do not seem to have existed in the 1st century) but against those who sought to *demonstrate* their membership in the covenant through obeying the Jewish law' (p. 360, italics his).

justification-by-faith versus works-of-the-law is at least partially grace versus works righteousness in Galatians and Romans.

I am guessing that part of Wright's rebuttal would be that the language of 'salvation' in Eph. 2:1-10 does not exactly match 'justification' elsewhere in Paul. But once works righteousness is admitted, the name that opposes it is irrelevant for my argument. It is hard to take this discussion further because I am not sure of Wright's meaning when he says that Eph. 2:1-10 is the 'old perspective.' Does he sees any works righteousness in Eph. 2:8-9 that is connected to Jewish Christians?

There are some NPP authors who see 'works' in Eph. 2:9 as shorthand for 'works of the law' based on Eph. 2:15. Hence, they see no works righteousness in the passage.[201] This would be consistent and matches Scenario 5 above. Few exegetes, however, conclude this. I assume this is not Wright's view.

Finally, a comment or two about Wright's statement that the old and new perspectives should be a 'both/and,' not an 'either/or.' Similar to Dunn, later in his works, Wright often notes that the old and new perspectives are not opposites. And again, similar to Dunn, it depends on what one means by 'old perspective.' Wright appreciates much about Reformed theology, including the third use of the law, redemptive-historical movement, covenants, and incorporating union with Christ ('in Christ') into soteriology.[202] He affirms broadly universal sin, Christ's atoning work, and salvation with past, present, and future aspects. However, similar to Dunn, it is in the specifics about 'law' and 'justification' that there are significant differences, at least from a traditional Reformed perspective. These differences, more or less, stem from the starting point of Sanders' covenantal nomism.

Wright views 'law' in Paul as always 'talking of the Jewish law, Torah. We cannot, without ruining his arguments, make *nomos* [law] into something universal.' This then, according to Wright,

---

201. Yinger notes two NPP authors (*The New Perspective on Paul*, 68 n. 26).

202. Wright, *Paul and His Recent Interpreters*, 29-33, 51-63, 67. There is even a mostly positive discussion of Herman Ridderbos (pp. 60-62).

destroys the Reformed 'covenant of works.' 'Make "the law" in Paul Israel-specific, and you shake a foundation of some branches at least of Reformed theology.'[203] Given this conclusion by Wright, the question of the relationship of 'works' to 'works of the law' is important in the NPP-versus-Reformed debate.

Wright's view of justification is problematic from a Reformed perspective. Initial justification is that one is declared in 'covenant membership' on the 'basis of the representative death and resurrection of Jesus,' which is 'on the basis of faith.' Final justification is on the 'basis of the total life' of Spirit-filled works.[204] During this life, faith is a 'badge of the sin-forgiven family.' 'Present justification declares, on the basis of faith, what future justification will affirm publicly (according to Rom. 2:14-16 and 8:9-11) on the basis of the entire life.'[205] Or again, future justification is 'on the basis of the entire life a person has led in the power of the Spirit—that is, it occurs on the basis of "works" in Paul's redefined sense.'[206] The righteousness of God is God's own righteousness that He is faithful to His covenant.[207] The righteous status that believers receive is '*not* God's own righteousness or Christ's own righteousness that is reckoned to God's redeemed people *but, rather,* the fresh status of "covenant member," and/or "justified sinner."'[208]

---

203. Wright, *Paul and His Recent Interpreters*, 94-95.

204. Wright, 'Justification,' in *New Dictionary of Theology*, 359-60. Note that Wright uses 'basis' for different aspects of justification. I assume, therefore, he does not mean 'basis' as ultimate ground for all of these. For a similar view as mine of Wright here, see Schreiner, *Faith Alone*, 242-43.

205. Wright, *What Saint Paul Really Said*, 129.

206. Wright, 'New Perspectives on Paul,' in *Justification in Perspective: Historical Developments and Contemporary Challenges* (ed. Bruce L. McCormack; Grand Rapids: Baker, 2006), 243-64, esp. 260. For a longer discussion of present and future justification, see *Paul and the Faithfulness of God*, 1026-32.

207. Wright, *What Saint Paul Really Said*, 100-10; and *Paul and the Faithfulness of God*, 799-800. So also Dunn, *The Theology of Paul the Apostle*, 342; and Hays, 'Justification,' 1131. For an extended critique of this view, see Charles Lee Irons, *The Righteousness of God*, 273-96.

208. Wright, 'New Perspectives on Paul,' in *Justification in Perspective*, 253, italics mine.

Given the above, Reformed theology especially has problems with (1) the inclusion of Spirit-filled works as part of final justification and (2) the denial of the imputed righteousness of Christ. These two combine to take the heart out of the once-for-all declaration that God in Christ has justified me, a sinner.

In addition to the definition of justification, Reformed theology, although not as much as Lutheran theology (!), disagrees with Wright's moderate downplaying of the importance of justification. Admittedly, part of this is semantic with Wright's insistence on emphasizing ecclesiology with justification and wanting to separate justification from conversion/call/initial-salvation.[209] Wright says, 'Salvation remains enormously important; conversion remains enormously important; "the gospel" remains central, powerful, vital; *but the language of "justification" is not the key term used by Paul to convey all this.*'[210] Similarly, 'All main NPP authors are quite clear that Paul was very concerned about the "universal human problem." They just do not think Paul's way of addressing that problem had "justification" as its primary focus.'[211]

In sum, Wright has minimal discussion of Eph. 2:8-10 and even less of Titus 3:4-7 and 2 Tim. 1:8-10. He *seems* to affirm that all three use 'works' as broader than 'works of the law,' but I am not sure of that. His discussion of Eph. 2:1-10 involves combining it with Eph. 2:11-22 and concluding that Eph. 2:1-22 supports both the old and new perspectives. Depending on what he means by the old perspective, he has undercut his own arguments about Galatians and Romans by admitting that works righteousness can be in the context of boundary markers. Also, he has admitted that works righteousness exists in the Second Temple period. However, it is not these considerations but his view of covenantal nomism that grounds his views of Galatians and Romans. Although I appreciate his wanting to see the old and new perspectives as 'both/and,' his definition of justification so significantly differs with traditional

---

209. Wright, 'New Perspectives on Paul,' in *Justification in Perspective*, 255-57.

210. Wright, *Paul and His Recent Interpreters*, 118, italics his.

211. Wright, *Paul and His Recent Interpreters*, 117 n. 39.

Reformed theology that I am obligated to say 'thanks, but no thanks' to his kind offer.

Partly because I am not sure of Wright's meaning of 'old perspective,' I hesitate to put him into one of the five standard scenarios above.

SUMMARY OF CHAPTER

The 'Deutero-Pauline' texts of Eph. 2:8-10, Titus 3:4-7, and 2 Tim. 1:8-10 include 'works' as works righteousness. The vast majority of scholars and I agree to this irrespective of authorship considerations. This prompts two related questions. How does this affect one's view of Galatians, Romans, and Philippians 3? How does this affect one's view generally of works righteousness existing in Second Temple Judaism?

This chapter considered in some detail three non-NPP authors, I. Howard Marshall, Michael Wolter, and John M. G. Barclay. These three concluded that 'works' was broader than 'works of the law' and did constitute works righteousness. Marshall saw the Deutero-Pauline texts as confirming that justification/righteousness in Galatians, Roman, and Philippians 3 was at least partially contrasted with works righteousness. Illogically from my perspective, Wolter and Barclay argued that one should not impose Deutero-Paul's views onto Paul. As to how this affects one's conclusions about the general existence of works righteousness in Second Temple Judaism, none of the three had much to say about this specifically.

Three NPP authors were considered, Sanders, Dunn, and Wright. Dunn clearly believes that 'works' in the three Deutero-Paul texts was broadened out from Jewish boundary markers and constitutes works righteousness. Sanders does not say much on the topic, but gives hints that he agrees that Eph. 2:8-10 and some Gospel passages indicate that the church was against works righteousness. Wright discusses Eph. 2:8-10 and does agree that here Paul represents the 'old perspective,' but he is not completely clear on the issue as he wants to combine this insight with Eph. 2:11-22 that confirms the 'new perspective.' Illogically from my perspective, the admission of works righteousness does not affect their readings of Galatians, Romans, and Philippians 3. Similarly, they do not appear to acknowledge that they are agreeing that some were concerned about work righteousness during the Second Temple period.

Based on the above exegesis of Eph. 2:8-10, Titus 3:4-7, and 2 Tim. 1:8-10, I conclude: (1) 'Works' is to be taken as works righteousness soteriology contrasted with God's saving activity. (2) 'Works' in all three texts refers to broad human effort that would be in conformity to God's moral law. (3) Works righteousness existed in the Second Temple period. (4) The works righteousness aspect of 'works' should be included in 'works,' 'works of the law,' and 'law' in Galatians, Romans, and Philippians 3 when these are contrasted conceptually with salvation/justification.

In my view, Eph. 2:1-10, Titus 3:4-7, and 2 Tim. 1:8-10 further confirm that NPP is misguided. Since I believe that Paul wrote all thirteen letters, it is not exegetically viable for me to conclude that these texts *do* refer to works righteousness and also conclude that Galatians, Romans, and Philippians 3 do *not*. Within a system that does not affirm Pauline authorship of all thirteen letters, it is theoretically viable, but I highly doubt it.[212]

Finally, in my view, it is not historically competent to conclude that these three texts refer to works righteousness and also conclude that covenantal nomism in Second Temple Judaism is universal. Even if one argued that Eph. 2:1-10, Titus 3:4-7, and 2 Tim. 1:8-10 only referred to Gentiles, and not Jewish Christians nor Jews per se,

---

212. So also Richard B. Gaffin, Jr. After arguing that Eph. 2:8-9, Titus 3:5-7, and 2 Tim. 1:9 have a soteriological antithesis similar to Galatians and Romans, he further concludes that 'even if we grant that denial [of Pauline authorship] for the sake of argument, that would still mean that already in the earliest post-Pauline generation of the church, including the sphere of Paul's particular influence, from which Ephesians and the Pastorals stem according to many who deny their Pauline authorship, the primary point of his teaching on justification in Galatians and Romans, according to the New Perspective, was missed or misunderstood' (*'By Faith, Not by Sight': Paul and the Order of Salvation* [Milton Keynes, England: Paternoster, 2006], 46).

works righteousness was 'in the air' and a group (Christians) that treasured the OT was concerned about it.

All this to say, Eph. 2:1-10, Titus 3:4-7, and 2 Tim. 1:1-10 crack the NPP's foundation of Sanders' covenantal nomism by showing that works righteousness did exist in Second Temple Judaism and Christian church contexts.

CHAPTER 5

SUMMARY

I remember the first time I saw Sanders' book, *Paul and Palestinian Judaism*. I was a Ph.D. student in January 1990. The book was being carried by another Ph.D. student. I had heard of the book, but I knew little about it. At that point, the student had only gotten through a few chapters of Sanders' book and was giving me his understanding of Sanders. While the other student was in the midst of explaining to me Sanders' covenantal-nomism thesis, it dawned on both of us that if what Sanders says is true, then major aspects of the traditional Protestant view of justification might be wrong. This made a significant impact on me—as can be seen by my remembrance of this conversation. Of course, Sanders and others had already made that connection, I was just not up-to-speed on it. My concern then and now has not changed. In a real sense, this book is the culmination of that initial conversation.

INTRODUCTION AND THESIS

The purpose of this chapter is to simply gather together my summaries and conclusions from the other chapters and have them in one convenient location. Much of this is verbatim from the previous chapters.

In brief, the NPP believes that the traditional Protestant view of justification is wrong or needs serious modification. The foundation of this NPP view is Sanders' covenantal nomism—Second Temple Judaism has a uniform soteriology that does *not* include works righeousness. Covenantal nomism is a soteriological system that 'getting in' the covenant is by grace/election, and 'staying in' is by obedience to the law along with atonement/repentance. To emphasize, from Sanders' perspective, these works to 'stay in' are not considered in any sense works righteousness. The whole system is grace oriented.

Given this starting point of covenantal nomism, the NPP concludes that Paul was not arguing against works righteousness and consequently develops a variety of understandings of justification that I find problematic for the church.

I disagree with Sanders' thesis and consider the Reformed view of justification to be biblical. However, Paul's presentation of justification is not the primary focus of this book. Instead, I focus on the foundation of the NPP view which is Sanders' covenantal nomism. Why this focus as opposed to evaluating Paul more directly? Compared to the many books that explicitly evaluate Paul's view of justification relative to NPP arguments, there are significantly less that evaluate the Second-Temple-Judaism portion of the arguments. I want to help the imbalance.

Ephesians 2:8-10, Titus 3:4-7, and 2 Tim. 1:8-10 is a secondary focus of this book. Because of the assumed Deutero-Pauline authorship of these texts, these three texts have not received as much attention. After my exegesis, I evaluate Sanders, Dunn, and Wright's views of these texts as to their implications on Sanders' thesis and to Paul's view of justification. Again, why this secondary focus? There is not as much discussion of these texts relative to the NPP as I think there should be, and in my view, the NPP is especially vulnerable here.

Now to state the formal thesis: *The primary thesis of this book is that there are many examples of works righteousness (Pelagian and semi-Pelagian versions) in Second Temple Judaism literature and*

Sanders' uniform covenantal nomism is mistaken. Hence, the new-perspective-on-Judaism foundation crumbles and the NPP house concerning justification comes crashing down. *The secondary thesis is that the NPP is especially vulnerable in its explanations and/or avoidance of Eph. 2:8-10, Titus 3:4-7, and 2 Tim. 1:8-10.*

I do not consider my arguments in this book as the complete vindication of the Reformed view of justification. A focus on all the relevant Pauline and biblical texts is required for that. However, the arguments in this book dovetail well with and support that vindication.

'FIVE POINTS' OF NPP

As described in Chapter 1, I summarize the NPP with five points. Note that except for the fifth point, NPP authors are all agreed. This book will not focus on all of these points.

1. NPP authors agree that Paul was not arguing against a legalistic works righteousness view because it did not exist—that is, they accept Sanders' covenantal nomism.

2. NPP authors agree on what justification is *not*—it is *not* the traditional-Protestant view.

3. NPP authors agree that 'works of the law' primarily refer to Jewish boundary markers, Sabbath, circumcision, and food laws.

4. NPP authors agree that Paul's mission to the Gentiles *is* the context for his teaching on justification.

5. NPP authors are not united on justification. One standard view: Initial justification is by faith and recognizes covenant status (ecclesiology) and final justification is partially by works, albeit works produced by the Spirit.

BROAD-BRUSH CRITIQUES OF COVENANTAL NOMISM

In Chapter 2 are included several broad-brush critiques of covenantal nomism. They are (1) covenantal nomism as defined includes a semi-Pelagian soteriology, (2) covenantal nomism's structure of 'getting in' and 'staying in' de-emphasizes the final judgment, (3) even election is not always clearly by grace in Second Temple Judaism sources, (4) the variegated nature of Second Temple Judaism argues against a uniform covenantal nomism, (5) the admission of Gentiles into Judaism and the admission of Jews into the Qumran community undercuts the supposed consistent grace emphasis of 'getting in,' (6) the halakah (law) emphasis tends toward works righteousness, (7) a soteriological system with repentance does not necessarily preclude a works righteousness component, and (8) the NT is not regarded as reliably providing important evidence.

Works Righteousness in Specific Jewish Documents

Chapter 3 is the heart of the book. Here I consider various Second Temple Judaism documents from both a Reformed perspective and from Sanders' perceptive (when available).

The documents considered were two works from the Apocrypha (4 Ezra and Sirach), three from the OT Pseudepigrapha (*2 Baruch*, *Testament of Abraham*, and *Psalms of Solomon*), three from the DSS (*Rule of the Community*, *Pesher Habakkuk*, and *Miqsat Ma'ase Ha-Torah*), and five Rabbinic literature tractates (*m. Abot, m. Sotah, t. Qiddushin, t. Sanhedrin*, and *b. Rosh Hashanah*).

I conclude that all of these documents have a works righteousness soteriology, whether Pelagian or semi-Pelagian. To be clear, I am not saying that all documents in Second Temple Judaism have a works righteousness soteriology; however, I am insisting that many do. Hence, I conclude that Sanders' conclusion that works righteousness did not exist in Second Temple Judaism is completely wrong.

Once given my conclusion that there is an abundance of works righteousness soteriology in Second Temple Judaism documents, the NPP foundation of covenantal nomism has crumbled. And with it, their new view of Pauline justification also crumbles as it is built upon that faulty foundation.

WORKS RIGHTEOUSNESS IN 'DEUTERO-PAUL'

The 'Deutero-Pauline'[1] texts of Eph. 2:8-10, Titus 3:4-7, and 2 Tim. 1:8-10 include 'works' as works righteousness. The vast majority of scholars and I agree to this irrespective of authorship considerations. This prompts two related questions. How does this affect one's view of Galatians, Romans, and Philippians 3? How does this affect one's view generally of works righteousness existing in Second Temple Judaism?

Three NPP authors were considered, Sanders, Dunn, and Wright. Dunn clearly believes that 'works' in the three Deutero-Paul texts were broadened out from Jewish boundary markers and constitute works righteousness. Sanders does not say much on the topic, but gives hints that he agrees that Eph. 2:8-10 and some Gospel passages indicate that the church was against works righteousness. Wright discusses Eph. 2:8-10 and does agree that here Paul represents the 'old perspective,' but he is not completely clear on the issue as he wants to combine this insight with Eph. 2:11-22 that confirms the 'new perspective.' Illogically for me, the admission of works righteousness by all three does not affect their readings of Galatians, Romans, and Philippians 3. Similarly, they do not appear to acknowledge that they are agreeing that at least some were concerned about work righteousness during the first-century A.D.

Based on my exegesis of Eph. 2:8-10, Titus 3:4-7, and 2 Tim. 1:8-10, I conclude: (1) 'Works' in all three texts are to be taken as works righteousness soteriology contrasted with God's saving activity. (2) 'Works' in all three texts refer to broad human effort that would be in conformity to God's moral law. (3) Works righteousness existed in the Second Temple period. (4) The works righteousness aspect of 'works' should be included

---

1. I accept all thirteen Pauline epistles in the canon as written by Paul. I am using ironic quotes for 'Deutero-Pauline' as the vast majority of critical scholars deny Pauline authorship here.

in 'works,' 'works of the law,' and 'law' in Galatians, Romans, and Philippians 3 when these are contrasted conceptually with salvation/justification.

In my view, Eph. 2:1-10, Titus 3:4-7, and 2 Tim. 1:8-10 further confirm that NPP is misguided. Since I believe that Paul wrote all thirteen letters, it is not exegetically viable for me to conclude that these texts *do* refer to works righteousness and also conclude that Galatians, Romans, and Philippians 3 do *not*. Within a system that does not affirm Pauline authorship of all thirteen letters, it is theoretically viable, but I highly doubt it.

Finally, in my view, it is not historically competent to conclude that these three texts refer to works righteousness and also conclude that covenantal nomism in Second Temple Judaism is universal. Even if one argued that Eph. 2:1-10, Titus 3:4-7, and 2 Tim. 1:8-10 only referred to Gentiles, and not Jewish Christians nor Jews per se, works righteousness was 'in the air' and a group (Christians) that treasured the OT was concerned about it.

All this to say, Eph. 2:1-10, Titus 3:4-7, and 2 Tim. 1:8-10 crack the NPP's foundation of Sanders' covenantal nomism by showing that works righteousness did exist in Second Temple Judaism and Christian church contexts.

CONCLUDING THOUGHTS

Yes, I see the denial of any works righteousness in Second Temple Judaism as historically wrong, and worse, the implications of this skew or deny important issues for the modern Church. I will just mention four.

(1) As has been mentioned numerous times, the doctrine of justification is significantly modified by the NPP to include Spirit-wrought human works in 'final' justification.[2] For me, keeping the Reformational insight that a human's works are *not* included in any sense as the ground for the declaration of justification is still worth *protesting* over. It is worth keeping this in the official church

---

2. The crux of this issue for NPP authors is Rom. 2, but this issue also turns on Christ's imputed righteousness and a host of other related doctrines.

creeds and requiring this be taught in the churches by the ordained ministry.[3]

(2) In Romans, Galatians, and Philippians 3, the NPP denies that Paul is primarily arguing against boasting in works righteousness. According to the NPP, yes, theoretically, if one were boasting in works righteousness, this would be wrong by implication from their view of justification, but it is not the primary point in Romans, Galatians, and Philippians 3. This denial affects the church's anthropology and the preacher's emphasis in proclaiming the Gospel. The modern church needs to have as part of her anthropology that a core sin for those outside of Christ is trying to achieve salvation through some sort of works righteousness. (For those in Christ, this sin is defeated, but its residual effects linger in Christians.) Given the importance of this sin, the preacher will address it appropriately with the full-orbed application of the Gospel.

With a NPP view of Romans, Galatians, and Philippians 3, however, the sin of boasting in one's differences or ethnocentrism is emphasized. Hence, the resulting counter emphasis of 'Christians' getting along,' although important, takes on disproportional importance for the NPP. For example, Wright at the end of his famous popular-level book, *What Saint Paul Really Said*, argues that the Reformation churches and Roman Catholic church are both wrong about justification and should not use justification to continue the separation.[4] This is not to say that ethnocentrism is to be taken

---

3. I am not dealing here with an individual believer and how much does one need to know about soteriology to be truly converted. At that level, I am quite broad.

4. N. T. Wright, '[They] have done themselves and the church a great disservice by treating the doctrine of "justification" as central to their debates, and by supposing that it describes the system by which people attained salvation. They have turned the doctrine into its opposite. Justification declares that all who believe in Jesus belong at the same table, no matter what their cultural or racial differences (and, let's face it, a good many denominational distinctions, and indeed distinctions within a single denomination, boil down more to culture than to doctrine). Because what matters is believing in Jesus, detailed agreement on justification itself, properly conceived, isn't the thing which

lightly in our day or that NT scholars should forget that Paul was many times dealing with Jew/Gentile issues in the context of works righteousness, it is instead a plea for proportionality on the issue.

(3) NPP authors deny the Covenant of Works, and more generally, they deny that Paul saw works righteousness as a theoretical option that portions of OT Israel were wrongly pursuing. That is, NPP authors do not admit that even Adam was under a works righteousness covenant, let alone that those outside of Christ in the OT and NT were/are still under the requirements of this covenant. This is a quasi-logical implication of Sanders' covenantal nomism. I assume NPP authors would argue that since no one in the first century A.D. was works righteousness oriented, then the whole history of OT Israel was not works righteousness oriented. In addition, other implications from Sanders' thesis are used by NPP authors to deny the Covenant of Works.[5] On the other hand, I would argue that Paul contends that Adam was under a Covenant of Works and portions of OT Israel wrongly pursued a works righteousness, 'righteousness of the law' salvation. Further, Paul is arguing that some in his day were also improperly pursing a works righteousness salvation.

As shown in Chapter 2 and elsewhere, the Covenant of Works has significant explanatory power for many specific exegetical 'problems.' For example, it dovetails well with the Bible's second use of the law—God demands perfect obedience and uses the law to show us our sin, which then shows us the futility of our attempt at achieving works righteousness, which then shows us our need for Christ— which is generally downplayed by NPP authors. The Covenant of Works also contributes to larger theological issues such as (a) the sinful anthropological impulse to earn salvation,

---

should determine eucharistic fellowship' (*What Saint Paul Really Said: Was Paul of Tarsus the Real Founder of Christianity?* [Grand Rapids: Eerdmans, 1997], 158-59).

5. N. T. Wright ties his denial of the Covenant of Works to Paul's use of 'works of the law' in Galatians and Romans; it only meant Torah, not a universalized law (*Paul and His Recent Interpreters: Some Contemporary Debates* [Minneapolis: Fortress, 2015], 94-95).

(b) the forensic background to justification, and (c) Adam/Christ parallels including Christ's fulfillment of the Covenant of Works and the connection to His imputed righteousness.

(4) Many, although not all, pro-Sanders and NPP authors have a 'low view' of the historical accuracy of the Bible. How does this evidence itself in NPP arguments? Primarily, it is the denial that Paul is the author of Ephesians, Second Timothy, and Titus and the conclusion that various statements in the Gospels about the Pharisees are historically suspect.

I sense that many in the broad evangelical church who are pro-NPP or are laissez-faire toward the NPP are not aware that (1) many NPP authors have a low view of the Bible and that (2) this low view significantly contributes to their arguments for the NPP. Since I consider a 'high view' of the Bible to be important for the health of Christ's church, these assumptions about the Bible by many NPP authors are a danger and need to be exposed. That is, even though critical scholarship has been arguing for a long time that Paul did not write all the letters attributed to him, I still consider it a danger to promote a theology in the church that includes the proposition that Paul did not write, for example, Titus. This leads to an erosion of confidence in God's Word for those in Christ's church.[6]

---

6. Of course, another reason I am against telling the church that Paul did not write Titus is because it is not true!

APPENDIX

OVERVIEW OF JUDAISM'S LITERARY SOURCES

While in my Ph.D. program I had several courses related to Second Temple Judaism. Although I had gone to an excellent seminary for my M.Div. degree, I was unprepared for my first course. My Hebrew and Aramaic language skills were fine, but my general knowledge was, shall we say, lacking. Who was Tobit again? Was Tobit a 'he' or a 'she'? There are how many Maccabees books! How many extant theological documents do we have from the Pharisees?—Oh, none. This first-course shock sent me on a long joyous journey that continues today of reading Second Temple Jewish and Rabbinic literature.

INTRODUCTION

As mentioned in Chapter 1, this appendix is designed to aid those not well aquainted with non-canonical ancient Jewish literature and current scholarship's general views about it. One reason to improve our grasp of first-century A.D. Judaism is to better understand and interact with the NPP arguments. The NPP authors are making honest arguments. A truth-in-love (Eph. 4:15) response requires that at least some of the rebuttals to the NPP address the Judaistic-background portion of their arguments. This is especially useful because the NPP perceives that the Judaistic-background portion of their argument is very important.

Yes, this appendix will present a lot of information, but the key is to get a sense of Second Temple Judaism and its literature.[1] A related angle is to appreciate the levels of scholarly uncertainty and disagreement about Second Temple Judaism. Getting a sense of Second Temple Judaism and scholars' levels of uncertainty about it will aid the reader in understanding at least one of my critiques about Sanders' covenantal nomism: His belief that it is uniform across all Judaisms in Second Temple Judaism. In sum, do not 'sweat' the details of this appendix, but take in the big picture.

LITERARY SOURCES CONSIDERED FOR THIS STUDY

DATING OF MAJOR LITERARY SOURCES

In theory, this study is primarily interested in the Judaism that existed during Paul's day, that is, first-century A.D. Judaism. Paul traveled in both Palestine and the greater Hellenistic world; hence, both Palestinian Judaism and Hellenistic Judaism are potentially important. Also, since Paul explicitly calls himself a former Pharisee (Phil. 3:5, Acts 23:6), knowing the views of the Pharisees would be especially helpful. Unfortunately, determining the views of first-century A.D. Judaism is not easy. Of course, Paul also interacted in the general Greco-Roman culture, but this aspect will not be included in this study.

---

1. For an up-to-date annotated bibliographic reference, see David W. Chapman and Andreas J. Köstenberger, 'Jewish Intertestamental and Early Rabbinic Literature: An Annotated Bibliographic Resource Updated (Part 1 and 2),' *JETS* 55 (2012): 235-72, 457-88.

Scholars are aware of a variety of Jewish parties (e.g., Pharisees) and groups of writings (e.g., OT Pseudepigrapha) that existed in the first century A.D. The problem is that many of the extant literary sources are not specific to the first century. Hence, one needs to evaluate documents written both before and after the first century A.D., and then make assumptions of the relevancy of the documents to the first century. Another problem is that for some first-century groups, we may have no literary documents (e.g., Sadducees). A final problem is that many of the written documents are difficult to date.

This difficulty in dating is one reason why scholars often use the term 'Second Temple Judaism,' as opposed to indicating more specifically, for example, second-century B.C. Judaism. The Second Temple existed from 520 B.C. to A.D. 70. However, the term 'Second Temple Judaism' usually refers to the varieties of Judaism that existed between 200 B.C. and A.D. 70 without designating a particular century. Or for some, the term is really used for Judaism from 200 B.C. to A.D. 135 (Bar-Kochba revolt) or even to A.D. 200 as some literature in Hellenistic Judaism appears to be unaffected by the A.D. 70 fall of the Second Temple.

Generally, when the literary sources of Second Temple Judaism are discussed, they are separated into literary groups.[2] For example, the OT Pseudepigrapha contains approximately sixty separate 'books,' with the books varying in length similar to biblical books. Below is a listing of the groups and approximate dates of the books within the large grouping. (These groups will be discussed in more detail later in this chapter.)

OT Pseudepigrapha (largely Apocalyptic
Judaism)...200 B.C.–A.D. 200

(OT) Apocrypha (history, tales, and
wisdom literature)...180 B.C.–A.D. 100[3]

---

2. Some include the canonical book of Daniel because of an assumed second-century A.D. dating. I hold to an early dating of Daniel.

3. Some date the *Letter of Jeremiah* to 317 B.C. although others put it in the second-century B.C.

Dead Sea Scrolls (Essenes/Qumran-
community)..150 B.C.–A.D. 68

Philo (Hellenistic Judaism).......................A.D. 10–50[4]

New Testament..A.D. 45–95

Josephus (Pharisee, but mostly non-
religious literature)...................................A.D. 75–100[5]

Rabbinic Literature (Mishnah to
Babylonian Talmud)..................................A.D. 200–600

To put these writings into some historical context, the following
key dates in Jewish history are provided:

Fall of Samaria (Northern Kingdom)................722 B.C.

Jewish exile to Babylon (multiple
deportations)..607–582 B.C.

Fall of Jerusalem and first Temple
destroyed..587 B.C.

Cyrus edict and return of Jewish
exiles...537 B.C.

Second Temple built....................................520–515 B.C.

Ptolemaic Egyptian—Greek rule of
Palestine begins...312 B.C.

Seleucid Syrian—Greek rule of
Palestine continues...................................198 B.C.

Judas Maccabees' revolt..............................166–160 B.C.

Second Temple rededicated.........................164 B.C.

---

4. Philo lived from approximately 20 B.C. to A.D. 50; the dates of his writings are
A.D. 10-50.

5. Josephus lived from approximately A.D. 37–100; the dates of his writings are
A.D. 75–100.

Hyracanus destroys Samaritan temple............128 B.C.

Rome takes Jerusalem—Roman rule of
Palestine begins..63 B.C.

Herod begins enlargement of Second
Temple ....18 B.C.

Christ's death..A.D. 30

Fall of Jerusalem and destruction of
Second Temple..A.D. 70

Bar-Kochba revolt and dispersion of
Jews from Judea......................................A.D. 132–135

As can be see from the above chart of the dates of various literary sources, excepting Rabbinic literature, all of the groups contain some writings that were written either before or during the first century A.D.[6] Therefore, these groups of writings are obviously useful for understanding first-century A.D. Judaism.

Some argue that a caveat to the above dating is needed for the OT Pseudepigrapha, Apocrypha, Josephus, and Philo.[7] With few exceptions, these texts were only preserved and transmitted by Christians, not Jews.[8] Only recently did traditional Jewish scholarship even concern itself with these texts. Did the Christians redact

---

6. The few writings in the OT Pseudepigrapha and the Apocrypha that are in the second century A.D. are not easy to date. In fact, they may be from the first century A.D.

7. M. de Jonge complains that most scholars interpret these texts as Jewish texts 'seemingly free from [Christian] contamination' and do not take into account that these writings were transmitted, redacted, and interpolated by Christians ('The So-Called Pseudepigrapha of the Old Testament and Early Christianity,' in *The New Testament and Hellenistic Judaism* [ed. Peder Borgen and Søren Giversen; Peabody: Hendrickson, 1997], 59-71, esp. 59). Also see James R. Davila, *The Provenance of the Pseudepigrapha: Jewish, Christian, or Other?* (Journal for the Study of Judaism Supplements 105; Leiden: Brill, 2005).

8. E.g., Sirach (from Apocrypha) is an exception. Portions of Sirach are extant in several Hebrew manuscripts, and Sirach is quoted in Rabbinic literature.

and/or add significant later interpolations into these texts? How does one tell if an ethical tract that uses OT characters is Jewish or simply a Christian using the OT? If these texts are Jewish, what accounts for only Christians preserving them and not Jews? Kraft has strongly argued that the 'default' position should be that vast majority of the OT Pseudepigrapha should be considered Christian until proved otherwise, that is, the 'burden of proof lies with claims of Jewishness.'[9]

Although I appreciate the caution that Kraft and others have exhibited, I do believe with the majority of scholars that generally the Christian community accurately transmitted texts that were not necessarily of their own making (e.g., the OT Scriptures!).[10] Hence, as to matters pertaining to our study, I will assume, with only a few exceptions, that Christians transmitted these texts faithfully.[11] Of course, this possible dating caveat due to Christian transmission of the texts does not apply to the DSS. They were discovered in caves near the Dead Sea in the late 1940s and early 1950s.

INCLUDE RABBINIC LITERATURE?

What about the Rabbinic literature? Should one use writings from A.D. 200–600 to help understand Second Temple Judaism, and more specifically, the first century A.D.?

Rabbinic Judaism is the name given to a Jewish religious party beginning immediately after the A.D. 70 fall of Jerusalem and

---

9. Robert A. Kraft, 'Setting the Stage and Framing Some Central Questions,' *JSJ* 32 (2001): 370-95, esp. 386, 373. Also see his well-known article 'The Pseudepigrapha in Christianity' in *Tracing the Threads: Studies in the Vitality of Jewish Pseudepigrapha* (ed. John C. Reeves; SBL Early Judaism and Its Literature 6; Atlanta: Scholars Press, 1994), 55-86.

10. See Richard Bauckham for an explicit critique of Kraft's 'default' position (*The Jewish World Around the New Testament* [Grand Rapids: Baker, 2010], 461-83). See John J. Collins for a good, short overview of this question ('Early Judaism in Modern Scholarship,' in *Early Judaism: A Comprehensive Overview* [eds. John J. Collins and Daniel C. Harlow; Grand Rapids: Eerdmans, 2012], 1-29, esp. 9-12).

11. If the topic of this study was the 'Messiah' or 'Jesus,' later interpolations are much more probable.

extending to present day. This party is the extension of the Pharisees and fairly quickly became the normative Jewish religion.[12]

First, two facts that create potential problems: (1) There are no extant explicit, Pharisaical religious-writings.[13] (2) There are no Rabbinic writings before A.D. 200. However, significant sections of Rabbinic literature purport to quote sayings and tell stories of rabbis from the first- and-second centuries A.D., including known Pharisees such as Gamaliel (Acts 5:34, 22:3, *m. Eduyyot* 3:10, *t. Berakhot* 2:6). Also, ideas that are attributed to even later rabbis may represent ideas that existed in the first century A.D. These ideas and purported quotes and stories are spread through various 'classic' Rabbinic documents. The classic Rabbinic literature starts with the Mishnah written in A.D. 200 and ends with the jewel of all Rabbinic literature, the Babylonian Talmud, in A.D. 600.

Potentially confirming that at least some information in the classic Rabbinic documents is useful for Second Temple Judaism study, it is true that various ideas and miscellaneous facts in the Rabbinic literature many times match to first-century A.D. information gleaned from the NT and elsewhere. For example, both Rabbinic literature and the NT contain a command to be reconciled with a friend before going to the altar (Matt. 6:23-24 // *m. Sukkah* 8:9). The 'corban' discussion in *m. Nedarim* 1:4-3:5 dovetails with and gives possible additional information for our understanding of corban mentioned in Mark 7:11. Also, the DSS document 4QMMT contains halakic discussions that parallel some in the Mishnah (e.g., 4QMMT B 55-58 // *m. Tohorot* 8:9).

---

12. There is archaeological evidence from synagogues from first to sixth centuries A.D. of non-Rabbinic Judaism, although there are no extant written documents. Drawings in these synagogues imply 'a Hellenistic-Jewish mystic mythology far closer to the Qabbalah—the mystical doctrine set forth in medieval Judaic books—than to the Judaism portrayed by Rabbinic literature. In a fairly limited time before the advent of Islam, these groups dissolved' (Jacob Neusner, *Judaism When Christianity Began: A Survey of Belief and Practice* [Louisville: Westminster John Knox, 2002], 10).

13. Occasionally, scholars will cite *Psalms of Solomon*, 4 Ezra, or *2 Baruch* as possibly Pharisaical. Josephus was a Pharisee, but his writings rarely deal with explicit religious themes.

The scholarly community is split on whether to use the Rabbinic literature for NT and first-century A.D. interpretation. Arguments against it include the Rabbinic literature's late date and the difficulty of distinguishing between a first-century A.D. Rabbinic/Pharisaic idea and a later Rabbinic one. Most scholars, however, do rely on at least some of the Rabbinic literature, while others do not use it at all.[14] My view is that the Rabbinic literature is certainly an extension of the pre-A.D. 70 Pharisees and is somewhat useful for interpreting the NT. This view matches well to the view of many NPP authors, including E. P. Sanders. Later in the 'Rabbinic Literature' section I will give qualifications as to which Rabbinic-literature documents are more likely to reflect first-century A.D. views than others.

INCLUDE NEW TESTAMENT?

Should one use the NT to determine views of first-century A.D. (non-Christian) Judaism? The Gospels, for example, have much to say about Pharisees. Since the NT is in fact a first-century A.D. document written by those who are ethnically Jewish (Luke is most likely an exception), and with few other documents available to us that are clearly written in the first century A.D.; it seems obvious

---

14. E.g., in favor of using Rabbinic literature for NT interpretation, see Sanders, *Paul and Palestinian Judaism*; and Martin McNamara, *Palestinian Judaism and the New Testament* (GNS 4; Wilmington, DE: Michael Glazier, 1983) esp. 177. In favor of not using it, see Raymond E. Brown, *An Introduction to the New Testament* (ABRL; New York: Doubleday, 1997), 79-83; Jacob Neusner, *Rabbinic Literature & the New Testament: What We Cannot Show, We Do Not Know* (Valley Forge: Trinity Press International, 1994); and George W. E. Nickelsburg, *Ancient Judaism and Christian Origins: Diversity, Continuity, and Transformation* (Minneapolis: Fortress, 2003). Neusner qualifies himself in a later book by noting that Rabbinic literature may provide some historical background information and examples for comparison (*Rabbinic Literature: An Essential Guide* [Nashville: Abingdon, 2005], 4). Note that although Nickelsburg is skeptical of the use of Rabbinic sources for NT interpretation, he is not in favor of a 'thoroughgoing skepticism' (*Ancient Judaism and Christian Origins*, 26). In any event, Nickelsburg does not use Rabbinic sources in his book to any substantive degree. Richard Bauckham is probably typical of many. He says 'Rabbinic literature, though of much later date, can be relevant when used with caution' (*The Jewish World Around the New Testament*, 2).

that the NT should be included. However, some object that one should not use the NT's portrayal of Judaism because (1) it is best to allow Judaism to explain itself and not to depend on an 'outsider's' view,[15] and (2) the NT's description of Judaism is often in a polemical setting that renders the description historically suspect.[16]

Concerning # 1, I agree that it is very helpful to note the portrayal that various Jewish documents make of their own religion. However, this does not necessarily exhaust the pertinent historical information as to the true nature of Judaism. Also, an 'insider's' view is not necessarily without its own distortions.

Concerning # 2, normally I am initially more cautious using a polemical source; however, since in this case the polemical source is the Bible and given the inspiration and inerrancy of the Bible, I take the NT descriptions of various Judaistic views as completely accurate. Although, this does not necessarily mean that the NT is describing, for example, the views of every single Pharisee and/or explaining every aspect of Pharisaic theology.

There is a second issue related to using the NT. Most critical NT scholars do not believe that Paul wrote Second Thessalonians, Ephesians, Colossians, First Timothy, Second Timothy, and Titus, the so-called 'Deutero-Paul' books. The remaining Pauline books are considered 'authentic' or 'undisputed': Romans, First Corinthians, Second Corinthians, Galatians, Philippians, First Thessalonians, and Philemon. Hence, when critical scholars conclude that Paul believes such-and-such, they are not including information from the Deutero-Paul books.[17] Most NPP authors, even if they believe

---

15. Sanders stresses this often (e.g., *Paul and Palestinian Judaism*, 426-27). In a historical survey, Moore traces the beginning of Christian scholars using only Jewish documents to portray Judaism to August Friedrich Gfroerer in 1831. Moore laments that this practice was still not firmly entrenched by his day (1921). See George Foot Moore, 'Christian Writers on Judaism,' *HTR* 14 (1921): 197-254, esp. 222-27.

16. Nickelsburg especially complains about using the polemical NT passages to historically understand the Pharisees (*Ancient Judaism and Christian Origins*, 5, 164-65).

17. Sanders is typical, 'I take the sources for studying Paul to be the seven letters

that Paul wrote some or all of the Deutero-Paul books, do not include these books in a substantial way in the argument because the vast majority of critical scholars do not accept their Pauline authorship.[18]Similarly, many anti-NPP authors also only substantively include the 'authentic' Paul books in their argument.[19]

I have included in Chapter 4 a special emphasis on the Deutero-Paul books because of their relative neglect related to the New Perspective issue. In my view, Paul did write all thirteen epistles attributed to him in the NT. However, even if a scholar does not believe that Paul wrote the Deutero-Paul books, he would have to agree that the writers of these books lived in the first century A.D. and were purportedly presenting the views of a Jewish man, albeit a Christian Jew. Therefore, even with the assumption that Paul did not write these books, the views in them are floating around the first century A.D. in Pauline circles and maybe even non-Christian Jewish circles. Also, critical scholars from their perspective should further agree that the Deutero-Paul books are an interpretation of Paul's views on 'works,' and it should be useful to determine what those close to Paul thought he said, even if they were wrong in their interpretation.

INCLUDE LXX, TARGUMS, ETC.?

Are there other Jewish writings in addition to the ones mentioned above that may shed light on Second Temple Judaism? Yes, but

---

whose authenticity is unquestioned: Romans, I and II Corinthians, Galatians, Philippians, I Thessalonians, and Philemon' (*Paul and Palestinian Judaism*, 431). Similarly, see Magnus Zetterholm, *Approaches to Paul: A Student's Guide to Recent Scholarship* (Minneapolis: Fortress, 2009), 30.

18. James D. G. Dunn has a slightly nuanced view as he includes Second Thessalonians as authentic (*The Theology of Paul the Apostle* [Grand Rapids: Eerdmans, 1998], 13 n. 39).

19. For example, Stephen Westerholm, *Perspectives Old and New on Paul: The 'Lutheran' Paul and His Critics* (Grand Rapids: Eerdmans, 2004), 263 n. 3; Cornelis P. Venema, *The Gospel of Free Acceptance in Christ: An Assessment of the Reformation and 'New Perspectives' on Paul* (Carlisle: Banner of Truth, 2006); and Francis Watson, *Paul and the Hermeneutics of Faith* (London: T & T Clark, 2004).

the impact of these is slight for our subject, and this book does has space limitations! Writings included here would be the LXX, a 250–150 B.C. Greek translation of the Hebrew OT. The LXX translation choices occasionally give insight into the thinking of the Jewish translators. Another source is the Targums. They are Aramaic translations/expansions of the Hebrew OT. Possibly, these were begun during the Babylonian exile.[20] Unfortunately, the vast majority of extant targums are assumed to be very late.[21] Also included would be the Elephantine papyri. These Aramaic writings, primarily letters and contracts, are from a fifth-century B.C. Jewish colony on the Egyptian island of Elephantine in the Nile River.[22] Another group would be the letters (written in Hebrew, Aramaic, and Greek) associated with the leaders of the Bar Kochba revolt in A.D. 132–35 (Bar Kochba, 'the son of the star,' was the name given to the leader of the revolt, Simon bar Kosiba). This was a Jewish revolt against the Roman rule in Judea.[23] Finally, some believe that

---

20. Among the DSS, Targums from two books were found, a several-chapter long section of Job and a few verses from Leviticus. Although, these Aramaic translations do not match later Targums in that they do not include the expansions that are so prevalent in the later, traditional Targums.

21. Craig A. Evans agrees to the lateness of the extant targums but does argue that 'the [extant] targums do preserve some tradition that dates to, and possibly before, the time of the NT' (*Noncanonical Writings and New Testament Interpretation* [Peabody: Hendrickson, 1992], 98). Paul V. M. Flesher and Bruce Chilton have fairly early dating. They date *Targum Onqelos*, the Palestinian Targums, and *Targum Pseudo Jonathan* as A.D. 150, 200, and 450, respectively. Flesher and Chilton also believe some of the expansions in the Targums do preserve first-century A.D. exegesis (*The Targums: A Critical Introduction* [Waco: Baylor University Press, 2011], 159, 404).

22. For a summary of the Elephantine writings, see Bezalel Porten, 'Elephantine Papyri,' *ABD*, 2:445-55.

23. On the surface, one would think that the Bar Kochba letters would provide useful information for our study. Especially given that Rabbinic literature does mention this revolt, including the horrible destruction of Bethar (e.g., *b. Gittin* 57a-58a). However, 'the letters for the most part concern relatively trivial matters' (Michael O. Wise, 'Bar Kokhba Letters,' *ABD*, 1:601-6, esp. 602).

the Jewish mysticism (Kabbalah) of the middle ages may contain speculations that extend back to Second Temple Judaism.[24]

Do the early church fathers shed light on first-century Judaism? To some degree they do, but for this study, the early church fathers will be used sparingly.

METHODOLOGY RELATED TO DATING PROBLEMS

How have the dating difficulties of many of the writings in the OT Pseudepigrapha, Apocrypha, DSS, and Rabbinic literature been handled in this study? How can documents of uncertain dating be used to determine views of first-century A.D. Judaism? Here, I am not talking about the writings of the NT, Philo, and Josephus.

All agree that in the past both Christian and Jewish scholarship simply combined pieces of information in similar Jewish writings without first intrepreting any of the individual documents on their own terms. This resulted in many over-statements such as 'Apocalyptic Judaism believes this' or 'Rabbinic Judaism has this view.'[25] While today this global mistake is rare, in current scholarship there is still significant disagreement as to how well we can date documents or date layers within a document to make accurate historical conclusions about the first century A.D.

The continuum of this scholarly disagreement depends partly on which group of literary writings is being examined. As mentioned above, the most extreme difference relates to the use of Rabbinic literature. This disagreement extends from no confidence to do this at all at the one end to a fair amount of confidence given the right historical-critical tools at the other.[26] Although not as extreme as

---

24. The 'early' books, *Sefer Yezirah* (third to sixth century A.D.?) and *3 Enoch* (fifth to sixth century A.D.?), are in this mystic tradition. For a sympathetic explanation of Jewish mysticism, see Isidore Epstein, *Judaism: A Historical Presentation* (New York: Penguin, 1990 [1950]), 223-51.

25. H. L. Strack and P. Billerbeck (*Kommentar zum Neuen Testament aus Talmud und Midrasch* [6 vols.; Munich: Beck, 1922-61]) is usually presented as exhibit 'A.'

26. E.g, Brad H. Young and Jacob Neusner are at the two ends of the spectrum.

the Rabbinic literature, scholars still disagree over the methodology of going from an individual document to a conclusion about the larger group for the OT Pseudepigrapha, Apocrypha, and the DSS. Since Philo and Josephus are individuals and the dating is good, there is not much disagreement.

From my perspective relative to the purpose of this study, I prefer to deal with most difficulties in dating by concentrating first on the theological views of individual Jewish books. That is, as I evaluate a document, my primary conclusion is that such-and-such a Jewish document presents such-and-such a theological view. Only after this document-specific evaluation do I compare and contrast this to views of other Jewish documents and Paul. This comparison is potentially useful without necessarily concluding whether the view actually existed in the first century A.D. or whether Paul himself actually interacted with the view. (Of course, some theological views are so pervasive across all types of Jewish literature that one can safely assume Paul was aware of it.) On the other hand, it is also important to remember the tentativeness of much of the dating because the comparisons, while interesting, may not be necessarily valuable to determining the views of Paul's opponents.

To restate my methodology, I will note a specific Jewish document's theological views along with the best guess of its dating. No matter the dating, it is potentially useful to compare and contrast with other Jewish writings and Paul.

My methodology is opposed to making conclusions by combining pieces of information from several documents supposedly written at approximately the same time or combining pieces of information from documents supposedly written from the same Jewish party. Even if others disagree with me as to the extent of the dating problems, I assume that all can agree that it is useful to tie specific theological views to a specific book. In fact, I have

---

Young has a high view of confidence in the Rabbinic literature to inform us about Jesus' parables. Jacob Neusner thinks that Young's views are virtual 'gibberish.' See Brad H. Young, *The Parables: Jewish Tradition and Christian Interpretation* (Peabody: Hendrickson, 1998) and Jacob Neusner, *Rabbinic Literature and the New Testament*, 188.

my own prejudices as to which Jewish books better represent the first century A.D., but for the purpose of this study, I do not need to invoke these. My methodology does not solve all difficulties, but I believe it is prudent given scholarship's current low level of certainty of dating for so many of the Jewish written documents. I am not unique here; many are following this general strategy for Second Temple Judaism studies.[27]

Since a major aspect of Sanders' view is the uniformity of covenant nomism, my methodology of emphasizing individual documents works well as I only need to show a lack of uniformity at the document level. I do not need to show that large groups, such as Hellenistic Judaism, are works righteousness oriented—this would involve many historical and dating assumptions.

SUMMARY OF LITERARY SOURCES CONSIDERED FOR THIS STUDY

To sum up this section, several groups of literary sources will be considered in order to aid us in understanding Second Temple Judaism, and more specifically, first-century A.D. Judaism. These sources are the OT Pseudepigrapha, the Apocrypha, the DSS Scrolls, the NT, and Rabbinic Literature. Also included are the writings of two individuals, Philo and Josephus.

VARIEGATED JUDAISM: PARTIES AND MOVEMENTS

It is now common in scholaship to emphasize that Second Temple Judaism included several Judaisms.[28] The current scholarly terminology is 'variegated' Judaism. Before looking more closely at the writings in the subsequent section, it is helpful to review some

---

27. E.g., S. Mason, 'Theologies and Sects, Jewish,' *DNTB*, 1221-30.

28. Jacob Neusner, William S. Green, and Ernst Frerichs, eds., *Judaisms and Their Messiahs at the Turn of the Christian Era* (Cambridge: CUP, 1987). At the other end of the spectrum emphasizing one Judaism with variations rather than Judaisms is E. P. Sanders (*Paul and Palestinian Judaism* [Minneapolis: Fortress, 1977]).

parties (e.g., Pharisees) and some movements (e.g., Hellenistic Judaism). This will give additional context to the writings. Also, the review will give the reader a sense of the level of certainty, or lack of it, that scholarship has about these parties and movements. Since NPP authors are making assertions about the character and theology of Second Temple Judaism, noting this uncertainty is useful especially if a reader of NPP material is not aware of it. Because of the uncertainty, I will make a special effort to cite and/or enumerate the available primary sources so that the reader himself can appreciate the various levels of confidence in the conclusions below. In the descriptions below, I will *not* include details about grace and works as that was the subject of Chapters 2 and 3.

RELIABILITY OF SOURCES TO DETERMINE PARTIES AND MOVEMENTS

Much of scholarship is moving toward less confidence in the former scholarly conclusions about parties and movements. This less-confidence trend is partially due to the general academic trend in all disciplines to distrust outsider's views of insiders. Dovetailing with this is another general academic trend to assume that most authors significantly twist historical information to fit the their point of view ('hermeneutics of suspicion'). A final trend is that many scholars now have a lower view of the historical accuracy of the NT than in the past.

It is true that much of the primary-source information for first-century A.D. parties and movements is from authors who are 'outsiders.' For example, for some scholars, Josephus' comments about Sadducees are suspect because (1) he is not a Sadducee and (2) he is biased to present a Jewish-Hellenistic priestly-aristocratic historian's view to a Roman audience.

Another factor that engenders less confidence is the realization that in the past many of the dating problems were simply ignored. For example, classic Rabbinic documents, which are all written post-A.D. 200, were assumed by some to always provide information relevant to first-century A.D. Pharisees.

A final factor interrelated with the dating problem is the current assumption that each party or movement in the Second Temple period was probably not monolithic during the same time frame and/ or through time. For example, to combine pieces of information from two apocalyptic books with debatable dating is potentially misleading.

I appreciate the above problems, but overall I have more confidence in some of the older conclusions than many others do. First of all, I consider the NT information as infallible. This gives me in many instances, but not all, a yard stick by which to measure the information in other sources. For non-canonical sources, yes, I do share some of the suspicions. However, once knowing an author's biases and some pertinent NT information, I have some confidence in using a source. The related problems of dating and monolithic assumptions are real.

PARTIES

A list of parties in Second Temple Judaism includes the Pharisees, Sadducees, Essenes, Zealots, Therapeutae, Herodians, Samaritans, 'Fourth Philosophy,' Sicarii, and the Qumran community. It is assumed that there are probably more parties; we just do not have information on them. Most of the information we have about the known parties is limited and comes from 'outsiders.' The large exception to this is the Qumran community. A second exception is the Pharisees as the Rabbinic material is closely tied to them.

Having an understanding of the size and influence of these parties is difficult. One gets a sense that the parties are relatively small groups with firm convictions, and that the majority of Jews do not belong to a specific party.[29] At least for first-century A.D. Palestine, Josephus and Hippolytus emphasize three parties: the Pharisees, Sadducees, and the Essenes. The NT emphasizes the Pharisees and Sadducees. Josephus explicitly states that the Pharisees have the most influence on the multitudes, and the NT implies this also.[30]

---

29. Bauckham agrees, although he is more firm in his conviction than I am. 'The vast majority of Jews, both in Palestine and in the Diaspora, did not adhere to such a group and did not think of themselves as following any particular interpretation of Judaism. They were just Jews' (*The Jewish World Around the New Testament*, 177).

30. B. D. Chilton believes that there was a 'radical pluralization of Judaism'

As the differences between the parties are emphasized below, it is helpful to remember that the vast majority of Jews of the first century A.D. did have much in common. They were monotheistic and believed that God spoke through the OT (or only Pentateuch). The majority practiced circumcision and some level of both Sabbath observance and food laws. At their best, they had an ethical code centered on the ten commandments. Idolatry was especially hated by most. Of course, there were probably also ethnic Jews in the Diaspora who were 'no longer remembering a single one of their ancient usages.'[31]

The conclusions presented below are fairly traditional. As stated above, some scholars are losing confidence in many of these older, traditional conclusions.

Pharisees

Our information about the Pharisees come from the NT,[32] Josephus,[33] the Church father Hippolytus (ca. A.D. 170–230),[34] and implications from the Rabbinic literature. The NT and Hippolytus are clearly outsiders. Although Josephus calls himself a Pharisee,[35] most scholars consider Josephus an outsider because his literary perspective is that of a Hellenistic historian. The Rabbinic literature has continuity with the Pharisees, but it is not Pharisaical literature per se.[36]

---

beginning 167 B.C. and the largest party was the Pharisees ('Judaism,' *DJG*, 398-405, esp. 401).

31. Philo, *On the Life of Moses* 1:31.

32. Pharisees are mentioned many places in the NT; some of the significant passages include Matt. 3:7, 5:20, 15:1-2, 23:13, 27:62, Mark 2:16, 8:15, 12:13, Luke 5:17, 11:37-43, 12:1, 15:2, 18:11, John 3:1, 7:32, 9:16, 11:47, 12:42, 18:3, Acts 5:34, 15:5, 23:6-8, 26:5, and Phil. 3:5.

33. See Josephus, *Ant.* 13 § 171-72, 13 § 288-98, 18 §11-15; *J.W.* 2 § 119, 162-66.

34. Hippolytus, *The Refutation of All Heresies* 9:13, 23 (*ANF*, 5:134, 137). Many discount Hippolytus as simply being dependent on Josephus and the NT.

35. Josephus claims that at age sixteen as a trial, he joined in succession the Pharisees, the Sadducees, and the Essenes. After the trial, he decided to become a Pharisee (*The Life*, 9-12).

36. Connecting the Pharisees to the Rabbinic literature is not straightforward. The Rabbinic literature does not mention the term 'Pharisees,' but does occasionally mention the term *perushim*, which probably refers to Pharisees (*m. Yadayim* 4:6-7, *t. Shabbat* 1:15). The writers of this literature do not

Bracketing out the question of the Pharisees' views of works righteousness, my view of the Pharisees is the older, traditional, scholarly consensus.[37] Most scholars believe that the Pharisees descended from the Hasidim, who were the primary supporters of the Maccabean revolt (166–160 B.C., 1 Macc. 2:42, 7:13, 2 Macc. 14:6). However, by the time of the first century A.D., the Pharisees did not seem to have political aspirations.

The Pharisees had an explicitly religious goal of having Jews follow the written law (OT) *and* the oral law (views of 'fathers'[38]). The oral law was the wisdom of various rabbis and presumably originated from oral statements by Moses (*m. Abot* 1:1, *m. Eduyyot* 8:7). The oral law took on more and more authority, and in many ways, the oral law in practice became greater than the written law.[39] Part of Pharisees' interpretative program through the oral law allowed modifications and nuances to the written law (and older, existing oral law) so that all the law (both written and oral) was still applicable

---

consider themselves to be, at least by name, the Pharisee/*Perushim* party. Sometimes the Rabbinic literature even mentions the *perushim* negatively (e.g., *m. Sotah* 3:4, *b. Sotah* 22b). On the other hand, several sages/rabbis who are otherwise known as Pharisees (e.g., Hillel, Shammai, Gamaliel) are positively mentioned in the Rabbinic literature.

37. This is similar to standard introductions by Helmut Koester, *History, Culture, and Religion of the Hellenistic Age*, vol. 1 of *Introduction to the New Testament* (2d ed.; New York: Walter de Gruyter, 1995), 227-30; Eduard Lohse, *The New Testament Environment* (trans. John E. Steely; Nashville: Abingdon, 1976), 77-83; Everett Ferguson, *Backgrounds of Early Christianity* (3d ed.; Grand Rapids: Eerdmans, 2003), 514-19; Bart D. Ehrman, *The New Testament: A Historical Introduction to the Early Christian Writings* (4th ed.; New York, OUP, 2008); and Menahem Mansoor, 'Pharisees,' *EncJud*, 13:363-66. However, there is currently a movement spearheaded by Neusner to question the confidence in the above Pharisaic picture because of the unreliability of the sources. See Jacob Neusner, *Rabbinic Tradition About the Pharisees Before 70* (3 vols.; Leiden: E. J. Brill, 1971); and an in-between view by Steve Mason, 'Pharisees,' *DNTB*, 782-87. Also see Jacob Neusner and Bruce D. Chilton, eds., *In Quest of the Historical Pharisees* (Waco: Baylor University Press, 2007). This volume does not seek to synthesize the data.

38. Josephus, *Ant.* 13 § 297; Hippolytus, *The Refutation of All Heresies* 9:23 (*ANF*, 5:137).

39. 'A more strict rule applies to the teaching of scribes than to the teachings of Torah' (*m. Sanhedrin* 11:3). Also see *b. Baba Metzi'a* 33a.

to any changing circumstances. Also, according to the Pharisees, certain requirements in the written law simply needed to be clarified no matter the circumstances (e.g., technicalities of tithes). This was done with oral laws. Another aspect of the oral law was to 'make a fence for the Torah.'[40] That is, the oral was sometimes purposely stricter than the written law to ensure that the written law was not violated. Jesus complained that some of the Pharisaical 'traditions of the elders' (oral law) actually violated the written OT (Mark 7:5-13).

The Pharisees believed in the immortality of the soul and the resurrection of the body. Josephus (and Hippolytus) is especially interested to tell us that they have a half-way view between fate and human responsibility (Josephus, *Ant.* 13 § 172).

The Pharisees included lay people, lawyers, scribes, and priests. They often came together for meals so that they could more easily observe various purity commandments. Apparently, they pressed that many of the OT purity laws for priests should apply to all. Josephus indicates that the Pharisees had sway over a significant portion of the Jewish masses (*Ant.* 13 § 288, 298, 18 § 16-17).

Sadducees

The primary sources for the Sadducees come from the NT,[41] Josephus,[42] Hippolytus,[43] and explicit references in the Rabbinic material.[44] All of this information is from outsiders. Most of it

---

40. *m. Abot* 1:1, 3:13. For an example application, see *m. Berakhot* 1:1.

41. There are less references to the Sadducees than to the Pharisees in the NT. The NT Sadducees references may be grouped into three: (1) Sadducees and Pharisees against Jesus without distinguishing the two parties (Matt. 3:7, 16:1, 6, 11-12), (2) Sadducees do not believe in the resurrection (Matt. 22:23, 24, Mark 12:18, Luke 20:27, Acts 23:6-8), (3) Sadducees connected to the Temple and High Priest (Acts 4:1, 5:17).

42. See Josephus, *Ant.* 13 § 171, 173, 13 § 293-97, 18 § 11, 16-17; and *J.W.* 2 § 119, 164-66.

43. Hippolytus, *The Refutation of All Heresies* 9:13, 24 (*ANF*, 5:134, 137).

44. Sadducees are referenced occasionally in Rabbinic literature, e.g., *m. Makkot* 1:6, *m. YADayim* 4:6-7, *m. Niddah* 4:2, *t.* Niddah 5:2-3, *t. Hagigah* 3:35, b. *Sanhedrin* 33b, 52b, *b. Niddah* 33b, *Sipre Numbers* 112:4. Gary

reflects points at which others disagree with the Sadducees. My view of the Sadducees presented below is the older, traditional scholarly consensus.[45]

The name Sadducees is probably related to the priestly name of Zadok or to 'righteous ones.' The Sadducees appear to be attached to the Temple. Their ranks include many priests and members of the aristocracy. Possibly they arose around 200 B.C. when the old Zadokite priestly-line ended. The Sadducees lost most of their influence after the Temple destruction in A.D. 70.

Several of the primary sources tell us the Sadducees did not believe in the bodily resurrection. Josephus tells us that they believed that one's soul ceased existence at death, and that God has no providential control over the humans and the world (*Ant.* 13 § 173, 18 § 16). There is no judgement for deeds, either good or evil. In the Rabbinic material, the Sadducees and the Pharisees differ on application of the purity laws. Several sources indicate that the Sadducees only accepted the written Law (or only the Torah) as opposed to the Pharisees with their high view of their oral law in addition to the written OT.[46]

G. Porton notes that 'in many instances the word "Sadducees" in later rabbinic texts [Babylonian Talmud and later] proves to be ambiguous, the intended reference in some contexts being to "heretics" and "gentiles" (i.e., Christians) in avoidance of medieval censors' ('Sadducees,' *ABD*, 5:892-95, esp. 892).

45. I am in substantial agreement with Helmut Koester, *History, Culture, and Religion of the Hellenistic Age*, 217-19; Eduard Lohse, *The New Testament Environment*, 74-77; Everett Ferguson, *Backgrounds of Early Christianity*, 519-20; Epstein, *Judaism: A Historical Presentation*, 96-100; and Ehrman, *The New Testament: A Historical Introduction to the Early Christian Writings*, 47-48. For a view that is more skeptical of the traditional view, see Porton, 'Sadducees,' ABD, 5:892-95.

46. E.g, Josephus, *Ant.* 13 § 297. Josephus never explicitly says that the Sadducees only believed in the Pentateuch as opposed to the entire OT; however, Hippolytus explicitly does say that the Sadducees only believed in the Pentateuch (Hippolytus, *The Refutation of All Heresies* 9:24 [*ANF*, 5:137]). F. F. Bruce believes that the Sadducees believed the entire OT, and that Hippolytus misunderstood Josephus (*New Testament History* [New York: Doubleday, 1980], 150).

Essenes and Qumran Community

The Essenes are explicitly mentioned by Philo,[47] Pliny the Elder,[48] Josephus,[49] and Hippolytus.[50] Since much of what these authors say matches to the practices of the Qumran Community as represented in the DSS,[51] most scholars believe that the Qumran community was the center of the Essene community even though the name 'Essenes' is not found in the DSS.[52] The Essenes are not mentioned in either the NT or the Rabbinic literature.

I will assume that the Essenes and the Qumran Community are the same. For the purposes of this book, nothing depends on whether the Essenes are a similar group to the Qumran Community or the same group. As opposed to the Pharisee and Sadducee descriptions, there is much more of a scholarly consensus on the Essenes. My brief description below is the standard scholarly view.[53] More will be said about the Qumran Community later in this chapter at the DSS section.

---

47. Philo, *That Every Good Man is Free* § 75-91; and *Hypothetica* 11 § 1-18.

48. Pliny the Elder, *Natural History* § 5.15.73, written in A.D. 77. Pliny is giving the geography of Palestine and mentions the Essenes (*Esseni*, Latin) in conjunction with his description of the Dead Sea. He says that the Essene community 'has no women and has renounced all sexual desire, has no money, and has only palm-trees for company' ([trans. H. Rackham; LCL 2; Cambridge, Mass.; Harvard University Press, 1969], 277).

49. Josephus, *Ant.* 13 § 171, 15 § 371-79, 18 § 18-22; and *J.W.* 2 § 119-161, 3 § 11.

50. Hippolytus, *The Refutation of All Heresies* 9:13, 22 (*ANF*, 5:134-37).

51. Especially 1QS and CD.

52. Nickelsburg agrees that the Qumran community is Essene; however, he believes it helpful to realize that there is not a complete overlap of religious practices in the DSS and information about the Essenes in Josephus and Hippolytus. Thus he suggests in 'the interest of clarity, ... rather than use the term "Essene" broadly and generically, it might be helpful to distinguish between Qumran belief and practice, as attested by the Scrolls, and Essene belief and practice, as attested by secondary sources' (*Ancient Judaism and Christian Sources*, 172).

53. For the standard view, see Todd Beall, 'Essenes,' *DNTB*, 342-48; Koester, *History, Culture, and Religion of the Hellenistic Age*, 223-30; and Geza Vermes, *The Dead Sea Scrolls: Qumran in Perspective* (collaboration with Pamela Vermes; rev. ed.; Philadelphia: Fortress, 1981), 87-130.

The Essenes began approximately 150 B.C. and probably ended near A.D. 100 with the A.D. 70 destruction of Jerusalem being the catalyst to their demise. Apparently, the group included two variations. One which was at Qumran and was male-only. The other variation was spread in villages throughout Palestine and could marry. Qumran was the headquarters for the two groups.

To join, one had to go through a probationary time (one year) and give one's possessions to the group. The Essenes were very ascetic as to their clothing and food. Their daily routine included prayers, washings, and menial labor. The DSS library shows that they were interested in studying the OT and other Jewish writings. The community was at odds with the current priestly line in Jerusalem during the first century A.D. because the current priests were not Zadokite. There was a significant priestly presence in the community. Philo mentions that there were 4,000 Essenes.[54]

The Essenes saw themselves as the true people of God as opposed to other Jewish parties. They were living near the end of time and interpreted eschatological biblical texts as referring to themselves. The Essenes had a higher view of God's providence than the Sadducees and Pharisees. They also had a significant dualistic tendency (e.g., Sons of Light versus Sons of Darkness). The Essenes were very interested in God's final judgment. Josephus notes that they believe in the immortality of the soul (*Ant.* 18 § 18). Hippolytus adds they believe in a bodily resurrection (*The Refutation of All Heresies* 9:22). However, the DSS are not as clear on either point.

Therapeutae

Philo discusses the group called the Therapeutae (θεραπεύω means 'to heal' or 'to serve').[55] They are so named because they are 'healers' of men's souls. Except for Eusebius (see below), the Therapeutae are not mentioned in any other early extant documents.

---

54. Philo, *Every Good Man is Free* § 75.

55. Philo, *On the Contemplative Life*.

Philo notes that the Therapeutae are a monastic group that lived alone in individual dwellings at a lake (Mareotic) near Alexandria, Egypt. Before joining the group, they gave their possessions to their families. They led a very ascetic lifestyle that was more extreme than the Essenes. On the Sabbath, they did meet together, both men and women. Philo says nothing explicit about their theology. He does say that they study the OT and other 'writings of ancient men.' Philo notes that they favor allegorical interpretations (*On the Contemplative Life* 29).

Philo explicitly contrasts the Essenes with the Therapeutae. The Essenes follow a 'practical course of life,' and the Therapeutae, a 'speculative life' (*On the Contemplative Life* 1). Some scholars believe that the Therapeutae are a branch of the Essenes of Judea, and others see no connection.[56] Either way, the existence of the Therapeutae is further evidence of variegated Judaism in the first century A.D.

The famous church historian, Eusebius, quotes and discusses Philo's description of the Therapeutae (*Ecclesiastical History* 2.17, written in A.D. 323). Eusebius argues that most likely the Therapeutae are (monastic) Christians. The 'writings of ancient men' that they studied were the writings of the NT apostles, and Philo did not use the term 'Christian' because it had not yet become common. Modern scholars believe Eusebius is mistaken in his identification of Therapeutae as Christians.

Zealots, Sicarii, 'Fourth Philosophy'

Josephus mentions 'Zealots,' the 'fourth philosophy,' and the 'Sicarii.' Scholars divide on whether Josephus presents these three as the same one group spanning from A.D. 6–74 or three different groups.[57] Part of the confusion is due to 'zealot/jealous'

---

56. In favor of a connection, see G. Vermes, 'Essenes and Therapeutai,' *RQ* 3 (1962): 495-504. Against a connection, see Joan E. Taylor and Philip R. Davies, 'The So-Called Therapeutae of *De Vita Contemplativa*,' *HTR* 91 (1998): 3-24.

57. In favor of one group, Bruce, *New Testament History*, 93-97. In favor of separate groups, R. Horsley, 'The Zealots: Their Origin, Relationships and

being used in two overlapping ways. (1) 'Zealot' was used as the official name of a party that wanted to overthrow Roman rule by force. (2) 'Zealot' was the semi-technical epithet of a person who was unusually 'zealous' for God's honor and laws, including the senses of being martyred, and/or actively committing violence, and/or actively doing non-violent good works. This second use has its fountain head in Phinehas (Num. 25:11-13) and is found often in Jewish and Christian literature (e.g., 1 Kings 19:10, 14, 1 Macc. 2:19-26, 54, 58, Jdt. 9:2-4, Sir. 45:23, 48:2, *2 Bar.* 66:5, Acts 21:20, 22:3, Gal. 1:14, Phil. 3:6, *m. Sanhedrin* 9:6).

In Josephus, the Zealots are clearly a party that fought against the Romans in A.D. 67–70. Josephus possibly implies that the Zealot party began in A.D. 6(?) under Judas the Galilean (Acts 5:37) as he protested the Roman imposition of a tax. The 'Sicarii,' so named for a type of dagger, were bandits who stealthily murdered in large crowds. They were against the Romans and plundered Jews who did not agree with them. They fought against the Romans and were the group that died at Masada in A.D. 74. Josephus tells us nothing explicitly about the theology of the Zealots or the Sicarii, unless one assumes they are connected to the 'fourth philosophy.'

Josephus connects the above Judas the Galilean to the 'fourth philosophy.' (The other three philosophies are the Pharisees, Sadducees, and Essenes.) He reports that this philosophy is similar to the Pharisees except that they have a strong attachment to liberty. The core of the philosophy is that only God is to be the Ruler and Lord of the Jews. The specific Roman offense that prompted Judas to incite a revolt in A.D. 6(?) was taxation.

The NT mentions the Apostle Simon the Zealot (Matt. 10:4, Mark 3:18, Luke 6:15, Acts 1:13). Apparently, 'the Zealot' is added

---

Importance in the Jewish Revolt,' *NovT* 28 (1986): 159-92. The key Josephus passages are *Ant.* 18 § 4-9, 23-25, 20 § 185-88; and *J.W.* 2 § 118, 4 § 160-61, 7 § 252-53. Hippolytus claims that the Essenes subdivided into four groups. One group is called either the Zealots or Sicarii; another group is clearly the 'fourth philosophy' described by Josephus even though Hippolytus does not use that term (*The Refutation of All Heresies* 9:21 [*ANF*, 5:136]).

in context to distinguish him from Simon Peter.[58] Here 'zealot' means either the official revolutionary Zealot party, assuming the party existed in approximately A.D. 30, or the semi-technical sense of one zealous for God's honor.

Herodians

Outside of the Gospels, there is no mention of a party named the Herodians.[59] The Gospels mention the 'Herodians' three times (Matt. 22:16, Mark 3:6, 12:13; some manuscripts include 'Herodians' in Mark 8:15). In the three verses, the Pharisees and Herodians are distinguished but are acting together against Jesus. By the name, it is evident that the Herodians are a party that favor the Herodian dynasty ruling Judea, and more specifically favor Herod Antipas.

Because of the associations with Herod, probably the Sadducees and Herodians had much in common politically. An interesting parallel exists between Matt. 16:6 and Mark 8:15. Jesus warns His disciples of the 'leaven of the Pharisees and *Sadducees*' in Matt. 16:6 and of the 'leaven of the Pharisees and *the leaven of Herod*' (some manuscripts, Herodians) in Mark 8:15. Although this parallel does not prove it, it is suggestive of some type of similarity between the Sadducees and Herodians.[60]

The NT tells us nothing about the theology of the Herodians. We can only make assumptions based on their name and that they were against Jesus. The Herodians are another example of variegated Judaism in the first century A.D.

Samaritans

The Samaritans were known for believing that proper worship of the OT God should occur at Mt. Gerizim, not Jerusalem. (Mt.

---

58. In Luke 6:15 and Acts 1:13, ζηλωτής is translated as Zealot. In Matt. 10:4 and Mark 3:18, καναναῖος is used. The Greek καναναῖος is a transliteration of the Aramaic קַנְאָנָא, which is similar to the Hebrew קַנָּאָה, which is used for 'jealous/zealous' related to Phinehas in Num. 25:11.

59. Josephus does not use the term 'Herodians,' but does mention group(s) that favored Herod (*Ant.* 14 § 450, *J.W.* 1 § 319).

60. For further discussion, see Harold W. Hoehner, 'Herodians,' *ISBE*, 2:698.

Gerizim is seven miles from Samaria, near ancient Shechem.) Jewish sources consider the Samaritans ethnically 'half-Jewish' at best. On the other hand, late Samaritan sources disagree and describe themselves as direct descendants from the tribes of Ephraim and Manaseh who survived the Assyrian destruction of northern Israel in 722 B.C.[61]

There are many references to the Samaritans in the NT,[62] Josephus,[63] and Rabbinic literature.[64] The Samaritans are also mentioned in Sir. 50:25-26 and 2 Macc. 5:22, 6:2; they are probably alluded to in *T. Levi* 5-7 and *Jub.* 30. These are all 'outsider' references, and most are antagonistic, excepting the NT. The only early 'insider' Samaritan sources are the Samaritan Pentateuch, written approximately 100 B.C., and the fourth-century B.C. Wadi Daliyeh Papyri that is related to selling slaves. Late Samaritan religious sources include the *Sayings of Marqah* (ca. A.D. 350) and the *Great Chronicle* by Abu'l-Fath (A.D. 1350).

In 2 Kings 17, the Assyrian king places various non-Jewish people in the Samaritan region and exiles the existing Jewish people. It is assumed that not all Jewish people left; hence, over time because of intermarriage, there would be some percentage of Jewish blood in the Samaritan descendants (see also Ezra 4). Josephus and the Rabbinic sources view the Samaritans of the first century A.D. as directly related to the events of 2 Kings 17, and they conclude that

---

61. For a comprehensive discussion of the Samaritans, see Robert T. Anderson and Terry Giles, *The Keepers: An Introduction to the History and Culture of the Samaritans* (Peabody: Hendrickson, 2002).

62. For important references, see Matt. 10:5-6, Luke 9:52, 10:33, 17:11-18, John 4:4-26, Acts 1:8, 8:14-17, 9:31, 15:3. Although a minority view, some scholars believe that there are implicit appeals to the Samaritans in John 4, Stephen's speech (Acts 7:37, 48-50), and the book of Hebrews (for a brief survey, see R. T. Anderson, 'Samaritan Literature,' *DNTB*, 1052-56).

63. E.g., *Ant.* 9 § 288-91, 11 § 84-119, 174, 340-46, 12 § 257-64, 13 § 74, 255-58, 18 § 29-30, 20 § 118, *J. W.* 2 § 232.

64. E.g., *m. Gittin* 1:5, *m. Qiddushin* 4:3, *m. Niddah* 4:1-2, *t. Pesahim* 2:3, *b. Qiddushin* 74b-76a, *b. Baba Mesia* 68a, *b. Niddah* 31b, *Genesis Rabbah* 81:3, *Masseket Kutim*. Many times the Samaritans are referred to as Cuthaeans or Kuteans, which is a pejorative term relating back to 2 Kings 17:24.

the first-century A.D. Samaritans are not ethnically fully-Jewish. Jesus implies agreement with this by referring to the Samaritans as 'not of the house of Israel' (Matt. 10:5-6) and as 'foreigner[s]' (Luke 17:18).

The Samaritan Pentateuch is written in Hebrew and includes the first five books of the OT. It predominantly matches the standard Jewish Hebrew OT text. Although there are several thousand differences between the two, the vast majority of them are simply minor spelling variants. The few important differences relate to Mt. Gerizim. For example, at the end of the ten commandments (Exod. 20:1-17) in the Samaritan Pentateuch is a command for Israel to build an altar on Mt. Gerizim.[65]

All sources agree and emphasize that the Samaritans worshiped at Mt. Gerizim and not Jerusalem. For example, in John 4, the woman at the well is a Samaritan from the town of Sychar (John 4:5), which is very near Mt. Gerizim. She notes that 'our fathers worshiped on this mountain [Mt. Gerizim], but you [Jesus] say that in Jerusalem is the place where people ought to worship' (John 4:20).

In addition to the ethnic and Mt. Gerizim disagreements, tensions between the Samaritans and the Jews also emanated from the Jewish John Hyrcanus' destruction of the 200 year-old temple at Mt. Gerizim in 128 B.C. As the NT and Josephus record, tensions were so high in the first century A.D. that many Jews avoided the Samaritan area when they traveled from Galilee to Jerusalem.

The Samaritans did not believe in a bodily resurrection, only accepted the five books of Moses as authoritative, anticipated a future Mosaic/Prophetic/Messianic figure based on Deut. 18:18 (called *Taheb*, 'the one who returns' or 'the one who restores'), and gave Moses an unusually special place of honor.

Interestingly, there is still a Samaritan religious community in modern Israel that lives near (modern Nablus) and worships at Mt. Gerizim.

---

65. For an extensive discussion, see Bruce K. Waltke, 'Samaritan Pentateuch,' *ABD*, 5:932-40.

Summary of Parties

The number of parties that early sources refer to confirms that Judaism was variegated in the first century A.D. The different emphases of the parties reflects some major differences between Jews. Emphases and interests include the Temple, proper priestly line, monasticism, relationship of Roman and Jewish power structure of Palestine, wisdom of past rabbis, application of OT food and Sabbath laws, eschatology, bodily resurrection, fate/free-will, and allegorical interpretation of OT.

MOVEMENTS

In addition to specific parties, scholars also use broader labels to describe Second Temple Judaism. I use the term 'movements' to describe these broader labels. The broadest of the labels is the distinction between Palestinian Judaism and Hellenistic Judaism. Less broadly, I will include another movement termed 'Apocalypticism.' As with the parties, current scholarship is in general becoming more and more uncomfortable with the older conclusions about these movements and is moving toward less certainty.

Palestinian Judaism and Hellenistic Judaism

One would think that Palestinian Judaism would refer to Jews who live in Palestine, and that Hellenistic Judaism would refer to Jews who live in the Hellenistic areas, that is the Greco-Roman world outside of Palestine. Unfortunately, the terms 'Palestinian Judaism' and 'Hellenistic Judaism' are confusing because Hellenistic Judaism does not simply refer to geography. It also refers to language, culture, and religious views.[66] Adding to the confusion is that

---

66. The term 'Hellenistic' with a cultural/religions aspect relates to 2 Macc. 4:13. Although much of Greek literature uses the terms ἑλληνισμός/ἑλληνιστής to simply mean Greek-speaking (e.g., Acts 6:1), ἑλληνισμός is used in 2 Macc. 4:13 to refer to Greek culture and aspects of Greek religion being adopted by Jews in Palestine. In context of 2 Macc. 4:13, ἑλληνισμός is paralleled by 'foreign religion/custom' (ἀλλοφυλισμός, also see 2 Macc. 6:24). Philo uses a cognate of ἑλληνισμός to refer to Caesar transforming barbarian areas by using Greek culture (*Embassy* § 147). For a discussion of the linguistic history of ἑλληνισμός, see Martin Hengel, *The 'Hellenization' of*

many Hellenistic non-Jews and Hellenistic Jews visited and/or lived in Palestine. Also, occasionally Palestinian Jews would go out into the Greco-Roman Hellenistic world (Matt. 23:15). Another confusion is that current scholarship is disagreeing as to the extent of the differences between Hellenistic and Palestinian Judaism and whether, in fact, this distinction is useful.

The distinction between Hellenistic and Palestinian Judaism is related to this study because one of the main NPP authors, E. P. Sanders, entitled his ground-breaking book, *Paul and Palestinian Judaism*. See the '*Paul and Palestinian Judaism* and Covenantal Nomism' section in Chapter 2 for a discussion on Sanders' book and what effect, if any, his decision to limit his book to only Palestinian Judaism makes on our study.

This distinction, or lack of it, between Hellenistic and Palestinian Judaism is related to our study in another way. Many connect this distinction to their view of Paul. For some, building upon the arguments about the size of the gulf between Palestinian Judaism and Hellenistic Judaism are implications about the gulf between first-century Jewish Christians centered in Palestine and Gentile Christians who follow Paul. These two 'gulfs' are not necessarily related, but many do assume a relationship. F. C. Baur's influential theory in the 1800s is that Christian Jews from Palestine with their champion Peter had a significantly different theology than Hellenistic Christians and their champion Paul. The NT covered up these differences, especially in the book of Acts.[67] Hence for some, the more they see a gulf between Hellenistic and Palestinian Judaism, the more they tend to see two different theologies in the early Church. The Baur theory, although currently modified, still influences portions of modern critical-scholarship.[68]

Judaea in the First Century after Christ (with Christoph Markschies; Eugene: Wipf and Stock, 2003), 7-18, 22.

67. Ferdinand Christian Baur, *Paul, the Apostle of Jesus Christ: His Life and Works, His Epistles and Teachings; A Contribution to a Critical History of Primitive Christianity* (2 vols.; London: Williams & Norgate, 1873-1875; repr., Peabody: Hendrickson, 2003), 1:1-14, 1:250-52.

68. For example, Michael Goulder is pro-Baur thesis (*St. Paul versus St. Peter: A Tale of Two Missions*, Louisville: Westminster John Knox, 1994).

So what is the distinction between Hellenistic and Palestinian Judaism? Palestinian Judaism usually refers to Jews who live in Palestine and whose first language is Aramaic, the language of Palestine at the time. These Jews were consciously against many of the influences of Hellenism. Scholars disagree significantly over how well Palestinian Judaism isolated itself from Hellenism (more on this below).

Before discussing the influence of Hellenism on Jews in Palestine, first it is useful to get a standard definition of Hellenistic Judaism as it would exist in the Greco-Roman world outside of Palestine, that is, Diaspora Judaism.

Hellenistic Judaism in the Diaspora refers to Jews whose first or second language is Greek and cannot speak the language of Palestine, Aramaic. Given the Greek language, the LXX would be their Scripture. Because these Jews lived outside of Palestine, they would have more interaction with Greco-Roman culture and religions and have had to face more directly cross-cultural challenges. Hellenistic Judaism is a type of Judaism that consciously and unconsciously adopted more Hellenistic ideas and cultural trends than their

---

George Strecker sees a strong distinction between Hellenistic Judaism and Palestinian Judaism. He believes that Paul primarily lived in the Diaspora. 'The roots of the thinking of the pre-Christian Paul are accordingly to be sought in Diaspora Judaism, i.e. in the realm of Hellenistic Judaism' (*Theology of the New Testament* [ed. Friedrich Wilhelm Horn; trans. M. Eugene Boring; Louisville: Westminister John Knox, 2000], 25). Hengel believes that his view of a small distinction between Palestinian and Hellenistic Judaism should be a problem for the Baur thesis (*The 'Hellenization' of Judea*, 1-5). Nickelsburg believes that the Palestinian and Hellenistic distinction for Judaism is a 'scholarly fiction' and 'requires that we rethink the implications that New Testament exegesis has drawn from these paradigms' (*Ancient Judaism and Christian Origins*, 150-52). W. D. Davies who downplays the distinction believes this invalidates Schweitzer's mysticism work (*Paul and Rabbinic Judaism: Some Rabbinic Elements in Pauline Theology* [New York: Harper & Row, 1948], vii-xii). For a conservative response to the Baur thesis and why it tends to influence modern critical-scholarship even though most of the Baur premises are no longer believed, see Andreas J. Köstenberger and Michael J. Kruger, *The Heresy of Orthodoxy: How Contemporary Culture's Fascination with Diversity Has Reshaped Our Understanding of Early Christianity* (Wheaton: Crossway, 2010).

counterparts in Palestine. Because of the Greco-Roman culture, it is assumed that Hellenistic Judaism is more open to syncretism, Greek philosophical views, allegorical interpretation of sacred texts, pro-Roman rule, etc.[69] (Of course, it is possible that being in the Greco-Roman culture drove some Jews to become even more isolated, but that is not how the term 'Hellenistic Judaism' is used.)

One problem for defining Hellenistic Judaism of the Diaspora is that there are few Jewish texts that we are certain came from the Diaspora. In fact, we are not sure of the provenance of most of the writings of the Apocrypha and OT Pseudepigrapha—that is, Were they written in or outside of Palestine?

Josephus is hard to categorize. He lived most of his life in Palestine but wrote his books in Rome. The primary witness of the Diaspora is Philo's writings. Philo's works are the only ones where we both know the name of the author and are sure he was in the Diaspora. Philo's works certainly show one trying to integrate Greek philosophy and the allegorical method with the OT.

Another witness to Diaspora Judaism is the OT Pseudepigraphic *Sibylline Oracles*.[70] These apocalyptic texts in Greek poetic style parallel the pagan versions of sibylline oracles. The Jewish *Sibylline Oracles* were written probably between the second century B.C. and the seventh century A.D. and our current version includes Christian interpolations. The *Sibylline Oracles* are supposedly written by different women, all named Sybil, of whom the first was a daughter-in-law of Noah (*Sib. Or.* Prologue 33, 1.289, 3.827). As in the pagan versions, each Sybil was an old prophetess who predicts future events. The use of this essentially pagan form by portions of Hellenistic Judaism (and early Christianity) is shocking.

Other likely Diaspora texts include Wisdom of Solomon, 3 Maccabees, 4 Maccabees, Tobit, additions to Esther, *Joseph*

---

69. For a discussion of Hellenistic Judaism in the Diaspora, see Nikolaus Walter, 'Hellenistic Jews of the Diaspora at the Cradle of Primitive Christianity,' in *The New Testament and Hellenistic Judaism* (ed. Peder Borgen and Søren Giversen; Peabody: Hendrickson, 1997), 37-58, esp. 41-51.

70. See J. J. Collins, *The Sibylline Oracles of Egyptian Judaism* (SBLDS 13; Missoula: Scholars, 1974).

and Aseneth, the *Testament of Abraham,* and the *Testament of Job.* 4 Maccabees is most likely a first-century A.D. Jewish text. It definitely is influenced by some type of stoic philosophical influence. The first verse is 'The subject that I am about to discuss is most philosophical, that is, whether devout reason is sovereign over the emotions' (4 Macc. 1:1). The *Testament of Abraham,* possibly written in Egypt c. A.D. 100, includes a final judgment of deeds that does not seem to distinguish between Gentile and Jew and never refers to any specific Jewish ceremonial laws.

The apocryphal text, the Wisdom of Solomon, is most likely from the Diaspora. In form, it is similar to Prov. 1–9 (Wis. 1–5) and Pss. 103–5 (Wis. 10–19). Its emphasis on 'wisdom' does not necessarily mean it is influenced by Hellenistic ideas (as the OT uses this motif), but its use may reflect a desire to compare and contrast Hellenistic wisdom with God's wisdom.

These Diaspora texts easily evidence that at some level Hellenistic ideas influenced Jews living in the Diaspora during the Second Temple period. On the other hand, most of the Rabbinic material was written at least in its final form by Jews living outside of Palestine, post A.D. 200. This shows that a 'more conservative' type of Palestinian Judaism could exist outside of Palestine in the Greco-Roman world.[71]

What about Hellenistic influences on Jews living in Palestine? First, it is noted that many Hellenistic cultural factors existed in Palestine during Second Temple Judaism. 2 Maccabees speaks of Greek gymnasiums and a Greek way of life (2 Macc. 4:9-14). Many coins and Jewish ossuaries (bone burial boxes) have been found with Greek writing. Acts 6:1 distinguishes between Greek-speaking and Aramaic-speaking widows in Jerusalem. Acts 6:9 refers to a synagogue of Jews from various Diaspora countries, which presumably is

---

71. This is not to say that there are no Hellenistic influences found in Rabbinic literature. For example, see David Daube, 'Rabbinic Methods of Interpretation and Hellenistic Rhetoric,' *HUCA* 22 (1949): 239-64. Also, the rabbis developed a legal document called a 'prosbol' that circumvented the OT requirement of eliminating debts in the seventh year. This allowed business interaction in the Greco-Roman world (*m. Shevi'it* 10:4, *b. Gittin* 36b).

Greek-speaking. The Roman rule and separate 'Greek' cities within Palestine influenced Jews who interacted with the government and business/trades.

As noted above, scholarship is significantly divided on the influence of Hellenism on Palestinian Jews. All agree that there was some limit to Hellenism in Palestine because the Jewish religion's monotheism was unusual in the Greco-Roman world. For example, there was only one Temple in Jerusalem.

Among scholars, concerning the influence of Hellenism on Jews in Palestine during the first century A.D., Bultmann is on one end of the continuum. 'There was no possibility there [in Palestine] of science and art, nor could there be any cultural intercourse with other nations. Israel (apart from Hellenistic Judaism) cut herself off from the outside world and lived in extraordinary isolation.'[72] Daube is in the middle of the continuum as he sees 'the sharp distinction between a Hellenistic and a Rabbinic Judaism in the New Testament period is being abandoned as it is found that many Hellenistic ideas had crept into, or been consciously taken over by Rabbinism.'[73] Hengel is on the other extreme from Bultmann arguing that Palestine was, within limits, significantly Hellenized in the first century A.D. He argues that the Greek language and the Hellenistic life-style, economy, technology, education, philosophy, and religions significantly affected most Jews in Palestine in A.D. 30-100.[74]

Now for some of my conclusions concerning the terms 'Palestinian Judaism' and 'Hellenistic Judaism.' Once qualified, I do believe that the distinction between Palestinian and Hellenistic Judaism is useful. I define Hellenistic Judaism as Greek-speaking and somewhat influenced by Hellenistic culture and ideas. I define Palestinian Judaism as Aramaic-speaking and significantly less

---

72. Rudolf Bultmann, *Primitive Christianity in Its Contemporary Setting* (trans. R. H. Fuller; London: Thames and Hudson, 1956), 60.

73. David Daube, *The New Testament and Rabbinic Judaism* (London: University of London, 1956; repr., Peabody: Hendrickson, 1988), ix. Also see W. D. Davies, *Paul and Rabbinic Judaism: Some Rabbinic Elements in Pauline Theology* (London: SPCK, 1948), 1-16.

74. Martin Hegel, *The 'Hellenization' of Judaea*, 5, 53-56.

influenced by Hellenistic culture and ideas. Hellenistic Judaism exists outside of Palestine and to some degree in Palestine. Palestinian Judaism exists in Palestine and to some small degree outside of Palestine in the Second Temple period. During the first century A.D. in Palestine, Hellenism in general is affecting all Jews at least minimally and many Jews to a significant degree. Some Jews were affected by Hellenism in the sense that they consciously isolated themselves from it. I do believe that past scholarship has not considered enough the way the Hellenistic culture, especially the Greek language, influenced religious leaders and tradesmen in Palestine.

This discussion of Palestinian and Hellenistic Judaism again shows the variety of Judaisms that existed in the Second Temple period. It also shows the deficiency of much of our knowledge about aspects of Second Temple Judaism.

Apocalypticism

All agree that there is a significant amount of apocalyptic literature from 200 B.C. to A.D. 200, most of it presumably from a Palestinian provenance. Is there behind this literature a social group or movement that may be termed 'apocalypticism' that is distinct from the Pharisees, Sadducees, etc.? Much of older scholarship assumed that there was.[75]

Before discussing the movement question, a quick summary of apocalyptic literature is useful. Apocalyptic literature is a genre of literature that the writer has special 'revealed' (ἀποκάλυψις = revelation) knowledge of past, current, and future events leading to the end of the current world, at which time God defeats the evil forces. The current time is pictured pessimistically with pain and suffering for true believers. Usually there is a messianic or prophetic figure involved. The events are described in highly symbolic language.

---

75. Sanders complains about older scholarship seeing virtually two Jewish religions in Palestine, legalism/Pharisees/Rabbinic and apocalypticism. He believes that his conclusions about a universal covenantal nomism and evidence from Qumran should dispel this view. For a summary of his conclusions concerning this, see *Paul and Palestinian Judaism*, 423-26.

Apocalyptic literature is found in the OT (e.g., Zechariah, Dan. 7-12, Isa. 24-27), the NT (e.g., Revelation, Matt. 24), the Apocrypha (4 Ezra), the OT Pseudepigrapha (e.g., *1 Enoch*, *2 Baruch*, *Sibylline Oracles*, *Testament of Abraham*, and many more), and Qumran (e.g., *War Scroll*, *Messianic Apocalypse*). Unfortunately for the Apocrypha and OT Pseudepigrapha apocalypses, it is very difficult to determine the date, provenance, and groups that produced this literature.

The older view thought that the social groups that produced apocalyptic literature were on the margins of Jewish society, both politically and economically. Apocalypticism had no power, so it developed literature to encourage the faithful to continue in the midst of suffering. Many of the apocalyptic texts see themselves as the true believers and others as not. Hence, it was assumed that apocalypticism was composed of many small groups. The Essenes being one example of an isolated group seemed to confirm this.

With the discovery of the DSS, it became obvious that a group could produce both apocalyptic literature and other types of literature. Also, the Qumran community included priests and those who voluntarily isolated themselves. In addition, both the OT and NT include apocalyptic literature along with other genres. Hence, the strong connection between apocalyptic literature and an isolated apocalypticism has been loosened. Were there separate groups or was apocalyptic literature one aspect of a more well-rounded group? Currently, scholarship is unsure of an answer.

How prevalent was the knowledge of OT Pseudepigraphic apocalyptic literature in Palestine to the average Jewish person in the first century A.D.? It is hard to know. Jude evidences knowledge of at least similar oral stories or the actual literature (Jude 9, 14-15). Philo, Josephus, and Pliny the Elder knew about the Essenes. Jesus does not seem to interact with anyone connected with isolated apocalypticism, but He uses apocalyptic speech (Matt. 24). Many Jews in Palestine were in a mood to revolt against the Romans. Rabbinic literature is not noticeably affected by it; however, some assume that the concepts of resurrection from the dead and messianic ideas came from apocalyptic literature to Rabbinic literature. There is much debate on how influential, if at all, non-canonical apocalyptic literature was on the eschatological views of the writers of the NT.[76]

Ferguson has a current, typical scholarly-view of this subject. He concludes that:

> More study is needed on the social setting of apocalypticism. It originated and recurred in times of oppression and among groups experiencing alienation, but its eschatological perspective was widely influential, affecting many Pharisees and rabbis as well as sectarian groups like the Qumran community.[77]

My view is that the concepts from non-canonical apocalyptic literature were certainly 'in the air' in first-century A.D. Palestine, although I am less sure that an average Jew would know about the specifics of actual literary documents.[78] Since there is evidence of at least one isolated group, the Qumran community, I assume that there were other isolated groups. I do not believe, however, that those producing an apocalyptic document were necessarily always part of an isolated group.

This discussion of apocalypticism again shows that there was a variegated nature of the ideas and/or movements in Second Temple Judaism. Also, this discussion shows again major uncertainties in current scholarship. Here scholarship is uncertain as to virtually any historical specifics behind the apocalyptic literature.

SUMMARY OF VARIEGATED JUDAISM: PARTIES AND MOVEMENTS

To give context to Judaism's literary documents, some background of Jewish parties and movements is required. Also, it is useful to

---

76. Koester claims that apocalypticism is the 'essential bridge between the Old and New Testaments' (*History, Culture, and Religion of the Hellenistic Age*), 219-20.

77. Everett Ferguson, *Backgrounds of Early Christianity*, 477.

78. My views here match well to McNamara's (*Palestinian Judaism and the New Testament*, 92-94).

know the confidence, or lack of it, that current scholarship has about our knowledge of the parties and movements.

As all agree, the religion of Judaism of the Second Temple period was variegated. There were many forms of Judaism in Palestine and in the Diaspora. Following the destruction of Judaism in A.D. 70 and the defeat of Bar-Kochba in A.D. 135, the various Judaisms moved primarily toward Rabbinic Judaism.

In Palestine, the parties of the Pharisees, Sadducees and Essenes were the most well known to the average Jew who himself probably did not belong to any specific party. The Pharisaical party engendered the most support from the Jewish people. Currently in general, scholarship is moving away from the traditional conclusions about the Pharisees and Sadducees to simply being uncertain about them. Part of this movement is because of a low view of the historicity of the Gospels about the Pharisees and Sadducees. For some, another part of this scholarly movement is related to a distrust of later Rabbinic sources to accurately reflect first-century A.D. Palestine. I maintain the traditional conclusions (for now, bracketing out questions about works righteousness) especially when they are confirmed in the NT. I have a middle view of the usefulness of Rabbinic sources between total confidence and no confidence (more on this in the next section).

A general distinction can be made between Hellenistic Judaism (Greek-speaking and more influenced by Greco-Roman culture) and Palestinian Judaism (Aramaic-speaking and less influenced by Greco-Roman culture). Even in Palestine itself, Hellenistic Judaism existed. Current scholarship has a continuum of views about the extent of the distinction between Hellenistic and Palestinian Judaism. This ranges from an extreme separation of the two at the one end of the continuum to a virtual denial that the distinction is even useful at the other. Properly qualified, I do believe the distinction is useful, but that past scholarship has underestimated the influence of Hellenistic Judaism in Palestine during the first century A.D.

Much of older scholarship assumed that there were many isolated apocalyptic groups that were on the margins of society. These groups produced the many extant apocalyptic texts. However, current scholarship and I are uncertain as to most historical assumptions about apocalyptic groups. I do believe that the apocalyptic texts were probably produced by both isolated and non-isolated groups. Also, I believe that apocalyptic ideas were 'in the air' of first-century A.D. Palestine.

JUDAISM'S LITERARY SOURCES

As noted above, scholars generally separate the extant Jewish literary writings of the Second Temple period into seven groups: Apocrypha, OT Pseudepigrapha, DSS, Josephus, NT (Jewish-Christian), Philo, and Rabbinic literature. Excepting the NT, Josephus, and Philo, below is a brief discussion of each group. The question of works righteousness in these writings will not be addressed here as it was in Chapters 2 and 3. The purpose of the discussions here is to give the reader a general orientation to these writings so that in Chapters 2 and 3 she may better appreciate the arguments for and against works righteousness being in these writings. Again, I am assuming that the reader has a reasonably good grasp of the NT (and OT) but not of the remaining Second Temple writings.

APOCRYPHA

For Western Christians over the last 450 years, the Apocrypha has referred to the debated ten books/additions that the Roman Catholic Church at the Council of Trent (A.D. 1546) officially declared as Scripture.[79] Typically, Protestants call these debated books/additions the 'Apocrypha,'[80] and Roman Catholics, the 'deuterocanonical' books. However, modern scholars have a slightly expanded number of books for what they define as the

---

79. Canons and Decrees of the Council of Trent, Fourth Session, Decree Concerning the Canonical Scripture.

80. Etymologically, *apocrypha* refers to 'hidden things.' Most likely this began as a positive term to refer to books that only wise people could understand (possibly related to 4 Ezra 14:44-47). During and after the Reformation, the term took on a negative connotation.

'Apocrypha.'[81] For purposes of this book, I will use the expanded definition.

As used by scholars today, the Apocrypha refers to sixteen books/ additions written between approximately 180 B.C. and A.D. 100. These books/additions were included in the LXX versions of the Christian era and the Old Latin translations (A.D. 200–400),[82] but were not included in the Hebrew OT. Most books are not extant in Hebrew.[83] Trying to back-track from the Greek, scholars disagree significantly as to which books were originally written in Hebrew (or Aramaic) or were originally written in Greek.

The canonical status of the books/additions and the exact number of which books/additions are considered part of the Apocrypha are complicated. Although these books were in the LXX and the Latin Vulgate, some in the Church considered none of the books/additions as canonical. Others considered most of them canonical with the remaining simply included in the LXX or Vulgate as an appendix. Eventually, Protestants came to call this group the Apocrypha and denied any were part of the canon.[84] Roman Catholics[85] and Eastern Orthodox[86] called the majority of

---

81. For example, the following excellent resources for the Apocrypha use the expanded definition, Bruce M. Metzger, ed., *The Oxford Annotated Apocrypha*, (New York, OUP, 1977); and David A. deSilva, *Introducing the Apocrypha: Message, Context, and Significance* (Grand Rapids: Baker, 2002).

82. The only exception is 4 Ezra, which is not in the LXX.

83. Portions of Tobit, Sirach, 3 Ezra, Letter of Jeremiah, and an expanded form of Ps. 151 are extant in Hebrew.

84. Several of the historic Protestant creeds acknowledge that it is useful to read the non-canonical Apocrypha. See Belgic Confession 6, Thirty-Nine Articles, and Irish Articles 3. The WCF 1.3 is more neutral.

85. It was not until the Council of Trent (A.D. 1540s–1550s) that the Roman Catholic church officially called the Apocryphal books 'Scripture' and part of the 'Old Testament' (Fourth Session). Also see the *Catechism of the Catholic Church* § 120 for the same list of canonical OT books.

86. Since the Eastern Orthodox churches follow the LXX for the OT, she affirms the Apocrypha as canonical. See for example, The Confession of Dositheus (A.D. 1672, also called the Synod of Jerusalem) Question 3. However, the Eastern Church is not completely uniform. The Longer Catechism of

the sixteen books/additions 'deuterocanonical' with the remainder as an 'appendix' to the Bible, although Roman Catholics and Eastern Orthodox disagree slightly on which are deuterocanonical and which are to be included in the appendix. Scholars take an inclusive approach to what they call the Apocrypha. They include all the deuterocanonical books and all the books considered an appendix by either the Roman Catholics or at least one of the Eastern Orthodox churches.

The following chart shows the slight differences of apocryphal books/additions among the modern scholars, Roman Catholics, and the Eastern Orthodox. For my purposes, I will be using the modern scholars' list.

APOCRYPHAL BOOKS

Modern Scholars	Roman Catholics	Eastern Orthodox
Tobit	Tobit	Tobit
Judith	Judith	Judith
Additions to Esther	Additions to Esther	Additions to Esther
Wisdom of Solomon	Wisdom of Solomon	Wisdom of Solomon
Sirach	Sirach (Ecclesiasticus)	Sirach
Baruch	Baruch	Baruch
Epistle of Jeremiah	Epistle of Jeremiah[87]	Epistle of Jeremiah

the Eastern Church 31-33 does not affirm the Apocrypha as canonical. Timothy Ware states that although the Eastern Orthodox churches affirm the deuterocanonical books, 'most Orthodox scholars at the present day ... consider that the Deutero-Canonical Books, although part of the Bible, stand on a lower footing than the rest of the Old Testament' (*The Orthodox Church* [rev. ed.; New York: Penguin, 1993], 200).

87. Chapter 6 of Baruch is the Epistle of Jeremiah.

APOCRYPHAL BOOKS

Modern Scholars	Roman Catholics	Eastern Orthodox
Additions to Daniel	Additions to Daniel	Additions to Daniel
Prayer of Azariah Song	Prayer of Azariah Song	Prayer of Azariah Song
Susanna	Susanna	Susanna
Bel and the Dragon	Bel and the Dragon	Bel and the Dragon
1 Maccabees	1 Maccabees	1 Maccabees
2 Maccabees	2 Maccabees	2 Maccabees
3 Maccabees		3 Maccabees
4 Maccabees		4 Maccabees (Appendix)
3 Ezra	3 Ezra (1 or 3 Esdras) (Appendix)	3 Ezra (1 Esdras)
4 Ezra	4 Ezra (2 or 4 Esdras) (Appendix)	4 Ezra (3 Esdras) (Appendix)
Prayer of Manasseh	Prayer of Manasseh (Appendix)	Prayer of Manasseh (Appendix)
Psalm 151		Psalm 151

If we are concerned with Second Temple Judaism, is the separation of the Apocrypha from the OT Pseudepigrapha arbitrary? Well, to some degree it is. It is not completely arbitrary, however, if it is true that the books of the Apocrypha were in the LXX because they were generally more well known during the Second Temple period.

In general, the Apocrypha books/additions include history, tales, wisdom literature, and one apocalypse. The following is a brief description and some quotes of a few of the Apocryphal books to give the reader a sense of the Apocrypha. Again, I will not include here any discussion about works righteousness.

Tobit

Tobit is a tale of romance and Jewish piety set primarily in Nineveh and the region of Media (Persia) in the early days of the exile of Northern Israel (710–680 B.C.). There are four main characters: Tobit, the pious Jew who has gone blind; Sarah, a Jewess who is prevented from marrying by a demon; Tobias who is Tobit's son and eventually marries Sarah; and Raphael, an angel who heals Tobit's blindness and causes Sarah and Tobias to marry. In addition to a good story, the tale promotes praying, almsgiving, marrying only Jews, and respect for parents.

The author of Tobit is unknown, and most scholars opt for a Diaspora setting. Tobit was written between 250–175 B.C.[88] The original language was either Aramaic or Hebrew as shown by DSS fragments that constitute about one fifth of the book. The primary Greek texts come in longer (e.g., NRSV) and slightly shorter (e.g., RSV) recensions. Tobit is 14 chapters long.

Toward the end of the book, the author summarizes Tobit's story. '[Tobit] was fifty-eight years old when he lost his sight, and after eight years he regained it. He gave alms, and he continued to fear the Lord God and to praise him' (Tob. 14:1).[89]

1 Maccabees

1 Maccabees is a historical account of Israel's struggle for freedom in 175–134 B.C. from the Seleucid-Syrian empire. The account begins with Antiochus IV Epiphanes, the Seleucid king and the 'sinful root' (1 Macc. 1:10). He brings Hellenization

---

88. For arguments about dating, see Carey A. Moore, *Tobit: A New Translation with Introduction and Commentary* (AB 40A; New York: Doubleday, 1996), 40-42.

89. All quotes of the Apocrypha are from the RSV unless otherwise noted.

to Israel and pollutes the Temple. The account then highlights three Hasmonean brothers, Judas, Jonathan, and Simon. The brothers lead a guerilla war and eventual achieve victory against the Seleucids. The book promotes national Jewish pride and emphasizes that ridding Israel of foreign powers should be a trait of a Jewish leader. There are no recorded miraculous events, but the author sees the events as part of the special providence of God. No explicit belief in the afterlife is mentioned, which contrasts sharply with the bodily resurrection mentioned in 2 Maccabees (e.g., 2 Macc. 12:43-45).

The name of the book is related to one of the brothers, Judas, who has the nickname of Maccabees (1 Macc. 2:4), with the probable etymology of 'the hammer.' 1 Maccabees has sixteen relatively long chapters. Josephus followed much of 1 Maccabees in his *Jewish Antiquities* and *Jewish War*.[90]

The author is unknown. Because of relatively accurate information of Palestinian geography, it is assumed that Palestine was the provenance. Although no Hebrew copies of the text are extant, most scholars assume that 1 Maccabees was originally written in Hebrew. The book was written after 134 b.c., which is the last event in the book; and before the Romans took over Palestine (63 b.c.), as they are viewed positively in 1 Maccabees (e.g., 1 Macc. 14:16). Hence, a date of about 100 b.c. is reasonable.[91]

Finally in 142 b.c. Simon achieves political independence for Israel. This concluded 170 years of Greek rule over Palestine (Greek rule began in 312 b.c.). 'In the one hundred and seventieth year the yoke of the Gentiles was removed from Israel, and the people began to write in their documents and contracts, "In the first year of Simon the great high priest and commander and leader of the Jews"' (1 Macc. 13:41-42).

---

90. Josephus was a descendent of Jonathan, the Hasmonean. For a discussion of Josephus related to 1 Maccabees, see Jonathan A. Goldstein, *I Maccabees: A New Translation with Introduction and Commentary* (AB 41; Garden City: Doubleday, 1976), 55-61, 558-74.

91. Some scholars see 1 Macc. 14-16 as a later addition in the first century A.D.

4 Maccabees

4 Maccabees is a Jewish philosophical treatise with the thesis that 'devout reason is sovereign over the emotions' (4 Macc. 1:1, 6:31, 13:1, 16:1, 18:2). The book conflates Greek philosophy with Judaism. It is a strong encouragement to follow OT food laws no matter the consequences.

To prove the thesis, the author expands upon the gruesome torture and martyrdom by the Seleucids of Eleazar, his wife, and seven sons from 2 Macc. 6:12-7:42. These pious Jews refused even under deadly torture to violate the food laws. A simple eating of the prohibited food would have stopped the torture and saved their lives. Therefore, their reason, based on divine reason from the OT, overcame their desires and emotions to have the torture stopped.

The author is unknown. He is well aware of various aspects of Greek philosophy and writes in very good Greek. Most likely 4 Maccabees was written between A.D. 25–50 in the Diaspora. The book is 18 chapters long and is so named because the torture of Eleazar and his family took place during the Maccabean revolt.

Within 4 Maccabees, Eleazar's wife is the last one tortured and has seen the torture of her sons. She gets the highest praise by the author because she had to overcome the most emotion. 'How great and how many torments the mother then suffered as her sons were tortured on the wheel and with the hot irons! But devout reason, giving her heart a man's courage in the very midst of her emotions, strengthened her to disregard her temporal love of her children' (4 Macc. 15:22-23).

Sirach (Ecclesiasticus, Wisdom of Jesus the Son of Sirach)

As to genre, Sirach is similar to Proverbs. Sirach consists mostly of shorter proverbs that contrast a wise person and a fool. Sirach has several topics that are similar to Proverbs such as concern for one's speech. Notable differences between Sirach and Proverbs are that Sirach includes comments about the sacrificial system and many more statements about women (a few are quite derogatory).

Sirach includes a prologue by the author's grandson. The grandson explains that while living in Egypt he translated his grandfather's original Hebrew into Greek.

The author is the grandfather, Jesus the son of Sirach (Sir. 50:27). This is the only Apocryphal book where the author identifies himself. The Hebrew was written in approximately 180 B.C. in Palestine; the Greek translation with prologue, approximately 125 B.C. in Egypt. About two-thirds of Sirach exists in extant Hebrew texts. The Greek text is fifty-one chapters long plus the prologue.

The following are a few quotes from Sirach to give the reader a feel for the book:

All wisdom comes from the Lord and is with him forever. (Sir. 1:1)

Be quick to hear and be deliberate in answering. (Sir. 5:11)

He who keeps the law makes many offerings: he who heeds the commandments sacrifices a peace offering. (Sir. 35:1)

Better the wickedness of a man than a woman who does good; and it is a woman who brings shame and disgrace. (Sir. 42:14)

OLD TESTAMENT PSEUDEPIGRAPHA

OT Pseudepigrapha is a scholarly name given to about sixty books primarily written between 200 B.C. and A.D. 200.[92] The books in the OT Pseudepigrapha are written by Jews (a few have obvious later Christian editing) and relate to themes in the OT and/or purport to be written by OT characters. These books have been preserved by Christians, and in virtually all cases, not by Jews. The DSS do include clear fragments of two books from the OT Pseudepigrapha (*1 Enoch, Jubilees*) and fragments that are similar to two books (*Testament of Levi, Testament of Naphtali*).

The exact number of books considered to be part of the OT Pseudepigrapha has historically varied in the scholarly community, but with the 1983-1985 publication of Charlesworth's edited work, *The Old Testament Pseudepigrapha*, this has stabilized.[93]

---

92. Etymologically, 'pseudepigrapha' refers to 'false title/superscription.' Many of the books and their associated titles purport to be written by OT characters, e.g., *1 Enoch, Testament of Adam, Prayer of Jacob.*

93. James H. Charlesworth, ed., *The Old Testament Pseudepigrapha* (2 vols.; Garden City: Doubleday, 1983-85). This is the standard resource and

The OT Pseudepigrapha consists of four primary genres. These are apocalyptic (e.g., *Apocryphon of Ezekiel*), testaments (e.g., *Testament of Job*), expansions of OT/legends (e.g., *Martyrdom and Ascension of Isaiah*), and prayers/psalms (e.g., *Prayer of Joseph*). The most noticeable aspect is the large number of apocalyptic books, and also many of the testaments have apocalyptic portions. This large percentage of apocalyptic material is somewhat jarring compared to the classic Rabbinic literature that has virtually no apocalyptic material.

For the books of the OT Pseudepigrapha, scholarship has no real knowledge of any authors and only guesses about the provenances. It is even very difficult to know what group the author was associated with. Also, as noted above, these Jewish books have been preserved by Christians, not Jews.

Past scholarship rarely used the OT Pseudepigrapha for NT interpretation; however, modern scholarship is very interested to use it. Some complain that the pendulum has swung too far to an overuse of the OT Pseudepigrapha for NT interpretation. Holland, for example, complains that too many scholars do not appreciate the problem of not knowing most of the authors and their theological background. Without this, the terminology and themes used in these documents are difficult to define adequately. Holland believes that many simply assume that the same technical term or theme in the OT Pseudepigrapha becomes the key for understanding how a NT writer used that term or theme.[94] Holland's warning is well taken.

Despite the above difficulties about authors and background, in my view, the OT Pseudepigrapha does provide us with at least a small window into the world of some Jews living in the Second Temple period.

---

consists of introductions and English translations of all the books in the OT Pseudepigrapha. Charlesworth considers sixty-three books as part of the OT Pseudepigrapha, but a few of these, others consider part of the Apocrypha, e.g., 4 Ezra, Prayer of Manasseh, 3 Maccabees, 4 Maccabees.

94. Tom Holland, *Contours of Pauline Theology: A Radical New Survey of the Influences of Paul's Biblical Writings* (Ross-shire: Mentor, 2009), 54-64, esp. 60.

The following is a brief description and quotes of one OT Pseudepigrapha book per genre to give the reader a beginning-sense of this literature. Again, I will not include any discussion about works righteousness here.

2 Baruch

On the surface, *2 Baruch* is written by Baruch, Jeremiah's scribe (Jer. 36:32), shortly after the destruction of Jerusalem in 587 B.C. However, the real author is writing in approximately A.D. 100 after the A.D. 70 destruction of the Temple. The author encourages his Jewish readers by noting that judgment by God upon Jerusalem/ Temple is due to Jewish sins, but those individuals who follow the Law in the aftermath of this disaster will ultimately be raised from the dead to live with God forever.[95]

2 Baruch has eighty-seven short chapters. The extant primary text is in Syriac, and there are some extant partial Greek texts. It is assumed that the original was in Hebrew or Aramaic. The early Christian document the *Epistle of Barnabas* appears once to quote *2 Baruch* (*Barn.* 11:9 // *2 Bar.* 61:7).

2 Baruch includes tales of Baruch's life, a long letter from Baruch to the Jewish faithful (*2 Bar.* 78-86), and several large apocalyptic sections in which Baruch sees visions primarily about the future that are then interpreted for him. In the apocalypse of the clouds section, Baruch sees a cloud that drops alternatingly black and bright waters, six times each (*2 Bar.* 53). An angel interprets this for Baruch. The alternating black (negative) and bright (positive) waters are Israel's history. The first black waters are Adam's sin, the following first bright water is Abraham, and so on until the end of the age (*2 Bar.* 55-73). Below is a quote related to the first black water and Adam with the angel speaking to Baruch:

> And you first saw the black waters on the top of the cloud which first came down upon the earth; this is the transgression which Adam, the first man, committed. For when he transgressed, untimely death

---

95. For a good summary of *2 Baruch*, see George W. E. Nickelsburg, *Jewish Literature Between the Bible and the Mishnah: A Historical and Literary Introduction* (rev. ed.; Philadelphia, Fortress, 1987), 281-87.

came into being, mourning was mentioned, affliction was prepared, illness was created, labor accomplished, pride began to come into existence, the realm of death began to ask to be renewed with blood, the conception of children came about, the passion of parents was produced, the loftiness of men was humiliated, and goodness vanished.[96] (*2 Bar.* 56:5-6)

Testaments of the Twelve Patriarchs

The *Testaments of the Twelve Patriarchs* contains twelve self-contained episodes, with each of the twelve Jewish patriarchs giving a farewell 'testament' just before he dies. This book is reminiscent of Gen. 49. Each episode has approximately ten short chapters and each follows the same general outline.[97]

Each episode includes an ethical exhortation that is usually related to an event in the patriarch's life and a prediction of the 'future.' Although the 'Law of God' is often mentioned (e.g., *T. Levi* 13:2), the ethical exhortations are not related to any specific Jewish requirements (e.g., circumcision, food laws) and are more general. They include encouragements to love your neighbor and warnings against lying, drunkenness, and many warnings against sexual promiscuity. The predictive sections include a 'future' exile due to sin and return from exile because of God's mercy. From the author's perspective (not the patriarch's), the eschatological events include two special eschatological figures, a Levite priest and a king from Judah; Gentiles coming to faith; the resurrection of the dead; and an eschatological New Jerusalem.

The primary text is in Greek and includes about 10-12 obvious Christian interpolations. Fragments of an Aramaic text of the *Testament of Levi* and the *Testament of Naphtiali* were found among the DSS, but these fragments differ significantly from the Greek. Scholars are divided as to whether the original was in Greek or

---

96. All quotes of OT Pseudepigrapha are from *OTP*.

97. Nickelsburg summarizes the outline as follows: (1) Setting the scene, (2) Narrative from patriarch's life, (3) Ethical exhortation, (4) Prediction of the future, (5) Brief second exhortation, (6) Patriarch's death, and (7) Patriarch's burial (*Jewish Literature Between the Bible and the Mishnah*, 232).

Aramaic/Hebrew, and consequently, differ over the provenance.[98] Most agree that it was written during the Maccabean period (166–107 B.C.), excepting the few later Christian interpolations.

Below are quotes from the *Testaments of the Twelve Patriarchs*:

> Now, my children, I tell you to keep the Lord's commands; show mercy to your neighbor, have compassion on all, not only human beings but to dumb animals. (*T. Zeb.* 5:1)

> And now, my children, I command you not to love money or to gaze on the beauty of women. Because it was on account of money and attractive appearance that I was led astray to Bathsua the Canaanite. (*T. Jud.* 17:1)

> And now, my children, be obedient to Levi and to Judah. Do not exalt yourselves above these two tribes. For the Lord will raise up from Levi someone as high priest and from Judah someone as king. He will save all gentiles and the tribe of Israel. (*T. Sim.* 7:1-2)

Joseph and Aseneth

Genesis 41:45 notes with no explanation that Joseph married Aseneth,[99] the daughter of an Egyptian priest (also see Gen. 41:50, 46:20). The book *Joseph and Aseneth* is a tale apparently to solve the dilemma of having one of the patriarchs marrying outside the appropriate blood line, and in addition, marrying the daughter of an idolatrous priest.

Joseph and Aseneth is a two-part story primarily focusing on Aseneth. The first part (*Jos. Asen.* 1-21) begins with Aseneth as a beautiful virgin who worships idols continuously. After a disastrous, chance meeting with Joseph, she repents of her idolatry and arrogance, and turns to the Lord God. An angel then visits her and promises her that she will marry Joseph, have eternal life, and be the paradigmatic proselyte, called the 'City of Refuge'

---

98. See discussion of various options by H. C. Kee, who ultimately favors an original Greek text written by a Hellenistic Jew in Syria ('Testaments of the Twelve Patriarchs: A New Translation and Introduction,' in *OTP*, 775-78).

99. The LXX Greek spelling transliterates as 'Aseneth,' and the Biblical Hebrew, 'Asenath.'

(*Jos. Asen.* 15:7, 17:6, 19;5, 8). Aseneth does marry Joseph and gives birth to Manasseh and Ephraim.

The second part (*Jos. Asen.* 22-29) concerns Pharaoh's son combining forces with Dan, Gad, Naphtali, and Asher to steal Aseneth from Joseph. In the end, God miraculously foils the plot. Aseneth then effectively intercedes for the evil brothers in order that the good brothers would forgive them. The book ends with Joseph reigning as king of Egypt for forty-eight years.

Most scholars believe *Joseph and Aseneth* was originally composed in Greek, and exists in four main recensions. There are no extant copies in Hebrew. The book was probably written between 100 B.C. and A.D. 200 in Egypt.[100]

The following are quotes from *Joseph and Aseneth*:

> The fame of [Aseneth's] beauty spread all over the land and to the ends of the inhabited world . ... Aseneth was despising and scorning every man, and she was boastful and arrogant with everyone. (*Jos. Asen.* 1:6, 2:1)

> And Aseneth hurried and took all her gods that were in her chamber, the ones of gold and silver who were without number, and ground them to pieces, and threw all the idols of the Egyptians through the window. (*Jos. Asen.* 10:12)

> And your name shall no longer be called Aseneth, but your name shall be City of Refuge, because in you many nations will take refuge with the Lord God. ... And the Lord God heard Aseneth's voice [cry for help], and at once their swords fell from their hands on the ground and were reduced to ashes. (*Jos. Asen.* 15:7, 27:11)

Psalms of Solomon

The *Psalms of Solomon* is a group of eighteen psalms related to the 63 B.C. Roman invasion of Jerusalem and desecration of the Temple. The author(s) delineates three groups: wicked Gentile invaders,

---

100. For a scholarly discussion of the introductory matters, see Christoph Burchard, *Untersuchungen zu Joseph und Aseneth* (WUNT 8; Tübingen: Mohr, 1965); and M. Philonenko, *Joseph et Asneth: Introduction, texte critique, traduction et notes* (SPB 13; Leiden: Brill, 1968).

wicked Jews, and righteous Jews. God's allowing the invasion is justified because it was due to the sins of the wicked Jews. The author also sees God vindicating the righteous by raising them to eternal life (*Pss. Sol.* 3:12) and eventually sending a special Messiah (*Pss. Sol.* 17). God is primarily shown as a righteous judge.

Past scholarship had uniformly assumed that the author was a Pharisee and the wicked Jews were Sadducees. Currently, some still hold to the author being a Pharisee, others believe he might be an Essene, while still others think we do not have enough historical information about the Pharisees to make a judgment.[101] The extant manuscripts are in Greek and Syriac, but most scholars assume the original was written in Hebrew while the author was in Jerusalem. It is not clear why the author used Solomon's name, maybe because of Ps. 72.

The most interesting aspect of this book is the psalm that presents the special, future Messiah (*Pss. Sol.* 17). This Messiah is called the 'son of David' (*Pss. Sol.* 17:21) and the 'Lord Messiah' (χριστὸς κυρίου, *Pss. Sol.* 17:32). He is 'free from sin' (*Pss. Sol.* 17:36) and will rule perfectly.

The following are quotes from *Psalms of Solomon*:

> Gentile foreigners went up to your place of sacrifice; they arrogantly trampled it with their sandals. Because the sons of Jerusalem defiled the sanctuary of the Lord. (*Pss. Sol.* 2:2-3)

> May God remove from the devout those who live in hypocrisy; may his flesh decay and his life be impoverished. (*Pss. Sol.* 4:5)

> Do not neglect us, Our God, lest the Gentiles devour us as if there were no redeemer. (*Pss. Sol.* 8:30)

> There will be no unrighteousness among them in his days, for all shall be holy, and their king shall be the Lord Messiah. (*Pss. Sol.* 17:32)

---

101. In favor of at least considering the Essenes, see R. B. Wright, 'The Psalms of Solomon, the Pharisees, and the Essenes,' *SCS* 2 (1972): 136-47. Larry Helyer argues for the traditional designations (*Exploring Jewish Literature of the Second Temple Period: A Guide for New Testament Students* [Downers Grove: Intervarsity, 2002], 389).

DEAD SEA SCROLLS

The Dead Sea Scrolls (DSS) are a collection of more than 850 documents (many fragmentary) found in eleven caves just northwest of the Dead Sea in an area called Wadi Qumran.[102] The initial cave discovery was made in 1947. The writings date from 150 B.C. (or maybe even 250 B.C.) to A.D. 68. As discussed previously, the Qumran community is identified with the Essenes.

Of the 850 documents, approximately 200 are copies of OT texts. Other types of documents include rules specific to the Qumran community, commentaries (pesher) on OT books, apocryphal expansions of OT books, targums, community hymns and psalms, halakah, calendars, prayers, benedictions, descriptions of a theoretical Temple, apocalyptic texts, etc. As mentioned in above sections, portions of a few previously known Apocryphal and OT Pseudepigraphic books are included. Most of the documents are written in either Hebrew or Aramaic. There are a few in Greek.

The DSS were housed in a library of sorts. The Qumran community did not necessarily compose all of these writings, although they obviously did compose many of them. Many of the documents have simply been re-copied and may not have in every instance necessarily represented the views of the community. Because of the nature of this archeological find, the dating and provenance of these texts are fairly fixed. This is in contrast to most other Jewish texts of Second Temple Judaism. For any of the DSS, one can be sure that the document existed in Palestine and was important enough for someone to compose or copy it. The DSS provide us with another window into the variegated nature of Second Temple Judaism.

To refer to various manuscripts, scholars have assigned the cave number, a 'Q' for Qumran, and then an abbreviated title. Sometimes a superscripted letter is added to the title to note various copies of the same document. Hence, 1QIsa[a] refers to cave 1, Qumran, OT

---

102. Other discoveries of ancient texts have also been made near these eleven caves, including finds at Masada and some Bar Kochba letters. However, I will not discuss these.

book of Isaiah, and copy 'a.' Some of the more famous documents are also known by their popular titles, e.g., *Temple Scroll* or 11QT. We do not have a completed version of the vast majority of these written works. For many there are several partial copies of the same work that scholars try and piece together to get as much of a whole work as possible.

For purposes of this chapter, we will look at three texts. Two of them are famous DSS documents. The third is one of the many short texts.

Rule of the Community (1QS)

The *Rule of the Community* (1QS) and the *Damascus Document* are the two major texts that give us an understanding of the Qumran community.[103] Both these texts give us the strict entrance requirements and rules for staying in the community. We also learn about the hierarchy of the community, along with aspects of daily life.

1QS is written in Hebrew and is a scroll 6.5 feet long by ten inches wide, with eleven columns of writing (each column appropriately equal in length to a biblical chapter). The estimated date of writing is 100–75 B.C.[104]

A simple outline for 1QS might be:

I-IV   Entrance into Community and Two Spirits
V-IX   Rules of the Community Per Se
X-XI   Hymn to God

Apparently, the process of admission was a two-year process that included probationary periods. The candidate 'shall not depart from any command of God concerning their times; they shall be neither early nor late for any of their appointed times, they shall stray neither to the right nor to the left of any of His true precepts'

---

103. The *Rule of the Community* is sometimes called the *Manual of Discipline*. The 'S' in 1QS stands for the Hebrew סרך ('rule'). In addition to 1QS, other recensions and fragments of this work include 4Q255, 4Q280, 286-7, 4Q502, and 5Q11, 13.

104. Nickelsburg, *Jewish Literature Between the Bible and the Mishnah*, 132; J. Murphy-O'Connor, 'Community, Rule of the (1QS),' *ABD*, 1:1110-12.

(1QS I, 14-16).[105] The requirements need to be strict because of the two 'spirits of Light and Darkness' that may rule men (1QS III, 12-IV, 27). Men may follow the spirit of Darkness and be denied entry into the Community and the afterlife.

Part of the Community's rules relate to their examination of candidates.

> When he [candidate] has completed one year within the Community, the Congregation shall deliberate his case with regard to his understanding and observance of the Law. And if it be his destiny, according to the judgment of the Priests and the multitude of the men of their Covenant, to enter the company of the Community, his property and earnings shall be handed over to the Bursar of the Congregation. (1QS VI, 18-19)

Other rules include:

> Whoever has deliberately lied shall do penance for six months. … Whoever has spoken foolishly: three months. Whoever has interrupted his companion whilst speaking: ten days. Whoever has lain down to sleep during an Assembly of the Congregation: thirty days. (1QS VII, 3-11)

After a long recitation of rules, 1QS ends with a heart-warming, long, psalm-like hymn praising God and His grace.

> I will sing with knowledge and all my music shall be for the glory of God. … Before I move my hands and feet, I will bless His Name. … If I stumble, the mercies of God shall be my eternal salvation. (1QS X, 8, 15, XI,12)

Genesis Apocryphon (1QapGen)

1QapGen is an apocryphal account of Noah and Abraham.[106] Most of the manuscript pertains to Gen. 12-14, with Abraham speaking in first person. The text is incomplete and actually may have

---

105. All quotes of the DSS are from Geza Vermes, *The Complete Dead Sea Scrolls in English* (rev. ed.; New York: Penguin, 2004).

106. J. A. Fitzmyer, *The Genesis Apocryphon of Qumran Cave I: A Commentary* (Rome: Biblical Institute, 1971).

begun with creation if the entire composition was extant. Scholars generally agree that the work was composed in the second century B.C., although the manuscript is probably from 25 B.C.–A.D. 50[107]

In addition to being an incomplete manuscript, the manuscript is damaged at many points. The best preserved portion relates to Abraham. There is no other copy of this work at Qumran, except possibly the fragment 1Q20. 1QapGen is written in Aramaic. The Noah portion has some loose parallels to Noah in *1 Enoch*. Overall, 1QapGen is closest in genre to *Jubilees*.

The most interesting sections of 1QapGen are the expansions to the biblical text related to Abram and Sarai in Egypt (Gen. 12:10-20 // 1QapGen XIX,11-XX, 34). Just as Abram and Sarai enter Egypt, Abram has a dream in which he is a cedar tree and Sarai, a palm tree:

> I saw in my dream a cedar tree and a palm tree … men came and they sought to cut down the cedar tree and to pull up its roots, leaving the palm tree alone. But the palm tree cried out saying, 'Do not cut down this cedar tree, for cursed be he who shall fell [it].' And the cedar tree was spared because of the palm tree and [was] not felled. (1QapGen XIX, 14-16)

Abram then tells Sarai the dream, and they both agree to tell others that Sarai is Abram's sister. As Evans remarks, 'Perhaps [this] is an attempt to justify the biblical account of Abraham's deceit.'[108]

4Q509 (fragment 3)

4Q509 is a short prayer to be made for one of the festivals. It is similar to several other prayers for festivals found in Cave 4 (4Q507-9). The actual festival that 4Q509 refers to is not known, although other prayers are related to the Day of Atonement (4Q508) and Day of Firstfruits (4Q509 [fragment 132]). The date of these manuscripts might be early first century A.D.[109]

---

107. Vermes, *The Complete Dead Sea Scrolls in English*, 481.

108. Evans, *Noncanonical Writings and New Testament Interpretation*, 52.

109. Vermes, *The Complete Dead Sea Scrolls in English*, 382.

I have included this brief text to give the reader the sense of the many short and fragmentary texts that are in the DSS. Below is the entire text of 4Q509 (fragment 3).

> For Thou has caused us to rejoice, removing our grief, and has assembled our banished ones for a feast of ... Thou shalt gather our dispersed women for the season of ... Thy [mer]cies on our congregation like ra[in -drops on the earth in the season of sowing ... and like showers on the gr]ass in the seasons of sprouting and ... We shall recount Thy marvels from generation to generation. Blessed be the Lord who has caused us to rejoice.

Rabbinic Literature

For our purposes, the classic Rabbinic literature beginning with the Mishnah and ending with the Babylonian Talmud (A.D. 200–600) will be considered. Rabbinic Judaism is the name given to the religious party after the A.D. 70 fall of Jerusalem that is the continuation of the Pharisee party. Before A.D. 200, there are no extant written documents for Rabbinic Judaism.

As discussed previously, I consider the Rabbinic literature useful to some degree to determine first-century A.D. views. The scholarly community is not in agreement on the methodology of how to use this literature, and for some, whether to use it at all. I will give my qualifications about the use of this literature at the end of this section.

Portions of Rabbinic material are usually termed either as *halakah* or *haggadah*. Halakah, related to the verb 'to walk,'[110] refers to interpretations that are legal or applying the law. Haggadah, related to the verb 'to tell, to draw out, to show,'[111] refers to interpretations that are general scriptural interpretations and homiletical material, that is, interpretations that are not legal. In the Rabbinic literature, there are no apocalyptic documents. This is in strong contrast to the OT Pseudepigrapha.

---

110. Related to the Hebrew root הלך (*halak*).
111. Related to the Hebrew root נגד (*nagad*).

The classic Rabbinic literature exists in two basic forms. One is a grouping *by topic* of various rabbis' views of *applied laws* (halakah) pertaining to, for example, proper oath making, sabbath observance, tithes, etc. The primary documents of this type are the Mishnah, Tosefta, Jerusalem Talmud, and the Babylonian Talmud. Included within this primarily halakah material is some haggadah material.

The other type of classic Rabbinic literature is a grouping *by continuous text of Scripture* of various rabbis' views of *applied laws, scriptural interpretations, and homiletical material* (halakah and haggadah). This is usually called 'midrash.' The text of a book of Scripture is used as the form to pull together all types of Rabbinic material. The primary documents of this type include *Mekilta* (of Rabbi Ishmael) (Exod. 12-23), *Sifra on Leviticus, Sifre on Numbers* (Num. 5-35), *Sifre on Deuteronomy*, and *Midrash Genesis*.

Of the above two basic forms of literature, Rabbinic Judaism held the grouping by topic as the preeminent one because it purports to have the older traditions, especially related to the Mishnah, and because the crown jewel of Rabbinic literature, the Babylonian Talmud, is also of this form.

To give a sense of dating, below are the primary documents and their estimated dates of consolidation into a book. Note, many of these books may have been edited long after the dates given.

Mishnah	A.D. 200
Tosefta	A.D. 300
Mekilta of Rabbi Ishmaeli	A.D. 350[112]
Sifre Numbers	A.D. 350–400
Sifre Deuteronomy	A.D. 350–400
Jerusalem Talmud	A.D. 400
Sifra Leviticus	A.D. 400
Genesis Rabbah	A.D. 425–450
Babylonian Talmud	A.D. 600

112. This date is highly disputed. Some date as early as A.D. 250; others as late as medieval times.

For purposes of this section, I will discuss the Mishnah, Tosefta, and the Babylonian Talmud. These three are very related as they are arranged per topic or 'tractate,' with all three many times covering the same topic. To refer to passages in these books, a prefix of either *m*, *t*, or *b* is used to refer to the Mishnah, Tosefta, or Babylonian Talmud, respectively. This prefix is used with the name of the tractate. For example, to refer to the Mishnah discussion of tractate *Berakot* (Benedictions), the reference *m. Berakot* is used.

Mishnah

The Mishnah is a large book (about half the size of the Bible) arranged in six major divisions that separate sixty-three topics.[113] These topics or tractates include, for example, 'Tithes,' 'Feast of Passover,' 'Bills of Divorce,' 'Oaths,' 'Meal Offerings,' and 'Hands.' The Mishnah is written in a non-expansive, choppy type of Hebrew, usually called Mishnaic Hebrew. The word 'mishnah' is related to the Hebrew verb 'to repeat.'

Again, the Mishnah was written in approximately A.D. 200 but includes purported quotes from rabbis who lived in 50 B.C. to A.D. 200. Some of the discussions appear to relate more to a theoretical Jewish community than to one that actually existed, especially considering the destruction of the Temple and absence of Jews controlling the government. Neusner comments that the Mishnah is an 'important statement of how humankind might in imagination create a world' and that it is a 'specimen of Utopia.'[114] Others simply see the Mishnah as a compendium of law and believe Neusner is overstating the case.[115]

Each tractate's discussion presents a problem of how to apply rules for living, for example, the proper method of making oaths. Then the tractate includes various rabbis making arguments against each other to determine the proper course of action. Many times

---

113. For a good overview of the Mishnah, see Ephraim E. Urbach, 'Mishnah,' *EncJud*, 12:94-110.

114. Jacob Neusner, *The Mishnah: A New Translation* (New Haven: Yale, 1988), xl.

115. Evans, *Noncanonical Writings and New Testament Interpretation*, 21.

the issue is left unresolved between the rabbis. Most tractates are related to issues from the OT, but the OT itself is only occasionally quoted or alluded to.

If the OT is not prominent, why does the Mishnah have such authority? A tradition developed that Moses gave both a *written* and *oral* Torah. The Pentateuch (Genesis through Deuteronomy) was the *written* Torah. The Mishnah then is the *oral* version that came from Moses that was passed down by memorization from prophet to prophet and from rabbi to rabbi until it was finally written down in A.D. 200 (*m. Abot* 1:1, *m. Eduyyot* 8:7, *m. Yadayim* 4:3, *b. Berakhot* 5a). However, at some level this is confusing because it appears that the rabbis in the Mishnah are often, although not always, contradicting each other.[116] Also, some topics could not have existed in Moses' day (e.g., 'Scroll of Esther').

Some scholars claim that during the Tannaitic period (50 B.C.–A.D. 200), the rabbis did not see the Rabbinic laws as coming from God through Moses, but rather the rabbis were given authority by God to legislate and even overturn OT laws. Then during the Amoraic period (A.D. 225–500), the idea that the whole Rabbinic tradition was divine and came from Moses developed as a response to those who were rejecting Rabbinic views and questioning their authority, such as Christians and non-Rabbinic Jewish groups.[117]

---

116. *m. Eduyyot* 1:4-6 asks why both majority and minority opinions are included in the Mishnah. It answers that a future court may prefer the minority opinion. However, in *t. Eduyyot* 1:4, the answer appears to be that the future court needs to be aware of the minority opinion so that if it is brought up again, it can clearly be shown to be wrong.

117. So Karin Hedner Zetterholm, *Jewish Interpretation of the Bible: Ancient and Contemporary* (Minneapolis: Fortress, 2012), 20-33, 182-83. She leans heavily on *b. Eruvin* 13b and *b. Baba Metzi'a* 59b. These passages certainly give the impression that the rabbis could alter God's laws. Although these texts are from the later Babylonian Talmud, she sees them as reflecting views during the earlier Tannaitic period. Interestingly, she ties this to modern Jewish denominations. She generalizes that the Orthodox denominations have a Amoraic view—Oral Torah is divine; and Reform and Conservative denominations have a Tannaitic view—Oral Torah is human interpretation.

If one has never read the Mishnah, it is difficult to convey the detail and apparent casuistry that the discussions often take. For example, I will use the tractate 'Oaths' (*Shabuot*).

In *m. Shabuot* 3:2, Rabbi Aqiba argues that if someone swears an oath that 'I won't eat,' and he eats a piece of wheat bread, a piece of barley bread, and a piece of spelt bread, then he is liable to one count of breaking an oath, not three. But if someone swears 'I won't eat a piece of bread made of wheat, a piece of bread made of barley, and a piece of bread made of spelt,' and eats these three, he is liable to three counts of breaking oaths.

A further discussion ensues concerning oaths about not eating in *m. Shabuot* 3:4:

> [Rabbi Aqiba] 'I swear I won't eat,' and he ate food which is not suitable for eating, or drank liquids which are not suitable for drinking—he is exempt.

> 'I swear I won't eat,' but he ate carrion and terefah meat, abominations and creeping things—he is liable. [But] Rabbi Simeon declares him exempt.

Here, after swearing one will not eat, Rabbi Aqiba distinguishes between eating non-food and eating food that violates Jewish food laws. One has not violated the oath if one eats dirt, but one has violated it if one eats pork. However, Rabbi Simeon disagrees with Rabbi Aqiba on the second issue and declares that one has not violated the oath if one eats pork.

In *m. Shabuot* 4:13, a distinction is made between positive oaths that are sworn 'by heaven and earth' versus those sworn 'by Adonai, or Yahweh, or by the Almighty, or by Hosts or by him who is merciful and gracious, or by him who is long-suffering and abundant in mercy, or by any other euphemism.' In the first case, the one who breaks an oath sworn upon 'by heaven and earth' is not liable; but in the second case, one is liable.

Tosefta

The Tosefta is very similar to and an expansion of the Mishnah. It is four times as large as the Mishnah, but it has the same six divisions and virtually the same tractate titles. The Tosefta was written approximately A.D. 300, one-hundred years after the Mishnah. Two extra generations of rabbis are included in addition to those quoted in the Mishnah. The word 'tosefta' is related to the Hebrew word 'supplement,' that is, an addition to the Mishnah. The Tosefta 'complements, explains, expands upon, identifies anonymous sayings, and at times explicitly comments on the Mishnah.'[118] The Tosefta is written in mishnaic Hebrew.

The following is a typical section of the Tosefta that expands upon the Mishnah. Again, I will use the oath section. In the Mishnah (*m. Shabuot* 3:7), the case is presented that if one swears by repeating three times that he will not eat, and then does eat, he is liable to only one count of a violation. The Tosefta expands upon this by giving a rationale for only violating one count, 'For he said the latter ones to back up the former ones' (*t. Shabuot* 2:4). That is, repeating the same oath is simply still referring to the one original oath.

The Tosefta also adds another scenario and a rationale to this discussion in *t. Shabuot* 2:4. What if the three-fold oath was not about future eating but about past eating?

> 'I swear that I didn't eat, that I didn't eat, that I didn't eat.' He is liable for each and every one of them [that is, three violations].

This rule is more strict concerning an oath involving what already has happened than it is concerning an oath about what is going to happen in the future.

As can be seen by these two examples of expansion, the Tosefta often explicitly includes a rationale that was implicit in the Mishnah.

Babylonian Talmud

Rabbinic Judaism produced two large talmuds, the Jerusalem Talmud and the Babylonian Talmud. The Babylonian Talmud is

---

118. Evans, *Noncanonical Writings and New Testament Interpretation*, 122. Similarly, Moshe D. Herr says, 'The aim of this anonymous compiler and redactor was obviously to produce a collection that would serve as a supplement to the *Mishnah*' ('Tosefta,' *EncJud*, 15:1284-85).

the more well known and is the dominant one. If one simply refers to the 'talmud,' he is referring to the Babylonian Talmud. The word 'talmud' means 'study' or 'learning.'

The Babylonian Talmud consists primarily of quotes of the Mishnah and then extended commentary about the quotes. This commentary is called the 'Gemera,' which translates as 'completion.' Not all of the Mishnah tractates are quoted and commented upon, only thirty-six of the sixty-three. Also, quotes of the Tosefta are often included.

The Gemera portion of the Babylonian Talmud was finalized approximately A.D. 600. Obviously, rabbis living after the Mishnah are responsible for the Gemera. However, they do refer often to the views of 'tannaite authority'—rabbis who lived from 50 B.C. to A.D. 200—in the Gemera. Therefore, taken at face value, we have additional information stretching back to the second temple time-period.

To give a sense of size, my version of the Babylonian Talmud is twenty-two volumes.[119] The language of the Babylonian Talmud includes mishnaic Hebrew for the quotes of the Mishnah, and both Aramaic and more normal Hebrew for the Gemera. Although the Babylonian Talmud is a halakah document, it contains much more haggadah material than the Mishnah and Tosefta do.[120] Also, a reader notes significantly more quotes of Scripture.

The Babylonian Talmud contains many intricate and fascinating arguments as it comments on the Mishnah. Neusner contends that these comments can be grouped into four categories: (1) exegeting and amplifying the meaning of the Mishnah, (2) giving additional scriptural proofs to defend the Mishnah's conclusions,

---

119. Jacob Neusner, *The Babylonian Talmud: A Translation and Commentary* (22 vols.; Peabody: Hendrickson, 2005).

120. Estimates vary as to what percentage of the Babylonian Talmud is haggadah material. Isidore Epstein concludes that about one-third is haggadah (*Judaism: A Historical Presentation* [New York: Penguin, 1990], 127). Eliezer Berkovits opts for two-thirds ('Talmud, Babylonian,' *EncJud*, 15:762). This percentage variation is due to the difficulty of defining haggadah material as it is included primarily as a subset of halakah discussions.

(3) harmonizing different Mishnah texts and texts in the Tosefta, and (4) deciding on the original wording of the Mishnah.[121]

The following are two examples from the Babylonian Talmud. The first is a short one from the tractate *Bekhorot* ('Firstlings'), which is related to the dedication of the firstborn male animals to God (Deut. 15:19-22). Included in the Mishnah is a discussion of 'blemishes' that disqualify a man from being a priest, and one of those 'blemishes' is being ambidextrous.[122] The Mishnah also simply states that there is disagreement as to whether being ambidextrous is truly a blemish (*m. Bekhorot* 7:6). Below is the short discussion of this in the Babylonian Talmud (*b. Bekhorot* 45b); the quotes of the Mishnah are in bold.

> **He who is ambidextrous, Rabbi declares invalid and sages declare valid.**
>
> Our rabbis have taught on Tannaite authority that if one is left-handed or left-legged, he is invalid.
>
> **He who is ambidextrous, Rabbi declares invalid and sages declare valid.**
>
> One authority takes the view that it is unusual weakness affecting the right hand. The other authority maintains that it is unusual strength affecting the left hand.

Above, the Gemera of the Babylonian Talmud first notes that it is not only being ambidextrous that discounts someone, but also if they are left-handed. The second point attempts to solve the disagreement between the rabbis as to whether being ambidextrous is a blemish. The answer is that the term ambidextrous may be confusing. Is it caused by an unusual weakness or unusual strength in one of the hands?

The second example also includes blemishes, but blemishes on women who were engaged to be married on the promise by the

---

121. Jacob Neusner, *Rabbinic Literature: An Essential Guide*, 34. Neusner notes that these same four items are also in the Jerusalem Talmud.

122. See Lev. 21:17-21 for biblical list of blemishes that disqualify priests.

father that his daughter had no blemishes. If these blemishes are found after the fact, the marriage is invalidated. This discussion is in tractate *Ketubot* ('marriage contracts'). In the Mishnah, there is little discussion of what actually constitutes a blemish, although it is noted that what invalidates a priest, invalidates a woman (*m. Ketubot* 7:7).

The Babylonian Talmud has a moderately long discussion on blemishes in women. I will give a truncated quote (*b. Ketubot* 75a); again the Mishnah quote is in bold.

> **All those blemishes which invalidate priests also invalidate women.**
>
> A Tannaite statement, they added to them one who perspires heavily, one with a mole, and one with bad breath.
>
> [. . .]
>
> Said Rabbi Yose son of Rabbi Hanina, 'There is no contradiction, the one speaks of excessive perspiration that is transitory, the other, excessive perspiration that is permanent.'
>
> Rabbi Ashi said, 'But are you contrasting perspiration and one who is filthy? There, in regard to the priests, it is possible to take away the sweat with sour wine, and it is possible to take away the bad breath by keeping pepper in one's mouth, and then the priest can do the Temple service. But in the case of a wife, these devices do not really do the job.'
>
> What is the definition of a mole? If there is hair in it, then in the case of the priest and in the case of the wife, it would invalidate. ... If there is no hair in it, if it is big, it is a blemish; if it is small [and no hair], it is no blemish. And what is the measure of a big one? Rabbi Simeon son of Gamaliel explained, 'As big as a big Italian issar coin.'
>
> [. . .]
>
> Said R. Hisda, 'A deep voice in a woman, lo, this is a blemish. "For sweet is your voice and your countenance is comely"' (Song 2:14).

Usefulness for First-Century A.D. Judaism?

As mentioned several times now, scholars disagree on the usefulness of Rabbinic literature for determining Jewish views in the first century A.D. As I argued earlier, I see some usefulness.

The Mishnah is the one Rabbinic document in which I have a modicum of trust. As shown previously in this appendix, information in the Mishnah and the Bible sometimes matches. Therefore, some of the information and ideas in the Mishnah were certainly floating around in the first century A.D. With even less trust, I do often consult the Tosefta. Other than these two documents, I have no confidence that the information in any other Rabbinic document is useful to make an argument about first-century views, although in theory, it is possible. In Chapters 2 and 3, I did include references to other Rabbinic literature, but these are presented more for information than an argument for Jewish views in the first century.

Even for the Mishnah and the Tosefta, should only the statements by rabbis who lived before A.D. 70 be used? My view is that by A.D. 200 various Rabbinic views were 'flattened out' so that it is equally probable that the purported views of any rabbi did exist before A.D. 70.[123]

SUMMARY OF CHAPTER

The above overview of Judaism's literary sources included a discussion with examples from OT Pseudepigrapha, Apocrypha, Dead Sea Scrolls, and Rabbinic literature (no examples were given for NT, Philo, and Josephus). Also included for more context was a discussion of parties (e.g., Pharisees) and movements (e.g., Palestinian Judaism).

The overview showed numerous interpretative difficulties as the provenance, author, party/movement, and dating are not known for many of the writings (the Dead Sea Scrolls, Josephus, and Philo are significant exceptions). Also, the overview showed a definite 'variegation' within Judaism. These difficulties with the writings

---

123. Some scholars are trying to develop methodologies to determine layers of historical development in Rabbinic literature. For instance, David Instone-Brewer is trying to isolate 'those rabbinic traditions which can be shown to originate before 70 C.E.' (*Prayer and Agriculture*, vol. 1 of *Traditions of the Rabbis from the Era of the New Testament* [Grand Rapids: Eerdmans, 2004], xviii). Whether this can be done is debatable.

and the variegation within Judaism should certainly caution one from making confident claims about what all of Second Temple Judaism believed.

Given the difficulties and variegation, however, I do believe that some general knowledge about Second Temple Judaism can be gleaned. Although, I feel much more confident about simply saying that such-and-such a document has such-and-such a view, as opposed to saying that all or large portions of Second Temple Judaism have such-and-such a view.

I must make one caveat to the above discussion. I consider the NT to be the Word of God; hence, when interpreted correctly, it provides inerrant information. My view of the Bible here will put me at odds with most, but not all, of the NPP authors and those who make conclusions about Second Temple Judaism. For example, I consider the NT's statements about the Pharisees to be accurate at least about those Pharisees in the specific NT context. Also, I will consider the 'Deutero-Paul' books as actually written by Paul and useful for our study whether one believes Paul wrote them or not.

BIBLIOGRAPHY

Abegg Jr., M. G. '4QMMT C 27, 31 and "Works Righteousness."' *DSD* 6 (1999): 139-47.

_____. 'Miqṣat Maʿaśey Ha-Torah (4QMMT).' *DNTB*, 709-11.

Alexander, Philip S. 'Torah and Salvation in Tannaitic Literature.' Pages 261-301 in *The Complexities of Second Temple Judaism*. Vol. 1 of *Justification and Variegated Nomism*. Edited by D. A. Carson, Peter T. O'Brien, and Mark A. Seifrid. Grand Rapids: Baker, 2001.

Allen, R. Michael. *Justification and the Gospel: Understanding the Contexts and Controversies*. Grand Rapids: Baker, 2013.

Anderson, R. T. 'Samaritan Literature.' *DNTB*, 1052-56.

Anderson, Robert T., and Terry Giles. *The Keepers: An Introduction to the History and Culture of the Samaritans*. Peabody: Hendrickson, 2002.

Arnold, Clinton E. *Ephesians*. ZECNT. Grand Rapids: Zondervan, 2010.

Barclay, John M. G. 'Why the Roman Empire Was Insignificant to Paul.' Pages 363-87 in *Pauline Churches and Diaspora Jews*. WUNT 275. Tübingen: Mohr Siebeck, 2011.

_____. *Paul and the Gift*. Grand Rapids: Eerdmans, 2015.

_____. Review of *Paul and the Faithfulness of God*, by N. T. Wright. *SJT* 68 (2015): 235-46.

Barcley, William Bayless. *A Study Commentary on 1 & 2 Timothy*. EP Study Commentary. Webster, NY: EP, 2005.

Barcley, William B., with Ligon Duncan. *Gospel Clarity: Challenging the New Perceptive on Paul*. Carlisle: EP, 2010.

Bauckham, Richard. *The Jewish World Around the New Testament*. Grand Rapids: Baker, 2010.

Bauer, Walter, Frederick William Danker, W. F. Arndt, F. W. Gingrich. *A Greek-English Lexicon of the New Testament and other Christian Literature*. 3rd ed. Chicago: University of Chicago Press, 2000.

Baugh, S. M. 'The New Perspective, Mediation, Justification.' Pages 137-63 in *Covenant, Justification, and Pastoral Ministry: Essays by the Faculty of Westminster Seminary California*. Edited by R. Scott Clark. Phillipsburg: P&R, 2007.

Baur, Ferdinand Christian. *Paul, the Apostle of Jesus Christ: His Life and Works, His Epistles and Teachings; A Contribution to a Critical History of Primitive Christianity*. 2 vols. London: Williams & Norgate, 1873-1875. Repr., Peabody: Hendrickson, 2003.

Bavinck, Herman. *Reformed Dogmatics*. Translated by John Vriend. Edited by John Bolt. 4 vols. 2d ed. Grand Rapids: Baker, 2003-08 [1906-11].

Beall, Todd. 'Essenes.' *DNTB*, 342-48.

Berkhof, L. *Systematic Theology*. 4th ed. Grand Rapids: Eerdmans, 1941.

Berkouwer, G. C. *Faith and Justification*. Translated by Lewis B. Smedes. Studies in Dogmatics. Grand Rapids: Eerdmans, 1954.

_____. *Sin*. Translated by Philip C. Holtrop. Studies in Dogmatics. Grand Rapids: Eerdmans, 1971.

Berkovits, Eliezer. 'Talmud, Babylonian.' *EncJud*, 15:762.

Best, Ernest. *A Critical and Exegetical Commentary on Ephesians*. ICC. Edinburgh: T&T Clark, 1998.

Bird, Michael. *The Saving Righteousness of God: Studies on Paul, Justification, and the New Perspective*. Paternoster Biblical Monographs. Eugene, OR: Wipf & Stock, 2007.

Blass, F., A. Debrunner, and Robert W. Funk. *A Greek Grammar of the New Testament*. Chicago: University of Chicago Press, 1961.

Bockmuehl, Markus. '1QS and Salvation at Qumran.' Pages 381-414 in *The Complexities of Second Temple Judaism*. Vol. 1 of *Justification and Variegated Nomism*. Edited by D. A. Carson, Peter T. O'Brien, and Mark A. Seifrid. Grand Rapids: Baker, 2001.

Bromiley, Geoffrey W., ed. *The International Standard Bible Encyclopedia*. 4 vols. Grand Rapids: Eerdmans, 1979-1988.

Bosman, Henkrik L. 'רֹאשׁ הַשָּׁנָה,' *NIDOTTE*, 3:1022-23.

Brown, Raymond E. *An Introduction to the New Testament*. ABRL. New York: Doubleday, 1997.

Brownlee, W. H. *The Midrash Pesher of Habakkuk*. SBLMS 24. Missoula: Scholars, 1979.

Bruce, F. F. *New Testament History*. New York: Doubleday, 1980.

Bultmann, Rudolf. *Theology of the New Testament.* Translated by Kendrick Grobel. 2 vols. New York: Scribner's, 1951, 1955.

_____. *Primitive Christianity in Its Contemporary Setting.* Translated by R. H. Fuller. London: Thames and Hudson, 1956.

Burchard, Christoph. *Untersuchungen zu Joseph und Aseneth.* WUNT 8. Tübingen: Mohr, 1965.

Caird, G. B. Review of *Paul and Palestinian Judaism: A Comparison of Patterns of Religion*, by E. P. Sanders. *JTS* NS 29 (1978): 538-43.

Calvin, John. *Institutes of the Christian Religion.* Translated by Ford Lewis Battles, Edited by John T. McNeill. Library of Christian Classics 20. Philadelphia: Westminster, 1960.

_____. *The Second Epistle of Paul the Apostle to the Corinthians and the Epistles to Timothy, Titus and Philemon.* Translated by T. A. Smail. Edited by David W. and Thomas F. Torrance. Calvin's Commentaries 10. Grand Rapids: Eerdmans, 1964.

_____. *The Epistles of Paul the Apostle to the Galatians, Ephesians, Philippians and Colossians.* Translated by T. H. L. Parker. Edited by David W. and Thomas F Torrance. Calvin's Commentaries 11. Grand Rapids: Eerdmans, 1965 [1556].

Cara, Robert J. Review of *Judgment & Justification in Early Judaism and the Apostle Paul*, by Chris VanLandingham. *WTJ* 70 (2008): 388-92.

_____. 'Redemptive-Historical Themes in the Westminster Larger Catechism,' Pages 3:55-79 in *The Westminster Confession into the 21st Century: Essays in Remembrance of the 350th Anniversary of the Westminster Assembly.* Edited by J. Ligon Duncan III. 3 vols. Ross-Shire, Scotland: Mentor, 2003-2009.

_____. *A Study Commentary on 1 & 2 Thessalonians*. EP Study Commentary. Webster, NY: EP, 2009.

Carson, D. A. 'Summaries and Conclusions.' Pages 505-48 in *The Complexities of Second Temple Judaism*. Vol. 1 of *Justification and Variegated Nomism*. Edited by D. A. Carson, Peter T. O'Brien, and Mark A. Seifrid. Grand Rapids: Baker, 2001.

_____. 'The Vindication of Imputation: On Fields of Discourse and Semantic Fields.' Pages 46-78 in *Justification: What's at Stake in the Current Debates*. Edited by Mark Husbands and Daniel J. Treier. Downers Grove: InterVarsity, 2004.

Carson, D. A., and Douglas J. Moo. *An Introduction to the New Testament*. 2d ed. Grand Rapids: Zondervan, 2005.

Carson, D. A., Peter T. O'Brien, and Mark A. Seifrid, eds., *The Complexities of Second Temple Judaism*. Vol. 1 of *Justification and Variegated Nomism*. Grand Rapids: Baker, 2001.

Carson, D. A., Peter T. O'Brien, and Mark A. Seifrid, eds., *The Paradoxes of Paul*. Vol. 2 of *Justification and Variegated Nomism*. Grand Rapids: Baker, 2004.

Chapman, David W., and Andreas J. Köstenberger. 'Jewish Intertestamental and Early Rabbinic Literature: An Annotated Bibliographic Resource Updated (Part 1 and 2).' *JETS* 55 (2012): 235-72, 457-88.

Charlesworth, James H., ed. *The Old Testament Pseudepigrapha*. 2 vols. Garden City: Doubleday, 1983-1985.

Chilton, B. D. 'Judaism.' *DJG*, 398-405.

Chrysostom, John. 'Homily V' in 'Homilies on Titus,' *NPNF*[1], 8:539.

Clark, R. Scott. 'Do This and Live: Christ's Active Obedience as the Ground of Justification,' Pages 229-65 in *Covenant, Justification, and Pastoral Ministry*. Edited by R. Scott Clark. Phillipsburg: P&R, 2007.

Clark, R. Scott, ed. *Covenant, Justification, and Pastoral Ministry: Essays by the Faculty of Westminster Seminary California.* Phillipsburg: P&R, 2007.

Cohen, J. D. *From the Maccabees to the Mishnah.* 2d. ed. Louisville: Westminster John Knox, 2006.

Collins, John J. *The Sibylline Oracles of Egyptian Judaism.* SBLDS 13. Missoula: Scholars, 1974

————. 'Early Judaism in Modern Scholarship,' Pages 1-21 in *Early Judaism: A Comprehensive Overview.* Edited by John J. Collins and Daniel C. Harlow. Grand Rapids: Eerdmans, 2012.

Collins, Raymond F. *1 & 2 Timothy: A Commentary.* NTL. Louisville: Westminster John Knox, 2002.

Davies, W. D. *Paul and Rabbinic Judaism: Some Rabbinic Elements in Pauline Theology.* London: SPCK, 1948.

Daube, David. 'Rabbinic Methods of Interpretation and Hellenistic Rhetoric.' *HUCA* 22 (1949): 239-64.

————. *The New Testament and Rabbinic Judaism.* London: University of London, 1956. Repr., Peabody: Hendrickson, 1988.

deSilva, David A. *Introducing the Apocrypha: Message, Context, and Significance.* Grand Rapids: Baker, 2002.

Davila, James R. *The Provenance of the Pseudepigrapha: Jewish, Christian, or Other?.* Journal for the Study of Judaism Supplements 105. Leiden: Brill, 2005.

Dibelius, Martin, and Hans Conzelmann. *A Commentary on the Pastoral Epistles.* Hermeneia. Philadelphia: Fortress, 1972.

Dunn, James D. G. 'The New Perspective on Paul.' *BJRL* 65 (1983): 95-122.

_____. *Jesus, Paul, and the Law: Studies in Mark and Galatians.* Louisville, KY: Westminster/Knox, 1990.

_____. 'The Justice of God: A renewed perspective on justification by faith.' *JTS* 43 (1992):1-22.

_____. *The Epistle to Galatians.* BNTC 9. Peabody: Hendrickson, 1993.

_____. '4QMMT and Galatians,' Pages 339-45 in *The New Perspective on Paul.* Rev. ed. Grand Rapids: Eerdmans, 2008. Repr. *NTS* 43 (1997): 147-53.

_____. 'Pauline Legacy and School.' *DLNT,* 887-93.

_____. 'Pseudepigraphy.' *DLNT,* 977-84.

_____. *Romans.* WBC 38A, 38B. Dallas: Word, 1988.

_____. *The Theology of Paul the Apostle.* Grand Rapids: Eerdmans, 1998.

_____. 'Ephesians.' Pages 1165-79 in *The Oxford Bible Commentary.* Edited by John Barton and John Muddiman. Oxford: OUP, 2001.

_____. 'The New Perspective: whence, what and whither?' Pages 1-97 in *The New Perspective on Paul.* Rev. ed. Grand Rapids: Eerdmans, 2008.

_____. 'Whatever Happened to "Works of the Law"?,' Pages 381-94 in *The New Perspective on Paul.* Rev. ed. Grand Rapids: Eerdmans, 2008. Repr. pages 107-20 in *Epitoayto: P. Pokorny FS.* Edited by J. Kerkovsky et. al. Praha: Mlyn, 1988.

_____. *Beginning from Jerusalem.* Vol. 2 of *Christianity in the Making.* Grand Rapids: Eerdmans, 2009.

_____. 'New Perspective View.' Pages 176-201 in *Justification: Five Views.* Edited by James K. Beilby and Paul Rhodes Eddy. Downers Grove: IVP Academic, 2011.

_____. 'The First and Second Letters to Timothy and the Letter of Titus: Introduction, Commentary, and Reflections.' Pages 371-460 in *The New Interpreter's Bible Commentary: Volume Ten*. Nashville: Abingdon, 2015 [2000].

Ehrman, Bart D. *The New Testament: A Historical Introduction to the Early Christian Writings*. 4th ed. New York, OUP, 2008.

Engberg-Pedersen, Troels. *Paul and the Stoics*. Louisville: Westminster, 2000.

Epstein, Isidore. *Judaism: A Historical Presentation*. New York: Penguin, 1990 [1950].

Eskola, Timo. 'Paul, Predestination and "Covenantal Nomism"— Re-assessing Paul and Palestinian Judaism.' *JSJ* 28 (1997): 390-412.

Evans, Craig A. *Noncanonical Writings and New Testament Interpretation*. Peabody: Hendrickson, 1992.

_____. 'Covenant in the Qumran Literature,' Pages 55-80 in *The Concept of the Covenant in the Second Temple Period*. Edited by Stanley E. Porter and Jacqueline C. R. de Roo. Supplements to the Journal for the Study of Judaism 71. Atlanta: SBL, 2003.

Evans, Craig A., and Stanley E. Porter, eds. *Dictionary of New Testament Background*. Downers Grove: InterVarsity, 2000.

Fairbairn, Patrick. *A Commentary on 1 & 2 Timothy and Titus*. Geneva. Carlisle: Banner of Truth, 2002 [1874].

Falk, Daniel. 'Prayers and Psalms.' Pages 35-51 in *The Complexities of Second Temple Judaism*. Vol. 1 of *Justification and Variegated Nomism*. Edited by D. A. Carson, Peter T. O'Brien, and Mark A. Seifrid. Grand Rapids: Baker, 2001.

Ferguson, Everett. *Backgrounds of Early Christianity*. 3d ed. Grand Rapids: Eerdmans, 2003.

Ferry, Brenton C. 'Works in the Mosaic Covenant: A Reformed Taxonomy.' Pages 76-106 in *The Law is not of Faith: Essays on Works and Grace in the Mosaic Covenant.* Edited by Bryan D. Estelle, J. V. Fesko, and David VanDrunen. Phillipsburg: P&R, 2009.

Fesko, J. V. *Justification: Understanding the Classic Reformed Doctrine.* Phillipsburg: P&R, 2008.

_____. *Beyond Calvin: Union with Christ and Justification in Early Modern Reformed Theology (1517-1700).* Reformed Historical Theology 20. Bristol, CT: Vandenhoeck & Ruprecht, 2012.

Fitzmyer, J. A. *The Genesis Apocryphon of Qumran Cave I: A Commentary.* Rome: Biblical Institute, 1971.

Flesher, Paul V. M., and Bruce Chilton. *The Targums: A Critical Introduction.* Waco: Baylor University Press, 2011.

Fowl, Stephen E. *Ephesians: A Commentary.* NTL. Louisville: Westminster John Knox, 2012.

Frame, John, M. *The Doctrine of the Knowledge of God.* A Theology of Lordship. Phillipsburg: Presbyterian and Reformed, 1987.

_____. *The Doctrine of the Christian Life.* Phillipsburg: P&R, 2008.

_____. *Systematic Theology: An Introduction to Christian Belief.* Phillipsburg: P&R, 2013.

Freeman, David Noel, ed. *The Anchor Bible Dictionary.* 6 vols. New York: Doubleday, 1992.

Gaffin, Jr., Richard B. *'By Faith, Not by Sight': Paul and the Order of Salvation.* Milton Keynes, England: Paternoster, 2006.

Garlington, Don B. *In Defense of the New Perspective on Paul: Essays and Reviews.* Eugene, OR: Wipf & Stock, 2005.

_____. 'Afterword by Don Garlington,' Pages 101-5 in *The New Perspective on Paul: An Introduction*, by Kent L. Yinger. Eugene, OR: Cascade, 2011.

Gathercole, Simon J. *Where is Boasting? Early Jewish Soteriology and Paul's Response in Romans 1-5*. Grand Rapids: Eerdmans, 2002.

Genderen, J. van, and W. H. Velema. *Concise Reformed Dogmatics*. Translated by Gerrit Bilkes and Ed. M. van der Maas. Phillipsburg: P&R, 2008.

Goldstein, Jonathan A. *I Maccabees: A New Translation with Introduction and Commentary*. AB 41. Garden City: Doubleday, 1976.

Gombis, Timothy G. *Paul: A Guide for the Perplexed*. New York: T&T Clark/Continuum, 2010.

Goulder, Michael. *St. Paul versus St. Peter: A Tale of Two Missions*. Louisville: Westminster John Knox, 1994.

Green, Joel B., and Scot McKnight, eds. *Dictionary of Jesus and the Gospels*. Downers Grove: Intervarsity, 1992.

Hamilton, James M. 'N. T. Wright and Saul's Moral Bootstraps: Newer Light on "The New Perspective."' *TrinJ* n.s. 25 (2004): 139-55.

Hawthorne, Gerald F., and Ralph P. Martin. eds. *Dictionary of Paul and His Letters*. Downers Grove: InterVarsity, 1993.

Hays, Richard B. 'Justification.' *ABD*, 3:1129-33.

Helyer, Larry. *Exploring Jewish Literature of the Second Temple Period: A Guide for New Testament Students*. Downers Grove: Intervarsity, 2002.

Herr, Moshe D. 'Tosefta.' *EncJud*, 15:1284-85.

Hendricksen, William. *Exposition of the Pastoral Epistles*. Grand Rapids: Baker, 1957.

_____. *Exposition of Ephesians*. NTC. Grand Rapids: Baker, 1967.

Hengel, Martin. *The 'Hellenization' of Judaea in the First Century after Christ*. With Christoph Markschies. Eugene: Wipf and Stock, 2003.

Hodge, Charles. *A Commentary on Ephesians*. Geneva Commentary. Carlisle: Banner of Truth, 1964 [1856].

_____. *A Commentary on Romans*. Geneva Commentary. Carlisle: Banner of Truth, 1972 [1864].

Hoehner, Harold W. 'Herodians.' *ISBE*, 2:698.

_____. *Ephesians: An Exegetical Commentary*. Grand Rapids: Baker, 2002.

Holland, Tom. *Contours of Pauline Theology: A Radical New Survey of the Influences on Paul's Biblical Writings*. Ross-shire: Mentor, 2009.

Horsley, R. 'The Zealots: Their Origin, Relationships and Importance in the Jewish Revolt.' *NovT* 28 (1986): 159-92.

Houlden, J. L. *The Pastoral Epistles: I and II Timothy, Titus*. TPINTC. Philadelphia: Trinity Press International, 1989.

Instone-Brewer, David. *Prayer and Agriculture*. Vol. 1 of *Traditions of the Rabbis from the Era of the New Testament*. Grand Rapids: Eerdmans, 2004.

Irons, Charles Lee. *The Righteousness of God: A Lexical Examination of the Covenant-Faithfulness Interpretation*. WUNT II/386. Tübingen: Mohr Siebeck, 2015.

Johnson, Luke Timothy. *The First and Second Letters to Timothy: A New Translation with Introduction and Commentary*. AB 35A. New York: Doubleday, 2001.

Jones, Mark. *Antinomianism: Reformed Theology's Unwelcome Guest?*. Phillipsburg: P&R, 2013.

Jonge, M. de. 'The So-Called Pseudepigrapha of the Old Testament and Early Christianity.' Pages 59-71 in *The New Testament and Hellenistic Judaism*. Edited by Peder Borgen and Søren Giversen. Peabody: Hendrickson, 1997.

Kampen, John, and Moshe J. Bernstein, eds. *Reading 4QMMT: New Perspectives on Qumran Law and History*. SBL Symposium Series 2. Atlanta: Scholars, 1996.

Kee, H. C. 'Testaments of the Twelve Patriarchs: A New Translation and Introduction,' in *OTP*, 775-78.

Kelly, J. N. D. *The Pastoral Epistles*. BNTC 14. Peabody: Hendrickson, 1960.

Kim, Seyoon. *Paul and the New Perspective: Second Thoughts on the Origin of Paul's Gospel*. Grand Rapids: Eerdmans, 2002.

Klijn, A. F. J. '2 (Syriac Apocalypse of) Baruch: A New Translation and Introduction,' in *OTP*, 1:619.

Knight, George W. *The Faithful Sayings in the Pastoral Epistles*. Grand Rapids: Baker, 1979.

————. *The Pastoral Epistles: A Commentary on the Greek Text*. NIGTC. Grand Rapids: 1992.

Koester, Helmut. *History, Culture, and Religion of the Hellenistic Age*. Vol. 1 of *Introduction to the New Testament*. 2d ed. New York: Walter de Gruyter, 1995.

Köstenberger, Andreas, and Michael J. Kruger. *The Heresy of Orthodoxy: How Contemporary Culture's Fascination with Diversity Has Reshaped Our Understanding of Early Christianity*. Wheaton: Crossway, 2010.

Kraft, Robert A. 'The Pseudepigrapha in Christianity.' Pages 55-86 in *Tracing the Threads: Studies in the Vitality of Jewish Pseudepigrapha*. Edited by John C. Reeves. SBL Early Judaism and Its Literature 6. Atlanta: Scholars Press, 1994.

_____. 'Setting the Stage and Framing Some Central Questions.' *JSJ* 32 (2001): 370-95.

Kümmel, Werner Georg. *Introduction to the New Testament.* Translated by Howard Clark Kee. Rev. ed. Nashville: Abingdon, 1975.

Lincoln, Andrew T. 'Ephesians 2:8-10: A Summary of Paul's Gospel?' *CBQ* 45 (1983): 617-30.

_____. *Ephesians.* WBC. Dallas: Waco, 1990.

_____. 'The Theology of Ephesians.' Pages 75-166 in *The Theology of the Later Pauline Letters.* NTT. Cambridge: CUP, 1993.

Lohse, Eduard. *The New Testament Environment.* Translated by John E. Steely. Nashville: Abingdon, 1976.

Longenecker, Bruce W. *Galatians.* WBC 41. Dallas: Waco, 1990.

_____. *Eschatology and the Covenant: A Comparison of 4 Ezra and Romans 1-11.* JSNTSup 57. Sheffield: Sheffield Academic Press, 1991.

_____. *2 Esdras.* Sheffield: Sheffield Academic Press, 1995.

_____. 'On Critiquing the "New Perspective" on Paul: A Case Study.' *ZNW* 96 (2005): 263-71.

Lusk, Rich. 'N. T. Wright and Reformed Theology: Friends or Foes?' *Reformation & Revival Journal* 11/2 (2002): 35-52.

Mansoor, Menahem. 'Pharisees.' *EncJud*, 13:363-66.

Marshall, I. Howard. 'Salvation, Grace and Works in the Later Writings in the Pauline Corpus.' *NTS* 42 [1996]: 339-58.

_____. *New Testament Theology: Many Witnesses, One Gospel.* Downers Grove: InterVarsity, 2004.

Marshall, I. Howard, with Philip H. Towner. *A Critical and Exegetical Commentary on the Pastoral Epistles*. ICC. Edinburgh: T&T Clark, 1999.

Martin, Ralph P., and Peter H. Davids, eds. *Dictionary of the Later New Testament & Its Developments*. Downers Grove: InterVarsity, 1987.

Mason, S. 'Theologies and Sects, Jewish.' *DNTB*, 1221-30.

Matera, Frank J. *Galatians*. SP 9. Liturgical: Collegeville, MN, 1992.

McGrath, Alister E. *Iustitia Dei: A History of the Christian Doctrine of Justification*. 3d ed. Cambridge: CUP, 2005.

McNamara, Martin. *Palestinian Judaism and the New Testament*. GNS 4. Wilmington, DE: Michael Glazier, 1983.

Metzger, Bruce M., ed. *The Oxford Annotated Apocrypha*. New York, OUP, 1977.

Montefiore, C. G. 'Rabbinic Judaism and the Epistles of St. Paul.' *JQR* 13 (1900-1901): 161-217.

Moo, Douglas J. *Galatians*. BECNT. Grand Rapids: Baker, 2013.

Moore, Carey A. *Tobit: A New Translation with Introduction and Commentary*. AB 40A. New York: Doubleday, 1996.

Moore, George Foot. 'Christian Writers on Judaism.' *HTR* 14 (1921): 197-254.

_____. *Judaism in the First Centuries of the Christian Era: The Age of Tannaim*. 3 vols. Peabody: Hendrickson, 1997 [1927-30].

Mounce, William D. *Pastoral Epistles*. WBC 46. Nashville: Thomas Nelson, 2000.

Mueller, James R. 'Abraham, Testament of,' *ABD*, 1:43-44.

Mueller, John Theodore. *Christian Dogmatics: A Handbook of Doctrinal Theology for Pastors, Teachers, and Laymen*. St. Louis: Concordia, 1955.

Murphy-O'Connor, J. 'Community, Rule of the (1QS).' *ABD*, 1:1110-12.

Murray, John. *Redemption: Accomplished and Applied*. Grand Rapids: Eerdmans, 1955.

Neusner, Jacob. *Rabbinic Tradition About the Pharisees Before 70*. 3 vols. Leiden: E. J. Brill, 1971.

_____. *The Mishnah: A New Translation*. New Haven: Yale, 1988.

_____. 'Mr. Sanders' Pharisees and Mine: A Response to E. P. Sanders, *Jewish Law from Jesus to the Mishnah*.' *SJT* 44 [1991]: 73-95.

_____. *Rabbinic Literature & the New Testament: What We Cannot Show, We Do Not Know*. Valley Forge: Trinity Press International, 1994.

_____. *The Tosefta: Translated from the Hebrew with a New Introduction*. Peabody, MA: Hendrickson, 2002.

_____. *Judaism When Christianity Began: A Survey of Belief and Practice*. Louisville: Westminster John Knox, 2002.

_____. *Rabbinic Literature: An Essential Guide*. Nashville: Abingdon, 2005.

_____. *The Babylonian Talmud: A Translation and Commentary*. 22 vols. Peabody: Hendrickson, 2005.

Neusner, Jacob, and Bruce D. Chilton, eds. *In Quest of the Historical Pharisees*. Waco: Baylor University Press, 2007.

Neusner, Jacob, William S. Green, and Ernst Frerichs, eds. *Judaisms and Their Messiahs at the Turn of the Christian Era*. Cambridge: CUP, 1987.

Nickelsburg, George W. E. *Jewish Literature Between the Bible and the Mishnah: A Historical and Literary Introduction*. Rev. ed. Philadelphia, Fortress, 1987.

_____. *Ancient Judaism and Christian Origins: Diversity, Continuity, and Transformation*. Minneapolis: Fortress, 2003.

O'Brien, Peter T. *The Letter to the Ephesians*. PNTC. Grand Rapids: Eerdmans, 1999.

O'Kelley, Aaron T. *Did the Reformers Misread Paul? A Historical-Theological Critique of the New Perspective*. Eugene, OR: Wipf & Stock, 2014.

Owen, John *The Doctrine of Justification by Faith through Imputation of the Righteousness of Christ: Explained, Confirmed, and Vindicated*. Grand Rapids: Reformation Heritage Books, 2006 [1677].

Perkins, William. *A Commentary on Galatians*. Edited by Gerald T. Shephard. Pilgrim Classic Commentaries. New York: Pilgrim, 1989 [1617].

Philonenko, M. *Joseph et Asneth: Introduction, texte critique, traduction et notes*. SPB 13. Leiden: Brill, 1968.

Piper, John. *Counted Righteous in Christ: Should We Abandon the Imputation of Christ's Righteousness?*. Wheaton: Crossway, 2002.

_____. *The Future of Justification: A Response to N. T. Wright*. Wheaton: Crossway, 2007.

Perkins, Pheme. 'The Letter to the Ephesians: Introduction, Commentary, and Reflections,' Pages 1-104 in *The New Interpreter's Bible Commentary: Volume Ten*. Nashville: Abingdon, 2015.

Porten, Bezalel. 'Elephantine Papyri.' *ABD*, 2:445-55.

Porton, Gary G. 'Sadducees.' *ABD*, 5:892-95.

Qimron, Elisha. 'Miqṣat Maʿase Hatorah,' *ABD*, 4:843-45.

Quinn, Jerome D. *The Letter to Titus: A New Translation with Notes and Commentary and An Introduction to Titus, I and II Timothy, The Pastoral Epistles*. AB 35. New York: Doubleday, 1990.

Quinn, Jerome D., and William C. Wacker. *The First and Second Letters to Timothy: A New Translation with Notes and Commentary*. ECC. Grand Rapids: Eerdmans, 2000.

Räisänen, Heikki. *Paul & the Law*. Philadelphia: Fortress, 1983.

Rast, Lawrence R. 'The Third Use of the Law: Keeping Up to Date with an Old Issue.' *CTQ* 69 (2005): 187-90.

Ridderbos, Herman. *Paul: An Outline of His Theology*. Translated by John Richard DeWitt. Grand Rapids: Eerdmans, 1975.

Saldarini, Anthony J. 'Sanhedrin,' *ABD*, 5:975-80.

Sanders, E. P. *Paul and Palestinian Judaism: A Comparison of Patterns of Religion*. Minneapolis: Fortress, 1977.

_____. *Paul, the Law, and the Jewish People*. Philadelphia: Fortress, 1983.

_____. *Jesus and Judaism*. Philadelphia: Fortress, 1985.

_____. 'Testament of Abraham,' in *OTP*, 1:877-78.

_____. *Judaism: Practice and Belief 63 B.C.E.-66 C.E.* Philadelphia: Trinity Press International, 1992.

_____. *Paul: the Apostle's life, Letters, and Thought*. Minneapolis: Fortress, 2015.

Schreiner, Thomas R. *The Law and Its Fulfillment: A Pauline Theology of Law*. Grand Rapids: Baker, 1993.

_____. *Paul Apostle of God's Glory in Christ: A Pauline Theology.* Downers Grove: InterVarsity, 2001.

_____. *Faith Alone: The Doctrine of Justification.* The Five Solas. Grand Rapids: Zondervan, 2015.

Schuller, E. M. 'Thanksgiving Hymns (1QH).' *DNTB*, 1214-18.

Schuller, Eileen M., and Carol A. Newsom, *The Hodayot (Thanksgiving Psalms): A Study Edition of 1QHa.* EJL 36. Atlanta: SBL, 2012.

Seifrid, Mark A. *Christ, our Righteousness: Paul's Theology of Justification.* NSBT 9. Downers Grove: InterVarsity, 2000.

Silva, Moisés. 'The Law and Christianity: Dunn's New Synthesis.' *WTJ* 53 (1991): 339-53.

_____. 'Faith Versus Works of Law in Galatians.' Pages 217-48 in *The Paradoxes of Paul.* Vol. 2 of *Justification and Variegated Nomism.* Edited by D. A. Carson, Peter T. O'Brien, and Mark A. Seifrid. Grand Rapids: Baker, 2004.

Slater, Thomas B. *Ephesians.* SHBC. Macon: Smyth & Helwys, 2012.

Smith, Barry D. *What Must I do to be Saved? Paul Parts Company with His Jewish Heritage.* New Testament Monographs 17. Sheffield: Sheffield Phoenix, 2007.

Spicq, C. *Saint Paul: Les Épîtres Pastorales.* EBib. Paris: Gabalda, 1947.

Sprinkle, Preston M. *Law and Life: The Interpretation of Leviticus 18:5 in Early Judaism and in Paul.* WUNT II/241. Tübingen: Mohr Siebeck, 2008.

_____. *Paul & Judaism Revisited: A Study of Divine and Human Agency in Salvation.* Downers Grove: IVP Academic, 2013.

Stendahl, Krister. 'The Apostle Paul and the Introspective Conscience of the West.' *HTR* 56 (1963): 199-215.

Stone, Michael Edward. *A Commentary on the Book of Fourth Ezra.* Hermeneia. Minneapolis, Fortress, 1990.

Strack, H. L., and P. Billerbeck. *Kommentar zum Neuen Testament aus Talmud und Midrasch.* 6 vols. Munich: Beck, 1922-61.

Strecker, George. *Theology of the New Testament.* Edited by Friedrich Wilhelm Horn. Translated by M. Eugene Boring. Louisville: Westminister John Knox, 2000.

Stuhlmacher, Peter. *Revisiting Paul's Doctrine of Justification: A Challenge to the New Perspective.* Downers Grove: InterVarsity, 2001.

Talbert, Charles H. 'Paul, Judaism, and the Revisionists.' *CBQ* 63 (2001): 1-22.

Taylor, Joan E., and Philip R. Davies. 'The So-Called Therapeutae of *De Vita Contemplativa.*' *HTR* 91 (1998): 3-24.

Thielman, Frank. *Paul & the Law: A Contextual Approach.* Downers Grove: InterVarsity, 1994.

_____. *From Plight to Solution: A Jewish Framework for Understanding Paul's View of the Law in Galatians and Romans.* NovTSup 61. Eugene: Wipf & Stock, 2007 [1989].

_____. *Ephesians.* BECNT. Grand Rapids: Baker, 2010.

Tipton, Lane G. 'Union with Christ and Justification.' Pages 23-49 in *Justified in Christ: God's plan for us in Justification.* Edited by K. Scott Oliphint. Ross-shire, Scotland: Mentor, 2007.

Towner, Philip H. *The Goal of Our Instruction: The Structure of Theology and Ethics in the Pastoral Epistles.* JSNTSup 34. Sheffield: JSOT Press, 1989.

Turretin, Francis. *Institutes of Elenctic Theology.* Translated by George Musgrave Giger. Edited by James T. Dennison, Jr. 3 vols. Phillipsburg: P& R, 1992-97 [1679-85].

Urbach, Ephraim E. 'Mishnah.' *EncJud*, 12:94-110.

Van Til, Cornelius. *The Defense of the Faith*. 3d ed. Philadelphia: Presbyterian and Reformed, 1967.

VanGemeren, Willem A. ed. *New International Dictionary of Old Testament Theology & Exegesis*. 5 vols. Grand Rapids: Zondervan, 1997.

VanLandingham, Chris. *Judgment & Justification in Early Judaism and the Apostle Paul*. Peabody: Hendrickson, 2006.

Venema, Cornelis P. *The Gospel of Free Acceptance in Christ: An Assessment of the Reformation and 'New Perspectives' on Paul*. Carlisle: Banner of Truth, 2006.

Vermes, Geza. 'Essenes and Therapeutai.' *RQ* 3 (1962): 495-504.

_____. *The Dead Sea Scrolls: Qumran in Perspective*. Collaboration with Pamela Vermes. Rev. ed. Philadelphia: Fortress, 1981.

_____. *The Complete Dead Sea Scrolls in English*. Rev. ed. New York: Penguin, 2004.

Vermigli, Peter Martyr. *Predestination and Justification*. Translated by and edited with introduction and notes Frank A. James III. Peter Martyr Library 8. Sixteenth Century Essays & Studies 68. Kirksville: MO, 2003 [1558].

Vickers, Brian. *Jesus' Blood and Righteousness: Paul's Theology of Imputation*. Wheaton: Crossway, 2006.

Vos, Geerhardus. *The Teaching of Jesus Concerning The Kingdom of God and the Church*. Phillipsburg: Presbyterian and Reformed, n.d. [1903].

_____. *Biblical Theology: Old and New Testaments*. Carlisle: Banner of Truth, 1975 [1948].

_____. *Soteriology: The Application of the Merits of the Mediator by the Holy Spirit*. Vol. 4 of *Reformed Dogmatics*. Translated and edited by Richard B. Gaffin, Jr. Bellingham, WA: Lexham, 2015.

Wallace, Daniel B. *Greek Grammar Beyond the Basics: An Exegetical Syntax of the New Testament.* Grand Rapids: Zondervan, 1996.

Walter, Nikolaus. 'Hellenistic Jews of the Diaspora at the Cradle of Primitive Christianity,' Pages 37-58 in *The New Testament and Hellenistic Judaism.* Edited by Peder Borgen and Søren Giversen. Peabody: Hendrickson, 1997.

Walther, C. F. W. *The Proper Distinction between the Law and the Gospel: Thirty-Nine Evening Lectures.* Translated by W. H. T. Dau. St. Louis: Concordia, 1928.

Waltke, Bruce K. 'Samaritan Pentateuch.' *ABD*, 5:932-40.

Ware, Timothy. *The Orthodox Church.* Rev. ed. New York: Penguin, 1993.

Warfield, B. B. 'Calvinism.' Pages 2:411-47 in *Selected Shorter Writings: Benjamin B. Warfield.* Edited by John E. Meeter. 2 vols. Phillipsburg: P&R, 1970-1973.

_____. *Plan of Salvation.* Boonton, NJ: Simpson, 1989 [1915].

Waters, Guy Prentiss. *Justification and the New Perspective on Paul: A Review and Response* (Phillipsburg: P&R, 2004).

Watson, Francis. *Paul and the Hermeneutics of Faith.* London: T & T Clark, 2004.

Wengert, Timothy. 'Biblical Interpretation in the Works of Philip Melanchthon.' Pages 319-40 in *The Medieval through the Reformation Periods.* Edited by Alan J. Hauser and Duane F. Watson. Vol. 2 of *A History of Biblical Interpretation.* Grand Rapids: Eerdmans, 2009.

Westerholm, Stephen. *Perspectives Old and New on Paul: The 'Lutheran' Paul and His Critics.* Grand Rapids: Eerdmans, 2004.

Wise, Michael O. 'Bar Kokhba Letters.' *ABD*, 1:601-6.

Wolter, Michael. 'The Development of Pauline Christianity from a "Religion of Conversion" to a "Religion of Tradition."' Translated by J. M. McConnell and D. P. Moessner. Pages 49-69 in *Paul and the Heritage of Israel*. Edited by D. P. Moessner, D. Marguerat, and M. Wolter. LNTS 452. London: T&T Clark, 2012.

_____. *Paul: An Outline of His Theology*. Translated by Robert L. Brawley. Waco: Baylor University Press, 2015.

Wrede, William. *Paul*. Translated by Edward Lummis. Eugene, OR: Wipf and Stock, 2001. Repr. Boston: American Unitarian Association, 1908 [German 1904].

Wright, N. T. 'The Paul of History and the Apostle of Faith.' *TynBul* 29 (1978): 61-88.

_____. 'Justification: The Biblical Basis and its Relevance for Contemporary Evangelicalism,' Pages 13-37, 109-19 in *The Great Acquittal: Justification by Faith and Current Christian Thought*. Edited by Gavin Reid. Glasgow: Collins, 1980.

_____. 'Justification.' Pages 359-61 in *New Dictionary of Theology*. Edited by Sinclair B. Ferguson and David F. Wright. Downers Grove: InterVarsity, 1988.

_____. *The Climax of the Covenant: Christ and the Law in Pauline Theology*. Minneapolis: Fortress, 1991.

_____. 'The Law in Romans 2.' Pages 131-50 in *Paul and the Mosaic Law*. Edited by James D. G. Dunn. WUNT 89. Tübingen: Mohr Siebeck: 1996.

_____. *What Saint Paul Really Said: Was Paul of Tarsus the Real Founder of Christianity?* Grand Rapids: Eerdmans, 1997.

_____. 'The Letter to the Romans: Introduction, Commentary, and Reflections.' Pages 393-770 in *The New Interpreter's Bible*. Vol. 10. Nashville: Abingdon, 2002.

_____. *The Resurrection of the Son of God*. London: SPCK, 2003.

_____. *Paul for Everyone: The Pastoral Letters: 1 and 2 Timothy and Titus*. 2d ed. London: SPCK, 2004.

_____. *Paul for Everyone: The Prison Letters: Ephesians, Philippians, Colossians and Philemon*. 2d ed.. London: SPCK, 2004.

_____. *Paul: In Fresh Perspective*. Minneapolis: Fortress, 2005.

_____. '4QMMT and Paul: Justification, "Works," and Eschatology,' Pages 104-32 in *History and Exegesis: New Testament Essays in Honor of Dr. E. Earle Ellis for His 80th Birthday*. Edited by Sand-Won Son. New York: T & T Clark, 2006.

_____. 'New Perspectives on Paul,' Pages 243-64 in *Justification in Perspective: Historical Developments and Contemporary Challenges*. Edited by Bruce L. McCormack. Grand Rapids: Baker, 2006.

_____. *Justification: God's Plan & Paul's Vision*. Downers Grove: IVP Academic, 2009.

_____. *Pauline Perspectives: Essays on Paul, 1978-2013*. Minneapolis: Fortress, 2013.

_____. *Paul and the Faithfulness of God*. Minneapolis: Fortress, 2013.

_____. *Paul and His Recent Interpreters: Some Contemporary Debates*. Minneapolis: Fortress, 2015.

Wright, R. B. 'The Psalms of Solomon, the Pharisees, and the Essenes.' *SCS* 2 (1972): 136-47.

Yinger, Kent L. *The New Perspective on Paul: An Introduction*. Eugene, OR: Cascade, 2011.

Young, Brad H. *The Parables: Jewish Tradition and Christian Interpretation*. Peabody: Hendrickson, 1998.

Young, Frances. *The Theology of the Pastoral Letters*. NTT. Cambridge: CUP, 1994.

Zetterholm, Karin Hedner. *Jewish Interpretation of the Bible: Ancient and Contemporary*. Minneapolis: Fortress, 2012.

Zetterholm, Magnus. *Approaches to Paul: A Student's Guide to Recent Scholarship*. Minneapolis: Fortress, 2009.

Ziesler, John. *Paul's Letter to the Romans*. TPINTC. Philadelphia: Trinity Press International, 1989.

SCRIPTURE INDEX

SUBJECT INDEX

Extra-canonical Texts

RABBINICAL WRITINGS

b. Bekhorot

b. Berakhot

b. Ketubot

b. Rosh Hashanah

b. Sanhedrin

b. Sotah

Genesis Rabbah

m. Abot

Other books of interest
from
Mentor

ISBN 978-1-78191-908-8

Death in Adam, Life in Christ
The Doctrine of Imputation
J. V. Fesko

The doctrine of imputation is the ground in which salvation is rooted. It is often seen as superfluous or splitting hairs, and yet, without it, redemption automatically becomes reliant on our own works and assurance of salvation is suddenly not so sure. J. V. Fesko works through this doctrine looking at its long history in the church, its exegetical foundation, and its dogmatic formulation. In exploring imputed guilt from the First Adam alongside the imputed righteousness from the Second, this volume offers a helpfully well-rounded explanation of the doctrine.

> Conversations over imputation are rarely informed by the history of interpretation. Fesko introduces us to seminal figures in this development and no engagement with original sin or justification should overlook his careful spade work.
>
> MICHAEL HORTON,
> J. Gresham Machen Professor of Systematic Theology and Apologetics,
> Westminster Seminary California, Escondido, California

> In classic Reformed fashion, and with grace and style, John Fesko brings confessional exposition, historical survey, and exegesis together in what is sure to become the standard Reformed work on Imputation for generations to come.
>
> BRIAN VICKERS,
> Professor of New Testament Interpretation and Biblical Theology,
> The Southern Baptist Theological Seminary, Louisville, Kentucky

J. V. Fesko is Academic Dean and Professor of Systematic and Historical Theology at Westminster Seminary in California.

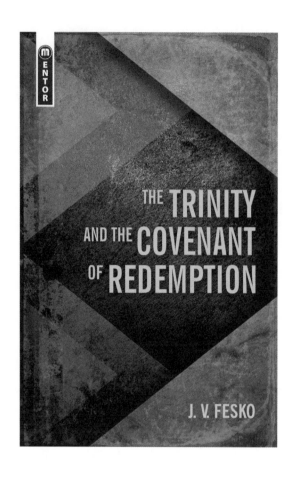

ISBN 978-1-78191-765-7

The Trinity and the Covenant of Redemption

J. V. Fesko

The doctrine of imputation is the ground in which salvation is rooted. It is often seen as superfluous or splitting hairs, and yet, without it, redemption automatically becomes reliant on our own works and assurance of salvation is suddenly not so sure. J. V. Fesko works through this doctrine looking at its long history in the church, its exegetical foundation, and its dogmatic formulation. In exploring imputed guilt from the First Adam alongside the imputed righteousness from the Second, this volume offers a helpfully well-rounded explanation of the doctrine.

... shows historical care, exegetical soundness, and doctrinal wisdom. I commend it heartily as a wonderful entryway to considering this most profound facet of the Christian confession.

MICHAEL ALLEN,
Associate Professor of Systematic and Historical Theology,
Reformed Theological Seminary, Orlando, Florida

Some books today exegete the shining truths of the Holy Scriptures, others mine the treasures of Reformed orthodoxy, and yet others interact with influential theologians of the modern era. This book is one of the few that does all three, and does them well.

JOEL R. BEEKES,
President, Puritan Reformed Theological Seminary, Grand Rapids, Michigan

... displays the vitality and richness of the covenant of redemption for other doctrines – not least, the Trinity. In both method and substance, this is an exemplary work that will edify as well as inform.

MICHAEL HORTON,
J. Gresham Machen Professor of Systematic Theology and Apologetics,
Westminster Seminary California, Escondido, California

J. V. Fesko is Academic Dean and Professor of Systematic and Historical Theology at Westminster Seminary in California.

CONTOURS OF PAULINE THEOLOGY
A RADICAL NEW SURVEY OF THE INFLUENCES ON PAUL'S BIBLICAL WRITINGS
TOM HOLLAND

"Challenging, unsettling and infuriating, Dr. Holland's tour de force cannot be ignored."
DR. PETER HEAD, CAMBRIDGE UNIVERSITY

ISBN 978-1-84550-625-4

Contours of Pauline Theology

A Radical New Survey of the Influences on Paul's Biblical Writings

Tom Holland

The Apostle Paul is a controversial church figure. Many theologians accuse Paul of starting a new religion: of hijacking early Christianity in a different direction. Is this a fair charge?

Tom Holland points us to a neglected fact, that the Jews in the first century AD would view concepts of salvation through the Exodus of Israel from Egypt to the promised land. Until now, a real elephant in the centre of the hermeneutical room.

Such a viewpoint opens up new understanding on Pauline studies – it is true of this book that it will change your view of the New Testament and deserves to radically alter New Testament studies in Universities, Theological Colleges and Seminaries around the world.

> Dr. Holland provides a timely emphasis on the corporate and communal structures of Paul's thinking as well as on its roots in the Old Testament ...it provides a fresh and useful treatment of Pauline theology, and many of its arguments offer corrections to widespread misunderstandings of Paul
>
> ANTHONY C. THISELTON,
> Emeritus Professor of Christian Theology in Residence,
> University of Nottingham, and Research Professor, University of Chester

> In constant critical engagement... Holland maps out new ways of understanding Paul and offers new insights into a range of absolutely vital issues from justification to Christology, and new insights into Pauline texts from Romans to Colossians. Challenging, unsettling and infuriating Dr. Holland's tour de force cannot be ignored.
>
> PETER HEAD,
> New Testament Tutor, Wycliffe Hall, University of Oxford

Christian Focus Publications

Our mission statement –

STAYING FAITHFUL
In dependence upon God we seek to impact the world through literature faithful to His infallible Word, the Bible. Our aim is to ensure that the Lord Jesus Christ is presented as the only hope to obtain forgiveness of sin, live a useful life and look forward to heaven with Him.

Our books are published in four imprints:

CHRISTIAN
FOCUS

Popular works including biographies, commentaries, basic doctrine and Christian living.

CHRISTIAN
HERITAGE

Books representing some of the best material from the rich heritage of the church.

MENTOR

Books written at a level suitable for Bible College and seminary students, pastors, and other serious readers. The imprint includes commentaries, doctrinal studies, examination of current issues and church history.

CF4•K

Children's books for quality Bible teaching and for all age groups: Sunday school curriculum, puzzle and activity books; personal and family devotional titles, biographies and inspirational stories – because you are never too young to know Jesus!

Christian Focus Publications Ltd,
Geanies House, Fearn, Ross-shire,
IV20 1TW, Scotland, United Kingdom.
www.christianfocus.com